Las Vegas

Jefferson Graham

Fodor's Travel Publications, Inc.
New York and London

**Copyright © 1990
by Fodor's Travel Publications, Inc.**

Fodor's is a trademark of Fodor's Travel Publications, Inc.

All rights reserved under International and Pan-American Copyright Conventions. Published in the United States by Fodor's Travel Publications, Inc., a subsidiary of Random House, Inc., New York, and simultaneously in Canada by Random House of Canada Limited, Toronto. Distributed by Random House, Inc., New York.

No maps, illustrations, or other portions of this book may be reproduced in any form without written permission from the publishers.

ISBN 0-679-01785-2

"Blackjack" (Chapter 2) reprinted from *Win at the Casino* by Dennis R. Harrison. Copyright © 1982 by Dennis R. Harrison. Used by permission of Fell Publishers, Inc., Hollywood, Florida.

"Casino Games and Slots" (Chapter 2) reprinted from *Gambling Times.* Copyright © 1982 by Gambling Times, Inc. Used by permission of the publisher.

Fodor's Las Vegas

Editor: Vernon Nahrgang
Associate Editor: Alison Hoffman
Editorial Contributors: Suzanne Brown, Dennis R. Harrison, Elliot S. Krane
Art Director: Fabrizio La Rocca
Cartographer: David Lindroth
Illustrator: Karl Tanner
Cover Photograph: Four by Five/Robert Llewellyn

Design: Vignelli Associates

About the Author

Jefferson Graham photographed and wrote about the neon jungle for *Vegas: Live and In Person* (Abbeville Press, 1989). A staff writer for *USA Today* whose articles and photographs have appeared in many national magazines, Graham is also the photographer and author of *Come on Down: The TV Game Show Book.* He lives in Los Angeles with his wife and son.

Special Sales

Fodor's Travel Publications are available at special discounts for bulk purchases (100 copies or more) for sales promotions or premiums. Special editions, including personalized covers, excerpts of existing guides, and corporate imprints, can be created in large quantities for special needs. For more information write to Special Marketing, Fodor's Travel Publications, 201 East 50th St., New York, NY 10022. Inquiries from the United Kingdom should be sent to Fodor's Travel Publications, 30-32 Bedford Square, London WC1B 3SG.

MANUFACTURED IN THE UNITED STATES OF AMERICA
10 9 8 7 6 5 4 3 2 1

iii

Contents

Foreword *v*

Highlights '90 *vii*

Fodor's Choice *x*

Introduction *xvi*

1 Essential Information *1*

Before You Go *2*

Visitor Information *2*
Tour Groups *2*
Package Deals for Independent Travelers *3*
Tips for British Travelers *3*
When to Go *4*
Festivals and Seasonal Events *5*
What to Pack *6*
Cash Machines *6*
Traveling with Film *7*
Traveling with Children *7*
Hints for Disabled Travelers *9*
Hints for Older Travelers *11*
Further Reading *13*

Arriving and Departing *13*

By Plane *13*
By Car *15*
Car Rentals *15*
By Train *15*
By Bus *15*

Staying in Las Vegas *15*

Important Addresses and Numbers *15*
Opening and Closing Times *16*
Getting Around Las Vegas *16*
Guided Tours *17*

2 Playing the Games *19*

"Blackjack," by Dennis R. Harrison *21*
"Casino Games and Slots," by *Gambling Times* *43*

3 Casinos *63*

4 Exploring Las Vegas *84*

Highlights for First-Time Visitors *85*
Tour 1: The Strip *85*

Contents iv

Tour 2: Downtown *91*
Las Vegas for Free *93*
What to See and Do with Children *94*
Off the Beaten Track *94*

Sightseeing Checklists *95*

Photographing Las Vegas *99*

Excursions from Las Vegas *102*

Excursion 1: Hoover Dam and Lake Mead *102*
Excursion 2: Valley of Fire *104*
Excursion 3: Laughlin, Nevada *104*
Excursion 4: Red Rock Canyon and Old Nevada *105*
Excursion 5: Mt. Charleston, Kyle and Lee Canyons *105*
Excursion 6: St. George, Zion National Park,
Bryce Canyon *106*

5 Shopping *108*

6 Sports and Fitness *115*

7 Dining *119*

8 Lodging *131*

9 Nightlife *147*

10 Reno and Lake Tahoe *158*

Index *183*

Maps

Nevada *xii*
Las Vegas *xiii*
World Time Zones *xiv–xv*
Las Vegas Strip Casinos *68*
Las Vegas Downtown Casinos *81*
Las Vegas Strip *86*
Las Vegas Downtown *92*
Lake Mead National Recreation Area *103*
Las Vegas Shopping *110*
Las Vegas Dining *122*
Las Vegas Lodging *134*
Reno *162*
Virginia City *165*
Reno Dining and Lodging *172*
Lake Tahoe *177*

Foreword

For a few weeks in 1989, when a major league baseball manager was accused of betting on sports events, Americans read and talked a lot about gambling, and many people realized for the first time that it had become a big business in the United States. In 1990 the racetrack and the bingo night have competition from statewide lotteries in 32 states, and economically troubled communities propose resolving their problems by introducing casino gambling or legalized sports betting.

Yet Nevada draws increasing crowds—and the principal share of the U.S. gambling dollar—with the great variety of its table games, the availability of sports betting, and the improved technology of video slot machines, which now account for almost 60% of casino gambling revenue. All-new casinos, with even newer slots, are preparing to open as this book goes to press, and another 12,000 hotel rooms are under construction.

What is the attraction of Las Vegas? Is it gambling alone, or is it the phenomenon of a city where gambling is a 24-hour production that colors and distorts the familiar activities of daily living? This year's completely rewritten edition of *Fodor's Las Vegas* may not answer that question for you, but it will help prepare you for the casinos, and it will suggest other activities and excursions for those who can tear themselves away from the slot machines.

This is an exciting time for Fodor's, as we continue our ambitious program to rewrite, reformat, and redesign all 140 of our guides. Here are just a few of the new features:

★ Brand-new computer-generated maps locating all the top attractions, hotels, restaurants, and shops

★ A unique system of numbers and legends to help readers move effortlessly between text and maps

★ A new star rating system for hotels and restaurants

★ Restaurant reviews by major food critics around the world

★ Stamped, self-addressed postcards, bound into every guide, give readers a chance to help evaluate hotels and restaurants

★ Complete page redesign for instant retrieval of information

★ FODOR'S CHOICE—Our favorite museums, beaches, cafes, romantic hideaways, festivals, and more

★ HIGHLIGHTS—An insider's look at the most important developments in tourism during the past year

★ TIME OUT—The best and most convenient lunch stops along exploring routes

★ A Traveler's Menu and Phrase Guide in all major foreign guides

★ Exclusive background essays create a powerful portrait of each destination

★ A mini-journal for travelers to keep track of their own itineraries and addresses

Foreword   vi

The author wishes to thank the following for their help and support: Stephen Allen, Dennis Michael, Tom Bruny, Paul Gilbert, George Knapp, Don Gugliemino, Debbie Munch, Melinda ("the First Lady of Magic"), Bonnie Saxe, Geno Munari, Sal Murillo, Steve Schiffman, "Nevada" Sam Graham, Ruth, Susan Weiss, Jack Curry, and Kitty Bean Yancey.

While every care has been taken to ensure the accuracy of the information in this guide, the passage of time will always bring change, and consequently the publisher cannot accept responsibility for errors that may occur.

All prices and opening times quoted here are based on information available to us at press time. Hours and admission fees may change, however, and the prudent traveler will avoid inconvenience by calling ahead.

Fodor's wants to hear about your travel experiences, both pleasant and unpleasant. When a hotel or restaurant fails to live up to its billing, let us know and we will investigate the complaint and revise our entries where the facts warrant it.

Send your letters to the editors of Fodor's Travel Publications, 201 E. 50th Street, New York, NY 10022.

Highlights '90 and Fodor's Choice

Highlights '90

A Gold Rush mentality in Las Vegas in the late 1980s led to the planning and construction of still more hotel-and-casino pleasure palaces and the expansion of several hotels.

The talk of the town at the end of 1989 was Steve Wynn's new $630 million showplace, **The Mirage,** which opened the day before Thanksgiving, hosted a $4.6 million Megabucks jackpot payoff on opening day, and two weeks later was the site of a super-middleweight title fight in a 16,000-seat stadium built for the occasion. Elsewhere on the 86-acre property are a 50-foot waterfall, palm trees and tropical plants, white tigers roaming a plastic-enclosed habitat, and lagoons that were scheduled to receive dolphins in the spring. The illusionists Siegfried and Roy have been signed for a long-term engagement in the Mirage showroom.

In June 1989 the Hilton organization opened the new two-story **O'Sheas Casino** to relieve crowding at the Flamingo Hilton next door; it has a Luck of the Irish motif and parking on the third story.

Rio Suites Hotel and Casino, the city's first all-suite hotel and casino, was readying 430 suites for inauguration in January 1990.

Spring 1990 was the target for the opening of the $300 million **Excalibur,** with 4,000 rooms, 100,000 square feet of casino space, and the appearance of a European castle. The Medieval motif extends to the shopping village, an entertainment dungeon, and roving performers.

New rooms have been added at the Sahara, Vegas World, the Lady Luck, the Flamingo Hilton, the Hacienda, Holiday Inn, Imperial Palace, and the Riviera.

Of the several casinos that have undergone changes in policy, the **Frontier Hotel and Gambling Hall** may have been the most transformed. A new owner instituted low minimums in the casino, closed the showroom and replaced it with a buffet, and added **Margarita's Mexican Cantina,** a new restaurant on the site of a former steak house.

One downtown casino, the Mint, simply disappeared when its next-door neighbor, **Binion's Horseshoe Hotel and Casino,** acquired it and expanded to incorporate it. The former Top of the Mint, a first-rate disco with great views, is now the **Skye Room.**

The city itself continues to pack in the visitors, with another 18 million expected in 1990. While automobile traffic is on the increase, however, city streets and roads remain as they were built, for a city half the size of today's Las Vegas, and there are frequent traffic snarls, especially during conven-

Highlights '90

tion weeks. The city fathers are trying to work out a solution to the problem; one possibility involves a central parking lot and shuttle bus service for hotel workers.

The long-delayed high-speed bullet train service between Los Angeles and Las Vegas won't be inaugurated until 1996 (at the earliest). The one-hour train ride will take passengers from downtown Los Angeles to downtown Las Vegas and back.

On the sports scene, the **Las Vegas Invitational** golf tournament has moved from spring to fall and now takes place in October on courses at the Desert Inn, the Las Vegas Country Club, and one other site.

Fodor's Choice

No two people will agree on what makes a perfect vacation, but it's fun and helpful to know what others think. We hope you'll have a chance to experience some of Fodor's Choices yourself while visiting Las Vegas. For detailed information about each entry, refer to the appropriate chapters in this guidebook.

Activities

Bowling at Sam's Town Hotel and Casino

Swimming in one of the biggest blue pools you'll ever see, at the Island of Vegas at the Tropicana

Moments

Watching the neon signs flicker as the sun goes down

Standing in the desert and looking back at metropolitan Las Vegas after you've gone five minutes west or east of the Strip

Wayne Newton saying, "You've been a very special audience"

Sights

The neon light show along Fremont Street downtown

Hoover Dam

Caesars Palace

One million dollars on display at Binion's Horseshoe

Circus Circus

Snacks

The Snickers ice cream concoction at Circus Circus

The $1 hot dog in the Dunes neon slot room

Free popcorn at the Slots-A-Fun casino

Hotels

Caesars Palace (*Very Expensive*)

Desert Inn Hotel and Casino (*Very Expensive*)

Barbary Coast Hotel and Casino (*Moderate*)

Gold Spike Hotel and Casino (*Inexpensive*)

Fodor's Choice

Restaurants

Ho Wan (Chinese, *Very Expensive)*

Alpine Village Inn and Rathskeller (German, *Moderate)*

Santa Fe (Mexican, *Moderate)*

The Flame (Steak house, *Moderate)*

Cafe Roma (Coffee shop, *Inexpensive–Moderate)*

The Golden Nugget (Buffet, *Inexpensive)*

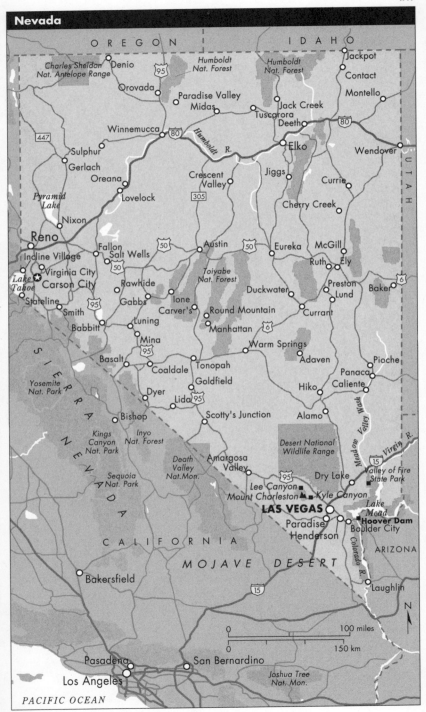

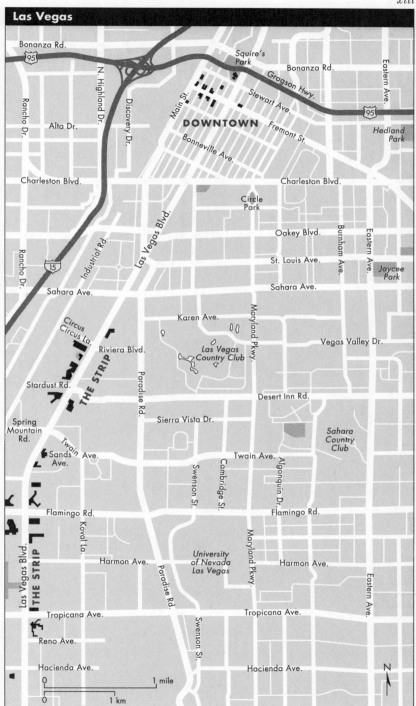

xiv

World Time Zones

Numbers below vertical bands relate each zone to Greenwich Mean Time (0 hrs.).
Local times may differ, as indicated by lightface numbers on the map.

Algiers, **29**	Berlin, **34**	Delhi, **48**	Istanbul, **40**
Anchorage, **3**	Bogotá, **19**	Denver, **8**	Jerusalem, **42**
Athens, **41**	Budapest, **37**	Djakarta, **53**	Johannesburg, **44**
Auckland, **1**	Buenos Aires, **24**	Dublin, **26**	Lima, **20**
Baghdad, **46**	Caracas, **22**	Edmonton, **7**	Lisbon, **28**
Bangkok, **50**	Chicago, **9**	Hong Kong, **56**	London (Greenwich), **27**
Beijing, **54**	Copenhagen, **33**	Honolulu, **2**	Los Angeles, **6**
	Dallas, **10**		Madrid, **38**
			Manila, **57**

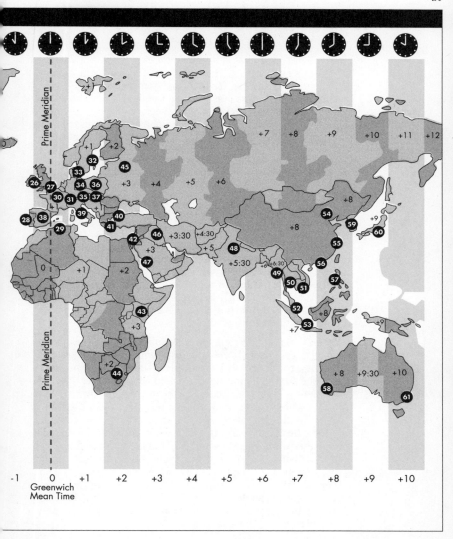

Mecca, **47**	Ottawa, **14**	San Francisco, **5**	Toronto, **13**
Mexico City, **12**	Paris, **30**	Santiago, **21**	Vancouver, **4**
Miami, **18**	Perth, **58**	Seoul, **59**	Vienna, **35**
Montreal, **15**	Reykjavík, **25**	Shanghai, **55**	Warsaw, **36**
Moscow, **45**	Rio de Janeiro, **23**	Singapore, **52**	Washington, DC, **17**
Nairobi, **43**	Rome, **39**	Stockholm, **32**	Yangon, **49**
New Orleans, **11**	Saigon, **51**	Sydney, **61**	Zürich, **31**
New York City, **16**		Tokyo, **60**	

Introduction

Let's recognize at the start that Las Vegas, a fantasy land for adults, exists for only one reason: *gambling*. Yes, there are museums and galleries here, but the truth is that everybody comes to Vegas to win or lose money, and as you walk or drive along Las Vegas Boulevard, you are constantly reminded of this. There are no supermarkets, post offices, movie theaters, or other familiar businesses of everyday life on the famous Strip; it's a place where you can buy a hamburger, get married, and lay a bet. In town you can stop in at a 7-Eleven or a supermarket at any hour and find people playing the slots across the aisle from the Cheerios and the Froot Loops.

While the Strip is the principal commercial area of the city, 700,000 people live—and lead normal lives—on the east and west sides of town. There you'll find rows and rows of three-bedroom houses, often with a mommy, daddy, two kids, and a car in a garage. What makes these homes a little different from those in other cities, however, is that in many of them Mommy is a show girl, Dad is a casino dealer, and both work nights rather than days.

Vegas is Sammy, Frank, and Dean, cards, dice, roulette wheels, and slots. It's cab drivers who have to know not only how to get around but who gives the best show in town. (It's the first question they're asked when visitors step off the plane and into the taxi.) The big men in this town, which has no widely known political leader, have been the flamboyant casino owners: Steve Wynn of the Golden Nugget, the late Benny Binion of the Horseshoe, and Paul Lowden of the Sahara. Vegas is show girls with smiles as bright as fireworks displays, a city where people make their living counting money or emptying coins from slot machines. And there are those who occupy the chairs in front of the slots, dropping countless coins into bottomless fountains, looking up only to accept a fresh drink from a cocktail waitress and to reward her with a quarter.

"Lost Wages" is a city of dreamers: gamblers hoping to beat the odds and get rich; dancers, singers, magicians, acrobats, and comedians seeking to "make it" in the Entertainment Capital of the World. At the same time, Las Vegas is a very religious town. The Utah border is just 90 minutes away, and the first major settler here was the Mormon leader Brigham Young. About one-third of the community is still Mormon, which is the largest organized religion in town, and consequently many community leaders frown on the concept of gambling, though they will agree to work in the "hospitality" industry.

Introduction   *xvii*

Gambling is not the only industry in Las Vegas—Nellis Air Force Base employs 8,000 people, and 6,000 more work at the Nevada Test Site—yet 80% of the Vegas work force labor in the "hospitality" industry. For all the local talk about Las Vegas citizens being average people who just happen to live and work in an unusual city, it must be admitted that there are differences here. Many people begin their day with breakfast at 2 PM. Others work virtually all day. A casino executive may start at noon, work through the afternoon dealing with management, go home for dinner, and return for the night shift, which is when the best customers arrive.

Some visitors may still believe that you can live in Vegas on gambling winnings and 49¢ breakfasts. While that can sometimes be the case, it's a rare occurrence. Most of those who work here choose to shut any thought of gambling out of their minds, for the odds are always against you, and everyone who lives here understands this. Gambling is the basis of the local economy, and for that reason the residents respect it, but they don't actively take part. Nevertheless there are those who will spend their loose change, their birthday money, even a paycheck at casinos built for locals; they just don't gamble for a living—or so they say.

Another popular misconception of Vegas concerns the ready availability of sexual favors. Bellhops are said to recommend call girls to guests, and one frequently hears thirdhand stories of unusual "room service" experiences. In fact, prostitution is against the law in Las Vegas, though a drive of less than an hour will take you to the town of Pahrump, due west of Vegas on Highway 160, where there are legal brothels.

The largest city in Nevada, Las Vegas is 2,162 feet above sea level. It is 45 minutes by car from the California and Arizona borders, 90 minutes from Utah. To the northwest, 448 miles away, is Reno, the city where gambling was first legalized, where the early casinos were built, and where the real power in the state lies.

The average daytime temperature in Las Vegas is 110 degrees during much of the year, and the colors of the sky can be quite rich in the afternoon, thanks to the western sun. At night the dark blue sky becomes a black background for the brightest lights in America: the red, turquoise, blue, pink, and green neon of the big casinos.

Las Vegas is also a small town, small enough that an entertainer with little experience can begin a career and go far. Melinda Saxe grew up wanting to be a magician. She worked for two years as a dancer in Siegfried and Roy's show "Beyond Belief." When she turned 21, she convinced the owners of the Bourbon Street Casino, a small property on Flamingo Road, to let her perform her magic in their 100-seat showroom. People came to see her. She worked the bugs out of her act. She became good. Today she stars at the Landmark in "Melinda's Follies Revue." All this happened

Introduction xviii

within a period of three years; could she have risen so fast in any other city?

Most people see Las Vegas as either the kitschiest place in the world or a town without rules where everyone can be free. The amazing success of the city has much to do with its appeal to those of all ages. Young people think the neon and the fantasy experience are "cool," and so do their parents and grandparents. For many, it's an adult Disneyland, where instead of climbing on fast, steep rides, they thrill to the fun of throwing dice, watching three 7s pop up on a slot, and being dealt a queen and an ace at the blackjack table.

Las Vegas sees itself as the Entertainment Capital of the World. Every hotel has nightly entertainment of some kind, whether it be a large-scale show ("Lido de Paris" at the Stardust), individual performers (Wayne Newton at the Las Vegas Hilton or female impersonators at the Sahara and Riviera), or lounge entertainment (everywhere). Those who want more active sport will find blackjack, craps, slot machines, roulette, baccarat, keno, red dog (acey-deucy), and even bingo offered at most gambling houses.

The food ranges from the cheapest—49¢ and 99¢ breakfasts, $3–$6 lunch buffets, $2 late-night steak dinners—to expensive "gourmet" fare, for which gentlemen wear jackets, ladies don gowns, and the chow may be Continental cuisine.

In Vegas you can find the tackiest souvenirs anywhere: dice clocks, inflatable Wayne Newton dolls, jack and queen playing-card earrings. You can take home gambling felt, decks of used casino cards, Vegas belt buckles, milk spouts in the shape of nipples. The Bally's men's shop has red, purple, green, even yellow blazers. At the same time, you'll find expensive furs, tuxedos, bikinis, and fashion clothing. That's Vegas—the cheesiest products sell almost side by side with the snazziest.

A drive through town will show you the greatest collection anywhere of neon sculpture and flashing light bulbs, especially on Fremont Street downtown. To the east, 25 minutes away, Hoover Dam is one of the seven man-made wonders of the world and Lake Mead is the largest man-made lake in the world. The desert nearby has yucca and Joshua trees galore; Mt. Charleston, Bryce Canyon, and Death Valley are a few hours out of town.

Before you enter the neon jungle of Vegas, you'll want to know a few important common local terms.

Toke. Short for token, or token of your esteem, a toke is a tip, and many of the folks you encounter will be expecting one. This may be the word you'll hear most often.

Introduction *xix*

Stiff. When you fail to toke your dealer or a cab driver, you might hear him mutter that you're a stiff. Not to worry; a contract has not been put out on you. You just happen to be the sort of person who doesn't believe in tipping.

Buy-in. The amount of cash money with which a player enters a game is the buy-in.

Checks. Everyone calls them chips but the dealers and the pit bosses; for some reason, casino personnel insist on calling casino chips "checks."

Click. This is the sound a pit boss makes, using a clicker, when he sees a player winning. The click is a signal to a cocktail waitress to deliver a drink to the player.

Juice. Juice is "influence," the ultimate Vegas intoxication. Politicians use juice daily to get what they want. "You scratch my back, and I'll scratch yours" is another way of putting it.

Comp. A gift from the casino of a complimentary drink, room, dinner, or show; a freebie.

RFB. Complimentary room, food, and beverage, courtesy of the casino. This is the ultimate Vegas status symbol.

High roller. A person with a good deal of money who looks for action (high-stakes games), and who drops thousands of dollars in a night without blinking.

Pit boss. The pit boss supervises the action on the gaming tables. His domain, called the pit, is an area surrounded by tables that is off-limits to the general public.

Shill. A shill is a person employed by the casino to sit at the tables and play games during the less busy hours. He poses as a player, but he plays with the casino's money. Casino bosses believe that gamblers are more comfortable playing at a table with other people rather than at an empty table.

Drop. When you exchange your folding money for checks at a gaming table, the dealer pushes the currency through a slot in the table, and it "drops" into a box beneath the table.

Grind joint. A grind joint is a gambling house that promotes cheap slots. It's a home no high roller would go near.

Las Vegas is a city in the middle of a desert. The nearest large city to the west, 90 minutes away, is Baker, California, with its row of motel rooms, fast-food restaurants, and gas stations. To the east, two hours away, is St. George, Utah, a gateway of sorts to Bryce Canyon. It's a small town of red rocks, gas stations, gift shops, and a mov-

Introduction xx

ie theater. Between the two, Las Vegas lives in isolation in the middle of the vast Nevada desert.

It's an amazing sight, on flying into Las Vegas, to watch a wide open space and see a cluster of glowing buildings appear out of nowhere. The sensation may be even greater for someone driving into the city: As you approach it, you'll first see the buildings of Vegas on turning a corner on Interstate 15, but you won't get there for another 20 minutes.

In the 1950s and 1960s Vegas had an atmosphere something like that of a resort: Men and women relaxed in the sun by day, changed for the evening, went out to dinner, then saw a show (and probably found opportunities to gamble during the day). In the nighttime they dressed in gowns and furs, jackets and ties. Those were the days of the high rollers, many of them oilmen who came to town without their wives and found that the hotel provided women to stand by them as they dropped their money at the tables through the night.

The days of the oilmen are over now, and what high rollers there are come chiefly from other countries, primarily from Asia. Las Vegas's widest appeal is to meat-and-potatoes, all-American visitors, all looking for cheap fun, pleasant accommodations, and maybe a show. These folks don't dress up, and no one expects them to. You can wear what you like in a Vegas casino, anything from a tux to T-shirt and shorts. (I once saw a barefoot woman playing roulette in bathrobe and curlers.) The casino bosses don't care what you look like, only what's inside your wallet.

L as Vegas is the largest American city founded in the 20th century (in 1905, though many would argue that the significant year was 1946, when Bugsy Siegel's Fabulous Flamingo opened for business). But the beginnings of Las Vegas lie in the 19th century, when Antonio Armijo led a party of 60 on the Old Spanish Trail to Los Angeles. While his caravan camped about 100 miles northeast of the present site of Las Vegas, a scouting party set out to look for water. Rafael Rivera, a young Mexican scout who left the main party and headed due west over the unexplored desert, discovered the oasis of the Las Vegas Springs. The abundance of the artesian spring water at Las Vegas shortened the Spanish trail to L.A. and eased the rigors of travel for the Spanish traders who used the route. Sometime between 1830 and 1848 the name Vegas, shown on maps of that day, became Las Vegas, Spanish for "the meadows." The area was named not for an abundance of meadows but for meadows that didn't exist!

The next major visitor to the Las Vegas Springs was John C. Fremont, leading his first overland expedition west. He was to lead four more expeditions between 1844 and 1854, and all of them stopped in Vegas. Today he is remembered

Introduction   *xxi*

fondly in the name of a hotel and the principal downtown thoroughfare.

The Mormons followed. In 1855, 30 Mormon settlers sent by Brigham Young from Salt Lake City began building a 150-square-foot adobe brick fort that still stands today. They intended to grow food and proselytize, but the desert heat killed all attempts at agriculture, and within two years they headed home.

Things didn't begin to start hopping here until 1905, when the northern Nevada mining boom shifted to the southern part of the state, in Tonopah, Goldfield, Rhyolite, and Searchlight, where silver and copper were abundant. A railroad stop that linked Las Vegas with Salt Lake and Los Angeles made Vegas the connection for trains to the four Nevada mining communities. By the end of the year Vegas had become a dusty railroad watering stop that consisted of tracks, tents, boardinghouses, stores, saloons, and Block 16—the only section of town where the sale of liquor was allowed and where the town's brothel was located.

The mining boom ended quickly, and the city fathers spent several years figuring out how to attract tourists. Their plans took shape in 1928 when the Boulder Canyon Project Act was signed into law, appropriating $165 million for the building of the world's largest antigravity dam.

Construction of the dam began in a historic year for Nevada. This was the year Governor Fred Balzar signed the "wide open" gambling bill that had been introduced by a Winnemucca rancher, Assemblyman Phil Tobin. Gambling had been legalized and outlawed many times since the beginning of Nevada, but Tobin was able to convince lawmakers to make it permanently legal. He maintained that it would be good for tourism and the state's economy; it was going to happen anyway, he argued, so why shouldn't the state tax gambling profits?

In the early 1930s Las Vegas was one of the rare towns that had lots of jobs when many Americans were looking for them. The construction of the dam on the Colorado River (bordering Arizona and Nevada) brought hundreds more job seekers to southern Nevada. Because the government didn't want dam workers to be distracted by the temptations of Las Vegas, it created a separate town, Boulder City, to house the workers. Today it remains the only city in Nevada where gambling is illegal.

At this time, with the state government located near Reno in Carson City and the major casinos (notably Harold's Club and Harrah's) in Reno, gambling power was based in northern Nevada. Then, with the dedication of the dam in 1936, came the electricity to light the neon signs that would become synonymous with Las Vegas. When the dam was finished, many of the workers stayed on, and gambling be-

Introduction xxii

gan to thrive on Fremont Street in Vegas, in the downtown area near the railroad station.

In 1941, on what is now Las Vegas Boulevard, the hotelier Tommy Hull had a flat tire. Watching all the cars go by, he realized it would be a great place for a hotel. He opened El Rancho Vegas, a western saloon with games and a home away from home for locals who wanted good, cheap chuck and blackjack. El Rancho's quick success led to the opening across the street of the Last Frontier the following year.

When the two gambling houses began making money, the gambling professionals—"the boys"—decided they wanted in. Benjamin "Bugsy" Siegel, who ran the New York mob's activities on the West Coast, saw Las Vegas in terms of legal speakeasies, places where gambling was legal and serious money could be made. He also saw that entertainment in a swank resort showplace could draw customers who would sample the heady wine of gambling and stay on through the night playing games and dropping money.

Siegel's Fabulous Flamingo was bankrolled by himself and his New York partners, Lucky Luciano and Meyer Lansky, for $6 million. It was a pink oasis surrounded by green palm trees in the middle of the desert. Siegel hired big-time entertainment; Jimmy Durante, Xavier Cugat, and Rose Marie opened the place on December 26, 1946. He figured the stars would attract his Hollywood friends, and others would come because they wanted to rub shoulders with the stars. Although the place was packed, business was terrible. Siegel paid out more money in winnings than he took in, and his New York partners got itchy. Six months later Bugsy Siegel was dead.

Ironically, once Siegel had been rubbed out, business at the Flamingo took off. Siegel's gangland assassination was front-page news across the country, and people wanted to see the house that Bugsy Siegel built.

The new success of the Flamingo led to the opening of other gambling houses, one after another. The Desert Inn, the Sands, the Sahara, the Riviera, the Dunes, the Fremont, the Tropicana, and the Stardust were all secretly financed at first with mob money. Every new hotel came on like a theme park opening for the summer with a new ride. Each was bigger, better, more unusual than the previous one. If the Riviera was the first nine-story building in town, the Sahara had the largest freestanding neon sign and the Stardust had the world's largest swimming pool.

The rumors of mob involvement and the sight of guys with Italian accents and big fedoras working the casinos added to the allure of Las Vegas. Customers loved to be around the boys, trying to decide whether or not they were mafiosi and

Introduction

knowing that trouble wouldn't start because Las Vegas was neutral territory. Fights would be bad for business.

In time the federal government cracked down, refusing to allow gangsters to run hotels as silent partners. It forced the state to take much firmer control of the regulation of gambling, and it threatened raids on casinos to weed out undesirables. Then, abruptly, in the middle of the night, an old man arrived on a train and soon revolutionized the nation's image of Las Vegas.

Howard Hughes had just sold TWA for $546 million and was considering what to do next. During a four-year stay in Vegas he bought the Desert Inn, Frontier, Landmark, and Silver Slipper hotels, a television station, and McCarran airfield. His presence in Las Vegas gave gambling its first positive image: As a former pilot, aviation pioneer, Hollywood mogul, and American folk hero, Hughes could in no way be connected with gangsters.

By 1969 the Hilton Corporation had continued the trend of legitimate corporate owners running gaming properties. With its purchase of the International (now the Las Vegas Hilton) and the Flamingo, Hilton became the first major hotel chain to join the gaming industry. Since then the Holiday Inn, Ramada, Viscount, Marriott, and Pratt Hotel chains have entered upon the Vegas playing field.

The bubble burst in the late 1970s with the legalization of gambling in Atlantic City. For the first time, gamblers had somewhere to play besides Las Vegas. Atlantic City was a much shorter trip for East Coast gamblers, most of whom were less than two hours away from New Jersey. Soon the Vegas economy was hurting; fewer folks were visiting at a time when airfares were rising and many hotels had decided to expand.

Then, as the recession of the early 1980s ended, airfares fell, more people came to Las Vegas, and the town thrived once more. Since 1988 Las Vegas has been enjoying a modern-day boom: Many new hotels have been constructed, and others have added new rooms. The city has deliberately diversified its appeal by promoting attractions that cater to families, and by marketing the lure of the showrooms more than that of the gaming tables. The tourism figures have been rising steadily—to 17 million visitors in 1988—and officials predict 20 million visitors and 2 million convention delegates in 1990.

At the start of the 1990s, Las Vegas has found a place for itself as a home for the young and the old, a destination for national and international tourists, and a weekend getaway for folks from California, Arizona, and Utah. The food's cheap, the entertainment's fun, and—who knows?— unlikely as we all know it is, you could go home a winner. In the back of everyone's mind is the thought that a trip to Las Vegas really doesn't cost anything, because if you win, the

Introduction

trip's paid for. And that's the kind of thinking that keeps the Vegas money men smiling as they add the finishing touches to their new multimillion-dollar hotels and renovations.

1 Essential Information

Before You Go

Visitor Information

For general information and brochures, contact the **Las Vegas Convention and Visitors Authority** (3150 Paradise Rd., Las Vegas, NV 89109, tel. 702/733–2323) or the **Las Vegas Chamber of Commerce** (2301 E. Sahara Ave., Las Vegas, NV 89104, tel. 702/457–4664). For maps and brochures on Las Vegas and the rest of Nevada, contact the **Nevada Commission on Tourism** (Capitol Complex, Carson City, NV 89710, tel. 800/638–2328).

Tour Groups

Joining a tour group has some advantages: Someone else worries about travel arrangements, accommodations, and baggage transfer; you are likely to save money on airfare, hotels, and ground transportation; and you will probably cover a lot of territory. The major disadvantages are that you'll have to adjust to someone else's schedule and pacing, and you won't be as free for independent explorations. Listed below are the major companies that serve the Las Vegas area; most of them offer combination Las Vegas/Grand Canyon packages. Consult your travel agent or the Las Vegas Convention and Visitors Authority (tel. 702/733–2323) for additional resources.

When considering a tour, be sure to find out (1) exactly what expenses are included, particularly tips, taxes, side trips, additional meals, and entertainment; (2) ratings of all hotels on the itinerary and the facilities they offer; (3) cancellation policies for both you and the tour operator; (4) the number of travelers in your group; and (5) if you are traveling alone, the cost of the single supplement. Most tour operators request that bookings be made through a travel agent, and in most cases there is no additional charge for doing so.

Many Las Vegas hotels offer package deals that can be even better than some tours.

General-Interest Tours
Affordable Las Vegas (400 W. Sahara Ave., Las Vegas, NV 89119, tel. 702/384–0026 or 800/999–9998).
American Express Vacations (Box 5014, Atlanta, GA 30302, tel. 800/241–1700 or, in GA, 800/282–0800).
AmeriWest Vacations (1150 E. University Ave., Tempe, AZ 85281, tel. 800/356–6611).
California Parlor Car Tours (515 S. Olive St., Los Angeles, CA 90017, tel. 800/227–4250).
Cosmos/Globus Gateway (150 S. Los Robles Ave., Suite 860, Pasadena, CA 91101, tel. 800/556–5454).
Domenico Tours (751 Broadway, Bayonne, NJ 07002, tel. 800/554–8687).
Far West Travel Corporation (4551 Glencoe Ave., Suite 205, Marina del Rey, CA 90292, tel. 800/553–1016).
Flair Tours, Inc. (6922 Hollywood Blvd., Suite 421, Hollywood, CA 90028, tel. 800/223–5247).
Great Escape (7855 Haskell Ave., Van Nuys, CA 91406, tel. 800/223–2929).

Special-Interest Tour
Casino Express (145 E. Reno St., Las Vegas, NV 89119, tel. 800/542–7433) offers a "Gambler's Maxi-Spree" that provides virtually free airline, hotel, food, drinks, and show packages

Tips for British Travelers 3

for gamblers who agree to play eight hours over the weekend on the dollar slot machines or at $5 per hand at the tables. (If you choose to play the slots and a slot calls for an investment of three coins in order to win the jackpot, you must insert all three coins.) The participating hotels are the Marina, Four Queens, and Landmark.

Package Deals for Independent Travelers

A wide range of packages is available for the independent traveler. Most airlines have packages that include car rental and lodging along with your flight. The major carriers offering these arrangements are American (tel. 800/433–7300), Delta (tel. 800/872–7786), Southwest (tel. 800/423–5683), TWA (tel. 800/438–2929), United (tel. 800/328–6877), and Piedmont/US Air (tel. 800/833–5436).

Hotels often have packages for weekends or during the off-season that include reduced airfare and room rates as well as complimentary meals and show tickets. Check with hotels when making reservations or consult the Las Vegas Convention and Visitors Authority (tel. 702/733–2323).

Tips for British Travelers

Passports and Visas You will need a valid, 10-year passport (cost £15) to enter the United States. You do not need a visa if you are staying for less than 90 days, have a return ticket, and are flying with a participating airline. There are some exceptions to this rule, so check with your travel agent or with the United States Embassy (Visa and Immigration Dept., 5 Upper Grosvenor St., London W1A 2JB, tel. 01/499–3443). No vaccinations are needed for entry into the United States.

Customs Visitors 21 and over can take in 200 cigarettes or 50 cigars or three pounds of tobacco; one U.S. quart of alcohol; and duty-free gifts to a value of $100. You cannot bring in meat or meat products, seeds, plants, or fruits. Avoid illegal drugs like the plague.

Returning to the United Kingdom, you may take home, if you are 17 or older: (1) 200 cigarettes or 100 cigarillos or 50 cigars or 250 grams of tobacco; (2) two liters of table wine and (a) one liter of alcohol over 22% by volume (most spirits), (b) two liters of alcohol under 22% by volume (fortified or sparkling wine), or (c) two more liters of table wine; (3) 50 grams of perfume and ¼ liter of toilet water; and (4) other goods up to a value of £32.

Insurance We recommend that you insure yourself against health and motoring mishaps. **Europ Assistance** (252 High St., Croydon, Surrey CRO 1NF, tel. 01/680–1234) is a firm that offers this service.

It is also wise to take out insurance to cover lost luggage (although check that such loss isn't already in any existing homeowner's policies you may have). Trip-cancellation insurance is also a good idea. **The Association of British Insurers** (Aldermary House, Queen St., London EC4, tel. 01/248–4477) will give you comprehensive advice on all aspects of holiday insurance.

Tour Operators The on-again, off-again price battle over transatlantic fares has meant that most tour operators now offer excellent budget packages to Las Vegas, usually in conjunction with tours to

Before You Go 4

other U.S. cities. Among those companies you might consider as you plan your trip are:

Albany Travel (Manchester) Ltd. (190 Deansgate, Manchester M3 3WD, tel. 061/833–0202).
American Airplan (Marlborough House, Churchfield Rd., Walton-on-Thames, Surrey KT12 2TJ, tel. 0932/246166).
Cosmosair (Tourama House, 17 Homesdale Rd., Bromley, Kent BR2 9LX, tel. 01/464–3400).
Jetsave (Sussex House, London Rd., East Grinstead, Sussex RH19 1LD, tel. 0342/312022).
Pan Am/Fly Drive (193 Piccadilly, London W1V 0AD, tel. 01/409–3377).
Speedbird (152 King St., London W6 0QU, tel. 01/741–8041).
Thomas Cook Ltd. (Box 36, Thorpe Wood, Peterborough PE3 6SB, tel. 0733/503202).

Airfares Airlines flying to Las Vegas include British Airways, TWA, Continental, and Virgin Atlantic. In the summer of 1989 a low-season return APEX fare was £424.

Thomas Cook Ltd. can often book you on very inexpensive flights. Ring the Cook branch nearest you and ask to be put through to the Airfare Warehouse. Be sure to ring at least 21 days in advance of when you want to travel.

Also check out the small ads in magazines such as *Time Out* and in the Sunday newspapers, where flights are offered for as low as £235 return.

Electricity 110 volts. You should take along an adaptor because American razor and hair-dryer socket outlets require flat, two-pronged plugs.

When to Go

The busy seasons in Vegas are in the spring and the fall. In April and May the daytime temperatures are in the comfortable 80s and the city is only semicrowded. The Las Vegas you've read about and seen pictured in the ads—women lying by the pools, saxophone players performing on the street, neon shining brightly—begins when the pools open in the spring.

In September, October, and November the summer crowds and the heat have abated and the pools remain open.

Winter is a distinctly different season, with snowcapped mountains in the distance, windy and chilly days, and a peace and quiet that will give you some idea of what Vegas was like in the days before the casinos. The week before Christmas finds most visitors gone, rooms at bargain rates, and never a traffic jam on the Strip.

Summer is a time of dry, uncomfortably hot weather (110 degrees in the shade) when lounging at an outdoor pool requires protection from the relentless desert sun. You'll probably find yourself thirstier than you can remember.

Climate What follows are the average daily maximum and minimum temperatures for Las Vegas.

Festivals and Seasonal Events 5

Jan.	60F	16C	May	89F	32C	Sept.	95F	35C
	28	-2		51	11		57	14
Feb.	66F	19C	June	98F	37C	Oct.	84F	29C
	33	1		60	16		46	8
Mar.	71F	22C	July	102F	39C	Nov.	71F	22C
	39	4		68	20		35	2
Apr.	80F	27C	Aug.	102F	39C	Dec.	60F	16C
	44	7		66	19		30	-1

Current weather information for more than 500 cities around the world may be obtained by calling the WeatherTrak information service at 900/370–8728 or, in TX, 900/575–8728. A taped message will tell you to dial a three-digit access code for the destination you're interested in. The code is either the area code (in the United States) or the first three letters of the foreign city. For a list of all access codes, send a self-addressed, stamped envelope to Cities, Box 7000, Dallas, TX 75209. For further information, phone 214/869–3035 or 800/247–3282.

Festivals and Seasonal Events

Las Vegas is not known for seasonal celebrations—the major gathering, on the Strip, is a continuous affair—yet there are a number of annual events that attract wide attention. For specific dates and information on other attractions, contact **Las Vegas Events** (tel. 702/731–2115) for the three-month calendar of events it publishes.

Apr.: Binion's Nissan Mint 400 is a daylong dirt road race in the desert that finishes with 400 cars zooming down Fremont Street. The prizes are awarded at a ceremony downtown on the following morning. *Tel. 702/366–7397.*

Apr.: Clark County Fair takes place 60 miles north of Las Vegas, in Logandale. *Tel. 702/477–0123.*

Apr. or May: World Series of Poker draws crowds to the Horseshoe casino to watch the poker faces of players from around the world, each investing $10,000 and participating for 22 days (or until their luck runs out) in the biggest poker game in the world. *Tel. 702/366–7397.*

Early May: Senior Classic golf tournament at the Desert Inn (four days), formerly a fall event, now takes place in the spring. *Tel. 702/382–6616.*

June: Helldorado Days and Rodeo celebrates the Old West with parades, contests, western costumes, and a championship rodeo at the Thomas and Mack Center. *Tel. 702/870–1221.*

Early Sept.: The Jerry Lewis Muscular Dystrophy Telethon on Labor Day weekend welcomes live audiences to the newly named Jerry Lewis Theater at Cashman Field. *Tel. 702/731–7110.*

Mid-Oct.: Las Vegas Invitational golf tournament, now a five-day fall event, is played on three courses, with television coverage. *Tel. 702/382–6616.*

Early Dec.: National Finals Rodeo brings together 15 finalists to compete in each of seven events; there are 10 performances in nine days at the Thomas and Mack Center. When the rodeo comes to town, the showrooms all feature country music, and it seems as though everyone on the street is wearing jeans, boots, and a cowboy hat. *Tel. 702/731–2115.*

Dec. 31: New Year's Eve is celebrated with fireworks over Fre-

Before You Go 6

mont Street in downtown Las Vegas, televised nationally. *Tel. 702/382–6397.*

What to Pack

Clothing When Bugsy Siegel first advertised his Fabulous Flamingo in 1946, he said, "Come as you are," and the advice is still good. The warm weather and informal character of Las Vegas make casual clothing appropriate all day long. Some people will prefer to dress for the evening—the women wearing cocktail dresses and the men jacket and tie. Lightweight clothing can be worn all year, but you'll want to have a light jacket for the cooler evenings and a sweater during the late fall and winter months.

Comfortable shoes for walking are a must; no matter what your intentions may be, you'll find yourself covering a lot of ground on foot. Those who pack light, using a small amount of luggage they can carry by themselves, will avoid long waits for the transfer of luggage to and from hotel rooms on arrival and departure.

Carry-on Luggage Passengers on U.S. airlines are usually limited to two carry-on bags. For a bag you wish to store under the seat, the maximum dimensions are 9″ x 14″ x 22″. For bags that can be hung in a closet or on a luggage rack, the maximum dimensions are 4″ x 23″ x 45″. For bags you wish to store in an overhead bin, the maximum dimensions are 10″ x 14″ x 36″. Any item that exceeds the specified dimensions may be rejected as a carryon and taken as checked baggage. Keep in mind that an airline can adapt these rules to circumstances, and on an especially crowded flight you may be allowed only one carry-on bag.

In addition to the two carryons, you may bring aboard a handbag (pocketbook or purse), an overcoat or wrap, an umbrella, a camera, a reasonable amount of reading material, an infant bag, crutches, cane, braces, or other prosthetic device, and an infant/child safety seat.

Note that these regulations are for U.S. airlines only. Foreign airlines generally allow only one piece of carry-on luggage in tourist class, in addition to handbags and bags filled with duty-free goods. Passengers in first and business class are also allowed to carry on one garment bag. It is best to call your airline in advance to learn its rules regarding carry-on luggage.

Checked Luggage Luggage allowances vary slightly from airline to airline. Many carriers allow three checked pieces; some allow only two. Again, it is best to check before you go. In all cases, each piece of check-in luggage cannot weigh more than 70 pounds or be larger than 62 inches (length + width + height).

Cash Machines

Virtually all U.S. banks now belong to a network of Automatic Teller Machines (ATMs) that dispense cash 24 hours a day. There are eight major networks in the United States; the largest are Cirrus, owned by MasterCard, and Plus, affiliated with Visa. Some banks belong to more than one network. Each network has a toll-free number you can call to locate its machines in a given city. The Cirrus number is 800/424–7787; Plus is 800/

Traveling with Children

843–7587. Note that these "cash cards" are not issued automatically; they must be requested at the branch at which you bank.

Cards issued by Visa, American Express, and MasterCard can also be used in the ATMs, but the fees are usually higher than the fees on bank cards (and there is a daily interest charge on the "loan"). All three companies issue directories that list the national and international outlets that accept their cards. You can pick up a Visa or MasterCard directory at your local bank. For an American Express directory, call 800/227–4669 (this number can also be used for general inquiries). Contact your bank for information on fees and the amount of cash you can withdraw on any given day. Although each bank individually charges for taking money with the card, using your American Express, Visa, or MasterCard at an ATM can be cheaper than exchanging money in a bank because of variations in exchange rates.

While cash and credit cards will be useful, don't expect to be able to cash a personal check in Las Vegas. Local merchants have been burned too many times by desperate gamblers to trust anyone.

Traveling with Film

If your camera is new, shoot and develop a few rolls before leaving home. Pack some lens tissue and an extra battery for your built-in light meter. Invest about $10 in a skylight filter and screw it onto the front of your lens; it will protect the lens and also reduce haze.

Film doesn't like hot weather. If you're driving in summer, don't store film in the glove compartment or on the shelf under the rear window. Put it behind the front seat on the floor, on the side opposite the exhaust pipe.

On a plane trip, never pack unprocessed film in checked luggage; if your bags are X-rayed, say goodbye to your pictures. Always carry undeveloped film with you through security and ask to have it inspected by hand. (It helps to isolate your film in a plastic bag, ready for quick inspection.) Inspectors at American airports are required by law to honor requests for hand inspection; abroad, you'll have to depend on the kindness of strangers.

The old airport scanning machines—still in use in some countries—use heavy doses of radiation that can turn a family portrait into an early morning fog. The newer models—used in all U.S. airports—are safe for anything from five to 500 scans, depending on the speed of your film. The effects are cumulative: You can put the same roll of film through several scans without worry; after five scans, though, you're asking for trouble.

If your film gets fogged and you want an explanation, send it to the National Association of Photographic Manufacturers (600 Mamaroneck Ave., Harrison, NY 10528). They will try to determine what went wrong. The service is free.

Traveling with Children

Publications   *Family Travel Times* is an 8- to 12-page newsletter published 10 times a year by TWYCH (Travel with Your Children, 80 8th

Before You Go 8

Ave., New York, NY 10011, tel. 212/206–0688). The $35 subscription includes access to back issues and twice-weekly opportunities to call in for specific information. Send $1 for a sample issue.

Great Vacations with Your Kids, by Dorothy Jordan (founder of TWYCH) and Marjorie Cohen, offers complete advice on planning a trip with children (toddlers to teens) and reports on special travel accommodations available to families ($9.95 paperback, E. P. Dutton, 2 Park Ave., New York, NY 10016, tel. 212/725–1818; a new edition was scheduled to appear in January 1990 for $11.95).

Family Travel Guides (Carousel Press, Box 6061, Albany, CA 94706, tel. 415/527–5849) is a catalogue offering guidebooks, games, diaries, and magazine articles geared to traveling with children. To receive the catalogue, send $1 for postage and handling.

Kids and Teens in Flight is a brochure on children traveling alone, developed by the Department of Transportation. To order a free copy, call 202/366–2220.

Getting There On domestic flights, children under 2 not occupying a seat travel free. Various discounts apply to children 2–12. Reserve a seat behind the bulkhead of the plane, which offers more legroom and can usually fit a bassinet (supplied by the airline). At the same time, inquire about special children's meals or snacks, offered by most airlines. (See "TWYCH's Airline Guide" in the February 1988 issue of *Family Travel Times* for a rundown on children's services furnished by 46 airlines; an update is planned for February 1990.) Ask your airline in advance if you can bring aboard your child's car seat. For the pamphlet "Child/Infant Safety Seats Acceptable for Use in Aircraft," write to the Community and Consumer Liaison Division (APA-200, Federal Aviation Administration, Washington, DC 20591, tel. 202/267–3479).

Hotels In addition to offering family discounts and special rates for children (for example, some large hotel chains don't charge extra for children under 12 when they stay in their parents' room), many hotels and resorts arrange for baby-sitting services and run a variety of special children's programs. If you are going to be traveling with your children, be sure to check with your travel agent for more information, or ask a hotel representative about children's programs when you make your reservations. The Nevada Commission on Tourism's accommodation guide lists Las Vegas hotels that have a children's game room (Capitol Complex, Carson City, NV 89710, tel. 800/638–2328).

Baby-sitting Services Make your child-care arrangements with the hotel concierge or housekeeper. Many hotels offer a licensed baby-sitting service (see the hotel directory), but the best deal may be that at the Las Vegas Hilton (3000 W. Paradise Rd., tel. 702/732–5111) and the Hilton Youth Hotel. While you visit the casino downstairs, your kids (ages 3–18) play, snack, and eat with counselors in a special dorm, where they can also spend the night.

Three local agencies are the Las Vegas Babysitting Agency (tel. 702/457–3777), which charges $6 an hour ($24 minimum); Reliable Babysitting (tel. 702/451–7507), which charges $4.50

Hints for Disabled Travelers

an hour ($22 minimum) for one or two children; and Sandy's Sitter Service (tel. 702/731-2086).

Hints for Disabled Travelers

Organizations   **Evergreen Travel Service** (19505L 44th Ave. W, Lynnwood, WA 98036, tel. 206/776-1184 or 800/435-2288) has been specializing in unique tours for the handicapped and blind for 33 years.

HELP of Southern Nevada (tel. 702/369-4357) refers callers to the proper social agency.

The Information Center for Individuals with Disabilities (Fort Point Place, 27-43 Wormwood St., Boston, MA 02217, tel. 617/727-5540) offers useful problem-solving assistance, including lists of travel agents who specialize in tours for the disabled.

Mobility International (Box 3551, Eugene, OR 97403, tel. 503/343-1284) is a membership organization ($20 annual fee) offering information on accommodations and organized study around the world.

Moss Rehabilitation Hospital Travel Information Service (12th St. and Tabor Rd., Philadelphia, PA 19141, tel. 215/329-5715) provides information on tourist sites, transportation, and accommodations in destinations around the world. The fee is $5 for up to three destinations. Allow one month for delivery.

The National Park Service provides a Golden Access Passport free of charge to those who are medically blind or have a permanent disability. The passport covers the entry fee for the holder and anyone accompanying the holder in the same private (non-commercial) vehicle and provides a 50% discount on camping, boat launching, and parking. All charges are covered except lodging. Apply for the passport in person at any national recreation facility that charges an entrance fee; proof of disability is required. For additional information, write to the National Park Service (U.S. Dept. of the Interior, 18th and C Sts. NW, Washington, DC 20240).

Nevada Association for the Handicapped (6200 W. Oakey Blvd., Las Vegas 89102, tel. 702/870-7050) refers callers to agencies serving the disabled.

The Society for the Advancement of Travel for the Handicapped (26 Court St., Brooklyn, NY 11242, tel. 718/858-5483) offers access information. Annual membership costs $40; $25 for senior travelers and students. Nonmembers may send $2 and a self-addressed, stamped envelope to obtain information on a specific country.

The Society for Nevada Sightless (1001 N. Bruce St., Las Vegas 89101, tel. 702/642-6000) provides general information and transportation assistance.

Travel Industry and Disabled Exchange (5435 Donna Ave., Tarzana, CA 91356, tel. 818/343-6339) is an industry-based organization with a $15 (per person) annual membership fee. Members receive a quarterly newsletter and information on travel agencies and tours.

Transportation   **Amtrak** (tel. 800/USA-RAIL) requests 72-hour notice to provide redcap service, special seats, or wheelchair assistance at stations equipped for this service. All handicapped and elderly passengers are entitled to a 25% discount on regular,

Before You Go 10

nondiscounted coach fares. A special children's handicapped fare is also available, offering qualifying children ages 2–11 a 25% discount on their already discounted children's fare. It should be noted that there are exceptions to these discounts on certain prescribed days on some routes. Always check with Amtrak first. For a free copy of "Access Amtrak," a guide to its services for elderly and handicapped travelers, write to Amtrak (National Railroad Corporation, 400 N. Capitol St. NW, Washington, DC 20001).

The Economic Opportunity Board (tel. 702/646–4203), a government-funded office, will transport handicapped and elderly passengers in Las Vegas from anywhere except the airport and the casinos. A small fee is charged, and 24-hour notice is required.

Greyhound Lines (tel. 800/531–5332) will carry a disabled person and companion for the price of a single fare.

Publications **Access America: An Atlas and Guide to the National Parks for Visitors with Disabilities** (Northern Cartographic, Box 133, Burlington, VT 05402, tel. 801/655–4321) contains detailed information about access for the 37 largest and most visited national parks in the United States. It costs $89.95 plus $5 shipping. Individuals or nonprofit organizations may order directly from the publisher for $67.45 plus $5 shipping.

Access to the World: A Travel Guide for the Handicapped, by Louise Weiss, offers tips on travel and accessibility around the world. It is available from Henry Holt & Co. (tel. 800/247–3912) for $12.95 plus $2 shipping; the order number is 0805 001417.

Access Travel, published in 1985 by the U.S. Office of Consumer Affairs, is a free brochure that lists design features, facilities, and services for the handicapped at 519 airport terminals in 62 countries. Order publication 570V by writing to S. James, Consumer Information Center-K, Box 100, Pueblo, CO 81002.

The Itinerary (Box 1084, Bayonne, NJ 07002, tel. 201/858–3400) is a respected bimonthly travel magazine for the disabled. Call for a subscription ($10 for one year, $18 for two); it's not available in stores.

Nevada Commission on Tourism (Capitol Complex, Carson City, NV 89710, tel. 800/638–2328) publishes an accommodations guide that includes access information for Las Vegas hotels.

Twin Peaks Press (Box 129, Vancouver, WA 98666, tel. 206/694–2462 or 800/637–2256 for orders only) specializes in books for the disabled. *Travel for the Disabled* ($9.95) offers helpful hints as well as a comprehensive list of guidebooks and facilities geared to the disabled. *Directory of Travel Agencies for the Disabled* ($12.95) lists more than 350 agencies throughout the world. *Wheelchair Vagabond* ($9.95) helps independent travelers plan for extended trips in cars, vans, or campers. Twin Peaks also offers a Traveling Nurse's Network that provides registered nurses trained in all medical areas to accompany and assist disabled travelers.

Accommodations Generally, the layouts of most hotels and casinos require that you walk long distances to get around in them. The following hotels take into account the special needs of the physically disa-

Hints for Older Travelers 11

bled with wheelchair-accessible accommodations: Bally's Casino Resort (3645 Las Vegas Blvd. S, tel. 702/739–4111), Barbary Coast Hotel and Casino (3595 Las Vegas Blvd. S, tel. 702/737–7111), Caesars Palace (3570 Las Vegas Blvd. S, tel. 702/731–7110), The Flamingo Hilton and Tower (3555 Las Vegas Blvd. S, tel. 702/733–3111), Four Queens Hotel and Casino (200 E. Fremont St., tel. 702/385–4011), Golden Nugget Hotel and Casino (129 E. Fremont St., tel. 702/385–7111), Hacienda Hotel and Casino (3950 Las Vegas Blvd. S, tel. 702/739–8911), Lady Luck Casino and Hotel (206 N. 3rd St., tel. 702/384– 4680), Las Vegas Club Hotel and Casino (18 E. Fremont St., tel. 702/385–1664), Las Vegas Hilton (3000 W. Paradise Rd., tel. 702/732–5111), Sam's Town Hotel and Casino (5111 W. Boulder Hwy., tel. 702/456–7777), and the Union Plaza Hotel (1 Main St., tel. 702/386–2110).

Hints for Older Travelers

Organizations **The American Association of Retired Persons** (1990 K St. NW, Washington, DC 20049, tel. 202/872–4700) offers independent travelers a Purchase Privilege Program that entitles members to discounts on hotels, airfare, car rentals, and sightseeing. The AARP Travel Service also arranges group tours in conjunction with two companies: Olson-Travelworld (100 N. Sepulvedo Blvd., El Segundo, CA 90245, tel. 800/227–7737) and RFD, Inc. (4401 W. 110th St., Overland Park, KS 66211, tel. 800/448–7010). AARP members must be at least 50 years old. Annual dues are $5 per person or per couple.

If you plan to use an AARP or another senior-citizen identification card to obtain a reduced hotel rate, mention it at the time you make your reservation, not when you check out. At restaurants, show your card to the maître d' before you are seated; discounts may be limited to certain set menus, days, or hours. Your AARP card will identify you as a retired person, but it will not ensure a discount in all hotels and restaurants. For a free list of hotels and restaurants that offer discounts, call or write to the AARP and ask for the "Purchase Privilege" brochure or call the AARP Travel Service. When renting a car, remember that economy cars, priced at promotional rates, may cost less than the cars that are available with your ID card.

The Economic Opportunity Board (tel. 702/646–4203) arranges transportation in Las Vegas for elderly passengers from anywhere except the airport and the casinos. A small fee is charged, and 24-hour notice is required.

Elderhostel (80 Boylston St., Suite 400, Boston, MA 02116, tel. 617/426–7788) is an innovative program for people 60 or over (only one member of a traveling couple has to qualify). Participants live in dormitories on some 1,200 campuses around the world. Mornings are devoted to lectures and seminars, afternoons to sightseeing and field trips. The fee for a trip includes room, board, tuition (in the United States and Canada), and round-trip transportation (overseas). Special scholarships are available for those in the United States and Canada who qualify financially.

The Golden Age Passport is a free lifetime pass to all parks, monuments, and recreation areas run by the federal govern-

Before You Go 12

ment. Any permanent U.S. resident over 62 may pick one up in person at any national park that charges admission. The passport covers the entrance fee for the holder and anyone accompanying the holder in the same private (noncommercial) vehicle. It also provides a 50% discount on camping, boat launching, and parking. Lodging is not included. Proof of age is necessary.

Mature Outlook (6001 N. Clarke St., Chicago, IL 60660, tel. 800/336–6330), a subsidiary of Sears, Roebuck & Co., is a travel club for people over 50 years of age that offers discounts at Holiday Inns and a bimonthly newsletter. Annual membership is $9.95 per person or couple. Instant membership is available at participating Holiday Inns.

National Council of Senior Citizens (925 15th St. NW, Washington, DC 20005, tel. 202/347–8800) is a nonprofit advocacy group with some 4,000 local clubs across the country. Annual membership is $10 per person or $14 per couple. Members receive a monthly newspaper with travel information and an ID for reduced rates on hotels and car rentals.

Saga International Holidays (120 Boylston St., Boston, MA 02116, tel. 800/343–0273) specializes in group travel for people over 60 and has a variety of tour packages at various prices.

September Days Club (tel. 800/241–5050) is run by the moderately priced Days Inns of America. The $12 annual membership fee for individuals or couples over 50 entitles them to reduced car-rental rates and reductions of 15%–50% at most of the chain's more than 350 motels. Members also receive *Travel Holiday Magazine Quarterly*, which contains updated information and travel articles.

Vantage Travel Service (111 Cypress St., Brookline, MA 02146, tel. 800/322–6677) offers land and cruise tours geared toward senior citizens. Nonsenior adult relatives and friends are welcome.

Transportation **Greyhound Lines** (tel. 800/531–5332) offers special fares for senior citizens; these fares are subject to date and destination restrictions.

Amtrak (*see* Hints for Disabled Travelers, above).

Publications *The Discount Guide for Travelers over 55,* by Caroline and Walter Weintz, lists helpful addresses, package tours, reduced-rate car-rental agencies, etc., in the United States and abroad. To order, send $7.95 to NAL/Cash Sales (Bergenfield Order Dept., 120 Woodbine St., Bergenfield, NJ 07021, tel. 800/526–0275).

The Senior Citizens Guide to Budget Travel in the United States and Canada, by Paige Palmer, is available for $3.95 plus $1 shipping from Pilot Books (103 Cooper St., Babylon, NY 11702, tel. 516/422–2225).

Travel Tips for Senior Citizens (U.S. Department of State Publication 8970, revised September 1987) is available for $1 from the Superintendent of Documents (U.S. Government Printing Office, Washington, DC 20402, tel. 202/783–3238).

By Plane

Further Reading

A. Alvarez's *The Best Game in Town* gives a vivid account of the Horseshoe's annual World Series of Poker and the guys who come from around the world to invest $10,000 in the tournament, hoping to walk away 22 days later as the "poker king of the year."

Mario Puzo's novel *The Godfather* describes the building of Las Vegas in the 1940s by the mob and the Corleone family's rubout of Moe Green, the character modeled on Bugsy Siegel.

Omar Garrison's *Howard Hughes in Las Vegas* tells the story of one of the city's most enterprising residents, the man who legitimized corporate investment in gambling, a man who lived for four years on the ninth floor of the Desert Inn, refusing to leave or to be seen in public.

Ovis Demaris and Ed Reid's *The Green Felt Jungle* shocked the nation in the early 1960s with its account of how the mob built Las Vegas and had a hand in virtually every hotel and casino built during the 1940s and 1950s.

Arriving and Departing

By Plane

When booking a flight, air travelers will want to keep in mind the distinction between *nonstop flights* (your destination is the only scheduled stop), *direct flights* (one or more stops are scheduled before you reach your destination), and *connecting flights* (you'll stop and change planes before you reach your destination).

Airport McCarran International Airport (tel. 702/739–5743), a large modern facility that is one of the 20 busiest airports in the country, is situated 5 miles south of the business district and immediately east of the southern end of the Strip on Las Vegas Boulevard. The principal approach to McCarran is Paradise Road (from the northeast), while the air-charter terminal is reached from Las Vegas Boulevard. Slot machines in the main terminal allow eager travelers to get right to work, but the airport slots don't return as much money as do slots in the casinos.

Airlines The principal airlines serving Las Vegas are Air Nevada (tel. 702/736–8900), American (tel. 702/385–3781 or 800/433–7300), America West (tel. 702/736–1737 or 800/247–5692), Braniff (tel. 800/272–6433), Continental (tel. 702/385–8291 or 800/525–0280), Delta (tel. 702/731–3111 or 800/221–1212), Hawaiian Air (tel. 702/739–0630 or 800/367–5320), TWA (tel. 702/385–1000 or 800/438–2929), United (tel. 702/385–3222 or 800/631–1500), and USAir (tel. 702/382–1905 or 800/428–4322).

Smoking Smoking is not allowed on domestic flights within the 48 contiguous states; within the states of Hawaii and Alaska; to and from the U.S. Virgin Islands and Puerto Rico; and on flights of under six hours to and from Hawaii and Alaska. The rule applies to both U.S. and foreign carriers.

On domestic and international flights where smoking is permitted, Department of Transportation regulations require that all U.S. airlines provide seats in a nonsmoking section for passen-

Arriving and Departing 14

gers who request them on booking their tickets or during an on-time check-in. The Department of Transportation does not have jurisdiction over foreign carriers traveling into or out of the United States.

Lost Luggage Loss of luggage is usually covered as part of a comprehensive travel-insurance package that includes personal accident, trip cancellation, and sometimes default and bankruptcy insurance. Several companies offer comprehensive policies:

Access America, Inc., a subsidiary of Blue Cross/Blue Shield (600 3rd Ave., Box 807, New York, NY 10163, tel. 212/490–5345 or 800/284–8300).

Near Services (1900 N. MacArthur Blvd., Suite 210, Oklahoma City, OK 73127, tel. 405/949–2500 or 800/654–6700).

Luggage Insurance Airlines are responsible for lost or damaged property only up to values of $1,250 per passenger for checked baggage on domestic flights, $9.07 per pound ($20 per kilo) for checked baggage on international flights, and $400 per passenger for carry-on baggage on international flights. If you're traveling with valuables, either take them with you on the airplane or purchase additional lost-luggage insurance. Some airlines will issue additional insurance when you check in, but many do not. Rates are $1 for each $100 of valuation, with a maximum $400 valuation per passenger. Hand luggage is not included.

Insurance for lost, damaged, or stolen luggage is available through travel agents or directly from insurance companies. Two companies that issue luggage insurance are **Tele-Trip** (3201 Farnam St., Omaha, NE 68131, tel. 800/228–9792), a subsidiary of Mutual of Omaha, and **The Travelers Insurance Co.** (Ticket and Travel Plans Dept., 1 Tower Sq., Hartford, CT 06183, tel. 201/277–2318 or 800/243–3174). Tele-Trip, which operates sales booths at airports and also issues policies through travel agents, insures checked luggage for up to 180 days, for valuations of $500 to $3,000. For one to three days, the rate for a $500 valuation is $8.25; for 180 days, $100. The Travelers Insurance Co. insures checked or hand luggage for valuations of $500 to $2,000 per person, also for a maximum of 180 days. Rates for a valuation of $500 are $10 for up to five days, $85 for up to 180 days. Both companies offer the same rates on domestic and international flights. Consult the travel pages of your local newspaper for the names of other companies that insure luggage.

Before you travel, itemize the contents of each bag in case you need to file an insurance claim. Be certain to label each piece of luggage, including carry-on bags, with your name and home address. If your luggage is stolen and later recovered, the airline must deliver that luggage to your home free of charge.

Between the Airport and Hotels *By Taxi* Metered taxicab service awaits your arrival at the airport. The fare is $1.70 for the first fraction of a mile and 20¢ for each additional ⅐ mile. When there are more than three passengers in the cab, there's an additional charge of 20¢ per mile. The trip to most hotels on the Strip should cost less than $10; the trip downtown should be around $15. Drivers are also a source of information on Vegas nightlife, and they can recommend shows, performers, and restaurants.

Important Addresses and Numbers   15

By Limousine   A limo from the airport to your hotel, shared with other riders, costs $3 per person to the Strip, $4.50 to downtown. The limos wait for passengers outside the terminal, along with the cabs. Private limousine service is available from Lucky 7 (tel. 702/739–6177), Bell Trans (tel. 702/736–4428), and Presidential (tel. 702/731–5577).

By Car

Approximately half of the visitors to Las Vegas arrive by automobile. The principal highway is Interstate 15, which brings motorists from southern California in the southwest and Utah in the northeast. U.S. 93 (Boulder Highway and Fremont Street in Las Vegas) extends into Arizona in the southeast, where it connects with Interstate 40. U.S. 95 brings traffic from northern California, Reno, and Interstate 80 in the northwest.

Drivers en route to Las Vegas should keep in mind, when there's an opportunity to fill up, that the next gas station can be an hour's travel time away. Arrival by car in Vegas allows you the pleasure of seeing the tall buildings rise out of a flat, empty desert about 15 minutes before you reach the city.

Car Rentals

Rental cars are available from Hertz (tel. 702/736–4900 or 800/654–3131), which has offices at the airport, the Desert Inn, and Union Plaza; Avis (tel. 702/739–5595 or 800/331–1212), which has offices at the airport, Bally's, Caesars Palace, and the Las Vegas Hilton; and Alamo (tel. 702/737–3111 or 800/327–9633), the only national chain that offers no mileage charge on rentals, so it may be a sensible choice if you plan an excursion to Bryce Canyon, Hoover Dam, Lake Mead, or Mt. Charleston.

By Train

Amtrak (tel. 800/USA–RAIL) offers nationwide service to Las Vegas's Union Station (1 N. Main St., tel. 702/386–6896), a railway station within a casino, where you can leave the train and head straight for the craps tables. Some trains travel overnight, and you can sleep in your seat or book a roomette at additional cost. When available, excursion fares may save you up to half the round-trip fare.

Los Angeles is eight hours from Las Vegas by train.

By Bus

Greyhound Lines (200 Main St., tel. 702/382–2292), one block south of the Union Plaza Hotel, has nationwide service.

Staying in Las Vegas

Important Addresses and Numbers

Tourist Information   Las Vegas Convention and Visitors Authority (3150 Paradise Rd., tel. 702/733–2323), next door to the Las Vegas Hilton, can provide brochures and general information.

Staying in Las Vegas   **16**

Las Vegas Chamber of Commerce (tel. 800/638–2328) gives show information 24 hours a day.

Hotels and gift shops on the Strip have maps, brochures, pamphlets, and free events magazines—*Today in Las Vegas, Fun and Gaming,* and *Tourguide*—that list shows and buffets and offer discounts to area attractions.

Emergencies Police, fire, ambulance (tel. 911).

Hospital Emergency Rooms **Southern Nevada Memorial Hospital** (1800 W. Charleston Blvd. at Shadow La., tel. 702/383–2000) has a 24-hour emergency service with outpatient and trauma-care facilities.

Humana Hospital Sunrise (3186 Maryland Pkwy. near Desert Inn Rd., tel. 702/731–8000) has an emergency room. You'll need your car or a cab to get here.

Doctors **Clark County Medical Society** (tel. 702/739–9989) will make referrals.

Dentists **Clark County Dental Society** (tel. 702/435–7767) will make referrals.

Late-night Pharmacies **White Cross Drug** (1700 Las Vegas Blvd. S, tel. 702/382–1733; 953 E. Sahara Ave., tel. 702/735–5189) is open 24 hours at both locations.

Opening and Closing Times

Banks are generally open Monday to Friday 10–3.

Most stores are open Monday to Friday 10–9, Saturday 9–6, and Sunday 11–6. The very expensive gift shops on the Strip remain open until midnight.

Getting Around Las Vegas

The best way to experience Las Vegas may be to drive it. A car gives you easy access to the attractions of the Strip as well as those that are several blocks away, it lets you make excursions to Lake Mead and elsewhere at your leisure, and it gives you the chance to cruise the Strip and bask in its neon glow.

By Car Las Vegas is an easy city to drive in, even for those who are terrible navigators. The principal north-south artery is Las Vegas Boulevard (Interstate 15 runs roughly parallel to it, less than a mile to the west). A 3½-mile stretch of Las Vegas Boulevard South is the Strip, where a majority of the city's hotels and casinos are clustered. Many of the major streets running east-west (Tropicana Avenue, Flamingo Road, Desert Inn Road, Sahara Avenue) are named for the casinos built on them, often at the intersection with the Strip.

Free parking is available at virtually every hotel. The one drawback is that the parking area is usually far to the rear of the property, and you may have to hunt for a space. Or you can have the valet park the car (have your $1 token ready). While parking space on Las Vegas Boulevard is nonexistent, you may find parking spaces on some side streets. The spaces on Fremont Street downtown are nearly always taken.

Because the capacity of the streets of Vegas has not kept pace with the incredible growth of the city, traffic can be heavy in the late afternoon, in the evening, and on the weekend. At

Guided Tours 17

those times you may prefer to drive the streets that parallel Las Vegas Boulevard: Paradise Road and Maryland Parkway to the east, Industrial Road to the west (which will deliver you directly to the parking lots of Caesars Palace or Circus Circus; take Tropicana Avenue to Industrial Road).

By Taxi Desert Cab (tel. 702/736–1702), Whittlesea Blue Cab (tel. 702/384–6111), and Yellow and Checker Cab (tel. 702/873–2227) are the principal taxi operators in Las Vegas. You may never need to call for a cab; you'll find cabs waiting at the airport and at every hotel in town. Cabs charge $1.70 for the first fraction of a mile and 20¢ for each additional ⅕ mile. When there are more than three passengers in the cab, there's an extra charge of 20¢ per mile. If you take a cab to a restaurant off the Strip, the restaurant will call a taxi to take you home.

By Bus Las Vegas Transit (tel. 702/384–3540) runs a Strip bus from the Hacienda Hotel at the south end of the Strip, stopping at all the major hotels, to the Casino Center downtown. The fare is $1 (exact change required); if you plan to get on and off the bus, buy a 10-ride commuter card ($6.65) from the driver. The Strip bus runs every 15 minutes, from 8:30 AM to 1 AM.

The downtown Glitter Gulch bus runs every 15 minutes from 7 AM to 12:45 AM, every 30 minutes from 12:45 AM to 2:45 AM, and every 60 minutes from 4:15 AM to 6:30 AM. Other routes serve the Meadows and Boulevard shopping malls, Sam's Town Hotel and Casino, and the western gift shop on Boulder Highway.

Guided Tours

Gray Line (1550 S. Industrial Rd., tel. 702/384–1234 or 800/634–6579) offers 16 bus tours of Las Vegas and environs. Itineraries include the Strip, Hoover Dam, Mt. Charleston, Bryce Canyon, and the Grand Canyon. The popular "Mini-City" tour (6½ hours) takes passengers to parks, museums, Siegfried and Roy's house, and downtown for sightseeing and gambling. Vegas tours last from 2 hours to 6½ hours; tours beyond the area are all-day affairs. Gray Line will pick you up at your hotel and return you to it at the end of the tour. Tours run from $14.50 to $115 (Bryce Canyon); city area tours average $25. Reservations can be made by telephone at any hour.

Ray and Ross Transport Inc. (300 W. Owens Ave., tel. 702/646–4661) has city tours, a nightclub tour (6 PM–1:30 AM, $62.85), and a dance tour (9:30 PM–3:30 AM, $38.10). Hotel pickup and return are included.

Martin Jettico (1928 Western Ave., tel. 702/382–1976) gives a six-hour Hoover Dam tour for $29.95. A bus collects you from your hotel, takes you past the homes of Las Vegas stars and to Ethel M Chocolates, the Botanical Gardens, the Liberace Museum, and finally the big dam, where champagne toasts are offered. The 4½ hour tour ($19.95) leaves out Liberace and the champagne.

Helicop-Tours (Landmark Hotel, 364 Convention Center Dr., tel. 702/736–0606) offers a 10-minute helicopter tour of the Las Vegas Strip for $35 per person.

2 Playing the Games

Like every visitor to Las Vegas, you're probably going to spend some time and money at the gaming tables or the slot machines. The key to having a good time may be to approach the casinos with the goal not of coming away a winner (that happens rarely) but of seeing that you get as much playing time as possible for your money. Your success will depend very little on luck and a lot on how well you understand the rules of the games you play and the strategies for playing them.

This chapter explains the rules, the play, the odds, and the strategy for each of the games played in the Vegas casinos. When you've found a game that appeals to you, take the time to learn the basics thoroughly—and go prepared.

Blackjack, or twenty-one, is the most popular table game in Nevada. Its rules are simple, the play is uncomplicated, and in the long run the odds are more favorable to the player than those of other games. Many players see it as a real challenge: With a basic understanding of strategy, you can stretch your gambling dollars over longer periods of play and even hope to hold your own or come out a bit ahead. In the following pages, Dennis R. Harrison explains the basics (and the intricacies) of blackjack and advises players on all aspects of the game, beginning with finding the right table and buying chips. Those who are new to blackjack need not be concerned about his discussion of card counting—it just shows how much work some people will put into gaining a further edge on the odds.

Many other casino games and machines hold fascination for players. Roulette, craps, baccarat, keno, bingo, Big Six (Wheel of Fortune), slot machines, and sports betting are widely available in Las Vegas gambling halls. The rules and strategies for each are outlined here in concise analyses prepared by *Gambling Times*, the premier publisher of gaming-related information.

The *Gambling Times* explanation of football betting is offered as just one example of how the sports books of the Nevada casinos operate. They will also take bets on baseball, basketball, boxing, horse racing, and other sports, but because these are not games that involve continuous play, we give no account of them in this chapter. Similarly, while there are poker rooms in Vegas casinos, poker is not a game the beginner will want to play for stakes with strangers, and there is no analysis of the game here.

Blackjack

by Dennis R. Harrison

I begin with blackjack for two very simple reasons: The odds can be more favorable for the player than in any other game, and it is my personal specialty. To my mind, anyone who does not select blackjack as his or her specialty is a masochist. The game is simple to play; the rules are clear and understandable. Properly played, the odds can actually be turned to the player's advantage.

Your first step is to find a table. Not just any table, but a table where the game is being played for stakes you can tolerate. It is quite embarrassing to rush up to a table, ask for $20 in chips, and then discover that the minimum bet at that table is $100.

You will usually find a small sign, to the dealer's right or left, which will indicate the minimum and maximum allowable wagers at that table. If the sign is obscured by ashtrays and empty drinks, don't hesitate to approach the dealer and inquire directly. Or simply check the bets being made by the players. If all you see are green chips, it is probably a $25 table (the minimum bet is $25). If all you see are red chips, it is undoubtedly a $5 table. If you see silver dollars or silver dollar tokens, it could be a $1, $2, or $3 table. Assuming that you are a novice, you'll want to start with low stakes; if your hotel casino does not offer a low-minimum table, go somewhere else.

The drawing shows a typical table. Your first preference should be to sit at the seat labeled "third base" (the reason for this will be explained later), but any seat will do. At any rate, I'll assume that you've found a table to your liking. Now it's time to dig into your wallet or purse and bring out the greenbacks. And let me emphasize that you will, indeed, be playing for money. In reality, you will be playing with the chips that your money has bought, but too many people forget that those red, green, and black chips represent authentic U.S. dollars; in many cases, hard-earned dollars.

Another suggestion: Purchase only a few chips. If you are playing at a $2 table, don't start with more than $20. If at a $5 table, don't start with more than $30–$40. Do not buy $100 worth of chips simply because you have a hundred dollar bill. You are not going to impress anyone; you will not intimidate the dealer by dropping a hundred dollar bill on the table. Go to the cashier, break your hundred dollar bill into five 20s and *then* buy chips at the blackjack table.

There are several reasons why I make this suggestion. First, having too many chips in front of you can create a false sense of security; as long as you can look down and see

---

Reprinted from Win at the Casino *by Dennis R. Harrison. Copyright © 1982 by Dennis R. Harrison. Used by permission of Fell Publishers, Inc., Hollywood, Florida.*

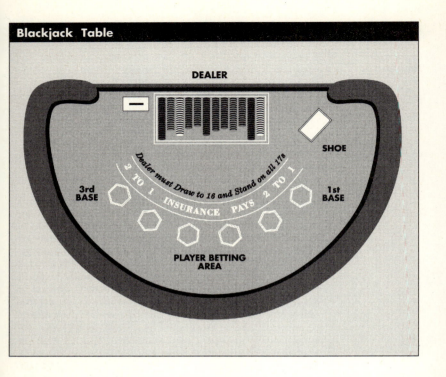

chips on the table, you will have a tendency to keep playing, even though you may be losing badly. Second, and conversely, if you start with only a small amount, and those chips suddenly vanish, you will have an automatic alarm clock to help make you aware that you are, indeed, losing money. There will be times when you can sit at a table and do everything right but still lose. The trick is to conserve your losses when you are losing. So, if that first $20 or $30 disappears, change tables! A new table can improve your morale and may help change your luck. In addition, your first time at the blackjack tables will be an experiment of sorts. You're going to find out if you really understand the game, so don't make it an expensive training session.

To purchase chips, simply wait until the dealer is finished with the hand being played, place your $20 in front of or behind your playing spot, and say "Change, please" or "Chips, please." Do not place the money *on* your playing (betting) area. This may lead the dealer to believe that you want to make a $20 cash bet. Some dealers will ask whether you want to bet that $20, others will go ahead and begin the deal. Don't leave any room for misunderstanding. Also, if the dealer does not give you the chips you want, tell her (I'll assume your dealer is female). If, for example, the dealer gives you four $5 chips and you only want to play for $2 a hand, push two of the chips back at her and request $1 chips.

Blackjack 23

Another point: The dealer can give you chips for your money, but the same is not true in reverse. She cannot buy back your chips when you leave the table. Chips can be exchanged for money only at the cashier's cage.

Okay, now you have your chips; probably two $5 chips and 10 $1 chips. To make your initial wager, place the minimum bet in your playing area. On some tables this area is rectangular; on others it is circular. Your chips should be stacked neatly, one on top of the other. When you see the dealer reminding people to stack their bets, it is not because she is a tidy person. It is because it is more difficult for a cheater to swindle the casino if the chips are stacked properly.

If you are making an odd wager, say $37, the chips should be stacked in the following manner: The largest-value chips on the bottom, the smallest-value on the top, and any others in the middle. If betting a green $25 chip, two red $5 chips, and two silver dollar tokens, the green would be on the bottom, the reds in the middle, the tokens on top. The casinos insist on this to help prevent cheating by the players. If this sounds a little strange, let me explain. Let's say you want to swindle the casino. You look at your first two cards, discover a total of 20, and decide you have a very good chance of winning the hand. So, with lightning-fast fingers, you quickly add a few more chips to your bet while the dealer is concentrating on another player. Yes, I know that sounds silly. Who could possibly move that fast? No one could possibly get away with such a trick. Right? Wrong. Dealers and pit bosses tell me that people try to do it all the time. In our $37 example, with your chips stacked properly, you'd only be able to add a few dollars to the top of your bet, which would hardly be worth the effort. But, were the chips stacked so that the $25 chip was on top of the pile, you could easily add another $50 or $100, which *would* be worth the risk of getting caught. And that's why you must stack your chips properly.

What happens next depends on how many decks are in use at your table. There are single-deck tables, double-deck tables, four-deck tables, and even six-deck tables. Who knows? One day we might even see eight- or 10-deck tables. The more decks, the more benefit to the casinos. Personally, I prefer single- or double-deck tables. Other gamblers will disagree with me, but I believe that anyone who plays at a four- or six-deck table is deranged. Though it is possible to win with four or six decks, it is much more difficult than it is playing with one or two decks. If your hotel casino does not offer single or double decks, go somewhere else.

If you are in doubt as to how many decks are being used, ask the dealer. If there is a *shoe* on the table, at least four decks are being used. A shoe is a small plastic box which holds all the cards. Instead of dealing from her hands, the dealer slides the cards out of the shoe.

Playing the Games 24

Now for the cards. It's a new shuffle. The dealer carefully mixes the cards, places them in front of your playing position, then stares at you as if she wants you to do something. Yes, that's right. She wants you to cut the cards. You comply, cutting the cards just as you do at home when you're playing bridge or poker. If you're playing at a two-, four-, or six-deck table, the dealer will pass you a small plastic card. That card is used to cut the deck. The dealer will extend all the decks so that you can insert the plastic card somewhere in the pile. The dealer then cuts the cards at that point.

After you've cut the cards, the dealer will discard the first one, two, or more cards into another small plastic tray to her right, called the discard tray. This action is called *burning* a card. Later I will explain its purpose.

The burning completed, the dealer starts dealing the cards from her left to her right, from first base to third base. In one- and two-deck games the player's cards are normally all dealt face down. In multiple-deck games, the player's cards are often dealt face up. In either case, the dealer always has one card face up, one face down. The dealer's face-down card is called the *down* card or the *hole* card.

You watch your two cards slide toward you, pick them up, and calculate the value of your hand. Don't be rushed. Take your time. Not all of us are mathematically inclined, so don't get nervous if the dealer gives you an annoyed look. Each card has a point value. Tens, Jacks, Queens, and Kings are worth 10 points each. Aces can be either one or 11. All other cards are face value; a Six is worth six points, a Two is worth two points, and so forth.

The object of the game is to obtain a total of 21, or as close to 21 as possible, without exceeding 21. If you exceed a total of 21, you bust (lose automatically). If you do not bust, and your total is higher than the dealer's total, you win even money. For example, a $2 bet would win $2. Should your total be the same as the dealer's total, you tie (or *push*), and neither win nor lose.

Assume your first hand is a Jack and an Ace. Rejoice! You have a natural blackjack, a total of 21 on your first two cards, which is an automatic winner. Not only do you win, but the payoff is three to two. A $2 bet would win $3, a $10 bet would win $15, and so forth. A natural blackjack is any two-card hand consisting of an Ace and any 10-value card. When you receive a natural, expose your cards immediately; turn them over and lay them down in front of your bet. If you don't immediately expose a natural, you may only be paid even money. Of course, if you're at a table where the cards are being dealt face up you needn't do anything but collect your winnings.

A natural blackjack cannot lose, but it can be tied by a dealer natural. If the dealer's up card is a 10-value or an Ace,

Blackjack 25

she must peek at her hole card to see if she has a natural. If she does, everyone loses except the players who also have naturals. Those players tie, or push.

Anyway, you won your first hand. Congratulations. You are smiling joyously, so the dealer grins at you and then turns to the player at first base. That player is the first to choose from several available options. Since you were dealt a natural you don't need to exercise any options, but you still need to understand your alternatives. Here they are:

- You can *stand* (or *stick*, or *stand pat*). This means that you are satisfied with your first two cards and don't want any more. To stand in a game where the cards are dealt face down, you simply slide your cards under the chips in your betting area. However, you *must not* actually touch the chips with your hands; the casino might think that you're cheating. If the cards are all dealt face up, simply wave your hand over the cards with your palm parallel to the table. You may also say, "I'm good," or "No more for me," or words to that effect.

- You may request additional cards (or *hit*, or *draw*). This means that you are not happy with your first two cards and want to improve your total. If the cards were dealt face down, hold the cards in your hand and brush them lightly against the top of the table. The dealer will give you another card every time you make this motion. If the cards were all dealt face up, you can accomplish the same by brushing one of your index fingers on the table. Or you may say, "Hit me," or "Give me another one," or words to that effect.

If, by taking additional cards, you exceed a total of 21, you bust. In that case you must expose all your cards by laying them face up on the table. The dealer will then collect your cards and your losing wager. You can take as many additional cards as you want as long as you do not exceed 21. When you are through taking cards, you then stand, as noted in the first example above.

- You can *double down*. Explained later.

- You can *split*. No, this doesn't mean you can grab your money and run for the exit, even though your initial two cards may inspire that reaction. I'll cover this one later, too.

- You can *surrender*. Later.

- You can buy *insurance*. Later.

As you watch the dealer move from player to player, you'll see your fellow gamblers exercising these options. When all the players have acted on their hands, it's the dealer's turn.

Ah, the poor dealer. While the players have several options, the dealer has only two:

- If the dealer's total is 16 or less, she *must* take additional cards until she reaches 17–21 or busts.

Playing the Games 26

- If the dealer's total is 17 or more, she *may not* take additional cards.

After acting on her hand, the dealer then settles all wagers, usually working from third base back to first base. Then the next round begins. You place your bet, receive your cards, decide which option to exercise, and win or lose. See, I told you this was simple.

What makes blackjack so interesting to play is that the gamblers have many options, the dealer only two. For the person who enjoys making quick decisions, no other casino game is as challenging or rewarding.

But how do you know when to exercise your options? Are there bad times to stand, good times to hit? And if you exercise your options properly, can you actually win? Yes, yes, and yes.

The following sections set forth the strategy you should use to win at blackjack. You *must* study the charts, memorize and practice them if you are serious about winning. You cannot win by exercising your options with decisions based on intuition or lucky feelings. You *must* know the basic strategies. They may seem difficult at first, so take your time. You can learn them!

Hard Holdings I don't know how the term *hard holding* originated, but it is quite descriptive. Often a hard holding of 12–16 puts you between a rock and a hard spot, creates a hard lump in your throat, or causes you to cast a very hard, disgusted look at the dealer.

A hard holding (also called *hard hand* or *stiff*) is a holding which can only be counted in one manner. A holding of Queen, Six can only be counted as 16. A holding of Eight, Seven can only be counted as 15. All hands are hard hands unless one or both of your cards is an Ace, since Aces can be one or 11.

What do you do if you have a total of 15 and the dealer's up card is an Ace? What if the dealer is showing a Two or a Six? Sometimes the decisions are agonizing.

The Hard Holding Strategy chart tells you what to do in every instance with hard holdings. Study it, memorize it, test yourself on it. Don't worry, you can learn it. I have tested this strategy in over a hundred thousand actual hands, plus used it in over a quarter million practice hands. It works.

There, that's not so difficult, is it? If you have 12 and the dealer is showing a Seven, you hit. If you have 12 and the dealer's up card is a Six, you stand. I give you an option on 16 versus a dealer Ten because this decision is never right, never wrong. If you have a total of 11 or less, hit. Stand on any total of 17 or more.

Hard Holding Strategy

The Dealer Is Showing:	2	3	4	5	6	7	8	9	10	Ace
Your Total Is: 4–11	H	H	H	H	H	H	H	H	H	H
12	H	H	S	S	S	H	H	H	H	H
13	S	S	S	S	S	H	H	H	H	H
14	S	S	S	S	S	H	H	H	H	H
15	S	S	S	S	S	H	H	H	H	H
16	S	S	S	S	S	H	H	O	H
17–21	S	S	S	S	S	S	S	S	S	S

S=Stand   H=Hit   O=Optional

Busting Percentages: Dealer's Hand

Dealer Is Showing:	2	3	4	5	6	7	8	9	10	Ace
% of Time Dealer Will Finish With 17–21	70	62	60	57	58	74	76	77	77	83
% of Time Dealer Will Bust	30	38	40	43	42	26	24	23	23	17

Busting Percentages: Your Hand

Your Total Is:	11	12	13	14	15	16	17	18	19	20
% of Time You Can Hit without Busting	100	69	62	54	46	39	31	23	15	8
% of Time a Hit Will Bust You	0	31	39	46	54	62	69	77	85	92

But, you also ask, why do I hit when I'm holding 12 and the dealer is showing an Ace, stand when the dealer is showing a Six, hit when the dealer is showing a Two? Good questions, all. The answers lie in the Busting Percentages charts.

The percentages will vary as the game progresses, but not much. Consequently, they are the percentages to use in determining whether to hit or stand. It is these percentages, combined with the rigid rules governing the dealer's options, which give you the basic strategy set forth in the Hard Holding Strategy chart. When the dealer has a high chance of busting, you do not want to hit. In those cases,

Playing the Games 28

you play for the dealer to bust. You want to shift the risk from your hand to the dealer's hand.

For example: Assume that your hand is 15. The dealer is showing a Nine. You have a 53.8% chance of busting, should you hit. However, the dealer will finish with 17–21 77% of the time. If you stand on your 15, you will probably lose. Therefore, in this case, you take the offensive in an attempt to improve your hand.

Now let's change the dealer's up card. Let's say she has a Five showing instead of a Nine. The percentages indicate that you should stand. The reasons are twofold: First, you have a 53.8% chance of busting if you hit. Second, the dealer has a 43% chance of busting. So why push your luck? Let the dealer risk busting *her* hand. You still may lose, but you've transferred the risk of busting to the dealer.

Similar examples can be drawn for all the other hard holding totals, but I'll let you figure them out for yourself.

The basic hard holding strategy does not change if your hand consists of more than two cards and you're playing against a shoe. If you have a three- or four-card total of 15, you should still hit against a dealer Nine. Assume you're playing against a shoe and you're dealt a Two and a Five. The dealer is showing a Queen. The basic strategy says to take a hit, so you do. You draw another Five, so now you've got a total of 12. The basic strategy says to hit a 12 against a dealer Queen; you do, and receive a Two, for a total of 14. Yes, I know you already have four cards, but that doesn't make any difference. Your lousy 14 will probably lose, so you must take another hit. You do, and receive an Ace. Now you have a 15 or 25, and since 25 is no good, you really have a hard 15. Now the sweat begins to trickle off your brow. The basic strategy says to hit a hard 15 when the dealer is showing any 10-value card. But you already have five cards, and you're convinced that if you take another hit you'll bust your hand. Your mind screams for you to stand pat. The other players are staring at you, waiting to see if you are stupid enough to draw a sixth card. It's decision time. And, since the basic strategy says to take a hit, you do so. Unfortunately, you receive a Ten and bust the hand, thereby losing your bet. Well, what can I say? You're not going to win every hand. The basic strategy is a guide which will help, but it will not miraculously cause you to win all the time. You might have caught a Six and won. That's why it's called gambling. Nothing ventured, nothing gained. However, in single and double deck games I prefer to stand on any three-card 15 or 16.

Whenever you are dealt an initial holding of 12, 13, 14, 15, or 16, your odds of winning are very slim. Again, that's why those totals are called hard holdings or stiffs. They are bad for your morale and bad for your pocketbook. Consequent-

Blackjack 29

ly, the hard holding strategy is designed to make the best out of terrible situations.

As I stated earlier, it is possible to do everything right and still lose. But if you use the basic strategy you will lose less than the other players at your table, who are relying solely on luck or whimsy. And I'm not discarding luck as being a valuable asset. What I'm saying is this: If you are using the basic strategy and you are still losing, you don't have any luck. Your karma is bad. Fate has decided to rob you of your money. You can't buck bad odds *and* bad luck. The basic strategy will help turn the odds in your favor and also protect you against the horrendous losses commonly associated with "bad luck." But if you sit down at a blackjack table and continually receive 12s, 13s, 14s, 15s and 16s, you are playing the wrong game. Leave the table and visit the hotel's steam room. If you use the basic strategy and still lose, you'll know fate is being unkind. If you *do not* use the basic strategy, there is no way to determine whether your losses are the result of bad luck or poor, foolish card play. On too many occasions to count, I have observed players making numerous ridiculous plays at the blackjack tables, and then heard those same gamblers complain about not having any luck. Play wisely, and you can create your own luck.

Yes, you will win some of the time when you have hard holdings. Yes, it is even possible to win a majority of those hands. However, the odds are against you, overall. If, in fact, you are winning a majority of those hands, you may wish to increase your bets. You could be on a hot streak, or the dealer could be on a cold streak.

In the next sections you'll see that there are ways for you to make up for all those terrible hard holding hands, options which will mean money in your pocket if utilized properly. On the hard holding hands, you are really striving to break even. On the other hands you swing the odds in your favor.

Doubling Down Perk up, your odds of winning are now improving. Pray that each new hand brings a double down opportunity. If you double down in the correct situations you can recapture the money you lost on all those miserable 15s and 16s. Here's your chance to get even with the dealer for giving you all those bad hands.

The term *doubling down* derives from two actions. First, you double your bet; second, you receive one additional card, normally dealt face down. Hence, you double down.

The rules governing doubling down vary from area to area. Most casinos allow you to double down on any two-card holding, others only on a holding of 10 or 11. It is to your advantage to play at casinos that allow you to double down on *any* two-card holding.

Doubling Down Strategy

The Dealer Is Showing:		2	3	4	5	6	7	8	9	10	Ace
Your Total Is:	**11**	D	D	D	D	D	D	D	D	D	D
	10	D	D	D	D	D	D	D	D	H	H
	9	D	D	D	D	D	H	H	H	H	H

H=Hit **D=Double Down**

To double down, you expose your cards to the dealer, placing them face up in front of your betting area. Then you match your original bet with a like amount placed *adjacent* to your original bet. If your original wager was $5, you must extend another $5. If all the cards were dealt face up, simply match your original wager. The dealer will then give you one card. You do not have the option of taking more cards. You receive one card, and one card only. Sound risky? It *is* if you do it at the wrong times; it *is not* if you do it at the right times. The Doubling Down Strategy chart will tell you when the time is right.

You should double down on 11 against every dealer up card, on 10 against every dealer up card except a Ten or an Ace, on nine only when the dealer is showing a Six or less. If you compare the Doubling Down Strategy chart with the Hard Holding Strategy chart, you'll see how the doubling down strategy was developed. In essence, you want to double down whenever the dealer has a high probability of busting. Doubling on 11 against a dealer Seven, Eight, Nine, Ten, or Ace is an offensive attempt. Remember that in a deck of 52 cards there are 16 10-value cards (four Tens, four Jacks, four Queens, and four Kings), so your chance of receiving a 10-value card on your double down is good. Also, you only want to double down on holdings which cannot be busted by the addition of one card; you would *not* double down on 12, 13, 14, or more.

I know one gambler who doubles down each time he has less than 12 and the dealer is showing a Five or a Six. Yes, I've seen him double down on a holding of three. And, believe it or not, he wins more than he loses. However, when I tried the same strategy I was massacred. In any case, you don't want to be too greedy. Don't forget: When you double down you double your winnings, but you can also double your losses. Use doubling down wisely and you'll give yourself an edge over the casino.

Soft Holdings A *soft holding* is any holding which can be counted in *more than one* manner. This can only happen when you have an Ace in your hand. Remember, an Ace can be counted as *ei-*

ther one or 11. If you have a holding of Ace, Five you have either six or 16. Since a holding of 16 is tantamount to certain death, you should count the Ace as one, for a total of six.

If you have a holding of Ace, Nine, you will want to count the Ace as 11, for a total of 20. You may also count it as one, for a total of 10, but why reduce a potential winning hand to an unknown?

Ace, Four could be five or 15. Ace, Seven could be eight or 18. Obviously, having a soft holding gives you more flexibility. It is virtually impossible to bust a soft holding. But ordinarily a soft holding does not stay soft very long.

Assume you're dealt Ace, Five. You treat the Ace as a value of one, so your total is six. You take a hit (you can't possibly bust) and catch a King. Your hand is no longer soft. Now you have a hard holding of $16 (1 + 5 + 10)$.

Another example: You are dealt Ace, Three. You have either four or 14. You take a hit, and get a Two. Now you have Ace, Three, Two, which is worth either six or 16. You take another hit, an Eight. Ace, Three, Two, Eight totals 14. It *must* total 14. You have no other choice. If you treat your Ace as 11, your total would be $24 (11 + 3 + 2 + 8)$!

Soft holdings can make for very interesting hands. I am sure that this has happened to all seasoned blackjack players, but I will relate this experience as an example. I was at a crowded casino on New Year's Eve, and all the two-deck tables were busy. I was possessed by gambling fever, so, in a fit of stupidity, I decided to play at a four-deck table. On one hand, my initial two cards were Ace, Two. The dealer was showing a Ten. I took a hit. I received another Ace, giving me either $4 (1 + 1 + 2)$ or $14 (1 + 11 + 2)$. My second hit was another Ace, as was my third. My hand was then Ace, Ace, Ace, Ace, Two for either six $(1 + 1 + 1 + 1 + 2)$ or 16 $(1 + 1 + 1 + 11 + 2)$. I then took another hit and received yet another Ace. Remember, I was at a four-deck table, so there were 16 Aces in the shoe. Anyway, my six-card total was still only seven or 17. I could have stopped at that point, but since the dealer was showing a Ten, and since I could not possibly bust my hand with another hit, I brushed my cards on the felt and received a Five, which gave me a total of $12 (1 + 1 + 1 + 1 + 1 + 2 + 5)$. At that point, my soft holding finally became a hard holding. The interesting point is that my hand stayed soft for six cards, which does not happen very often.

In case you're interested in whether I won or lost that hand, I suppose I should finish the story. I had to take two more hits to complete my hand. One was a Two, the other was a Five. My final hand was Ace, Ace, Ace, Ace, Ace, Two, Five, Two, Five for a total of 19. The dealer had 18. Hooray for our side!

Soft Holding Strategy										
The Dealer Is Showing:		2	3	4	5	6	7	8	9	10 Ace
You Have:	Ace, 9	S	S	S	S	S	S	S	S	S S
	Ace, 8	S	S	S	S	S	S	S	S	S S
	Ace, 7	S	D	D	D	D	S	S	H	H S
	Ace, 6	H	D	D	D	D	S	H	H	H H
	Ace, 5	H	H	D	D	D	H	H	H	H H
	Ace, 4	H	H	D	D	D	H	H	H	H H
	Ace, 3	H	H	D	D	D	H	H	H	H H
	Ace, 2	H	H	D	D	D	H	H	H	H H
S=Stand **H=Hit** **D=Double Down**										

The Soft Holding Strategy chart shows you what to do with various soft holdings against all dealer up cards. With soft holdings you really have three options: stand, hit, or double down.

The reasons for doubling down a soft holding are threefold: First, you cannot possibly bust your hand. Second, in each of the situations depicted in the chart there is an excellent probability of the dealer busting. Finally, there is a good chance that you will receive a card that will improve your hand. So you have just enough of an edge to make it worthwhile to double your bet.

You always stand on Ace, Eight and Ace, Nine, because those hands are worth 19 and 20, respectively. You could double down on either of those hands against a dealer Five or Six, but again I caution you against becoming greedy. Explore this chart, study it, memorize it. You'll see that some of the situations call for defensive action, others for offensive action by the player. As with the chart for doubling down, astute use of soft holdings will increase your winnings.

Splitting When you split your initial two cards you actually turn one hand into two, with each treated as a separate hand that must be played. This can only happen when your first two cards are a pair. If your first two cards are Two, Two, you can split them. You can split Three, Three or Four, Four, or any pair including any two 10-value cards (Ten, Jack, Queen, or King).

When you split your hand you must double your bet because you will be playing two separate hands. The procedure is the same as that for doubling down; expose your cards to the dealer and match your bet with a like amount. If the cards were dealt face up, simply match your bet. But unlike doubling down, take care to create a space between your cards when you expose them. If you are splitting a pair and you lay them down so that one card is on top of the other, the dealer may think you want to double down. In any case, make sure the dealer understands that you want to split.

Splitting Pairs Strategy

The Dealer is Showing:	2	3	4	5	6	7	8	9	10	Ace
You Have: 2, 2	H	Sp	Sp	Sp	Sp	Sp	H	H	H	H
3, 3	H	Sp	Sp	Sp	Sp	Sp	H	H	H	H
4, 4	H	H	H	H	H	H	H	H	H	H
5, 5	D	D	D	D	D	D	D	D	H	H
6, 6	Sp	Sp	Sp	Sp	Sp	H	H	H	H	H
7, 7	Sp	Sp	Sp	Sp	Sp	Sp	H	H	H	H
8, 8	Sp	Sp	Sp	Sp	Sp	Sp	Sp	Sp	Sp	Sp
9, 9	Sp	Sp	Sp	Sp	Sp	S	S	Sp	S	S
10, 10	S	S	S	S	S	S	S	S	S	S
Ace,Ace	Sp	Sp	Sp	Sp	Sp	Sp	Sp	Sp	Sp	Sp

S=Stand   H=Hit   Sp=Split   D=Double Down

The dealer will deal a hit to the first card of your pair (the first of your two separate hands) and wait to see if you want additional cards on that hand. The hand is played like any other, using the strategies discussed. You can hit or stand, and certain casinos will allow you to double down or resplit. Once the first hand is completed, the dealer moves to your second hand.

There are rule variations for splitting, but one rule is the same at all casinos. If you split a pair of Aces, you will receive only *one* card, usually dealt face down, on each of your Aces. You have no options. You live or die with the single card that you are dealt on each Ace. In addition, should one or both of your Aces be dealt a 10-value card, you do not have a natural blackjack. You simply have a total of 21 and are paid even money if you win. Remember, the only time you can have a natural blackjack is on your initial two cards.

Here is the basic strategy for splitting:

You should *always* split Ace, Ace and Eight, Eight. You should *never* split Ten, Ten or Five, Five. When holding Five, Five, you should use the rules for doubling down on Ten. It is not a good idea to split Fours, but, if you feel lucky, you can split them against a dealer Five or Six.

Playing the Games 34

You will note that at times you are taking the offensive, at other times the defensive. Holding Seven, Seven is no great joy. By splitting Sevens you may draw cards which will improve your chance of winning (nearly anything is better than 14). Splitting Nines is an offensive attempt when the dealer is showing a card worth less than a Six. Yet we do not split Nines against a dealer Seven for the simple reason that if the dealer has 17, you will beat her with your 18. Against a dealer Eight you should stand on Nine, Nine, hoping for a tie. Against a dealer Ten or Ace assume that your 18 will lose, so you split and try to save the bet by making at least one of the hands a winner. If one of the Nines draws a Two and a Ten you are in good shape even if you bust the other hand (you win one, lose one, and break even).

Splitting opportunities do not present themselves very often, but you should know how to handle them when they occur.

Insurance   *Insurance* is one of the least understood of all the player options. Yet it can be quite beneficial once you know what buying insurance really means.

The only time you can buy insurance is when the dealer's up card is an Ace. In that case the dealer will ask all the players whether they want to buy insurance. If you want to buy insurance, place an amount equal to half your original wager into the area marked insurance. The dealer then peeks at her hole card to see if she has a 10-value card for a natural blackjack. If she does have a blackjack, you lose your original wager (unless you also have a natural blackjack), but you win two to one on your insurance bet. If the dealer does not have a blackjack, you lose your insurance bet and the game continues in the normal manner, with each player then acting on their hands.

But you are *not* really buying insurance. In essence, you are simply making another bet. You are *betting* on whether or not the dealer has a natural blackjack. And unless you are a card counter (explained later) this is a bad bet to make! Unless you are a card counter, there is only one possible instance when you *might* want to buy insurance—if you have a holding of 20. In that case, even if you lose the insurance bet, you stand a good chance of winning your original wager. If you had bet $5 you would lose $2.50 on the insurance bet but win $5 on the original wager, for a net gain of $2.50.

No matter what the dealers try to tell you, no matter what other players try to tell you, buying insurance is not a good bet unless you are a card counter. Some people will tell you that if you have a natural blackjack as your holding you should always buy insurance if offered. Nonsense! Don't do it—again, unless you are a card counter.

Blackjack 35

Surrender Yes, the *surrender* option is exactly what the word implies. You surrender your hand to the dealer. You give up. You wave a white flag over your head. And the result is that the dealer takes only *half* your bet. If you are a card counter this option can be very beneficial. If you are not a card counter, this option may not be as great as it sounds.

To surrender your cards, simply turn them over and expose them to the dealer. If the cards were all dealt face up, simply say, "Surrender" or "I surrender." In either case, *do not* touch your bet. The dealer will take half your wager. The casino does not want you fooling around with your chips; they are always on guard for cheaters.

You may only exercise this option *before* acting on your hand. You cannot take a hit, bust, and then surrender. You must surrender your original two cards.

If you are not a card counter, there are only a few situations in which you *might* want to surrender. If your hand is 15 or 16 and the dealer is showing a 10-value card; or if your hand is a 14 made up of Seven, Seven and the dealer is showing a 10-value card. Otherwise, take your chances and try to beat the dealer.

Not all casinos offer this option, so always ask the dealer about surrendering.

Card Counting *Card counting* means counting certain cards in order to ascertain whether the deck is in favor of the players or the dealer. Yes, a deck of cards can fluctuate quite a bit in favor of one or the other. It has been proven by several people that the deck is favorable to the players when the ratio of high cards remaining in the deck is greater than the ratio of low cards. When the deck contains a high ratio of low cards, Twos through Sixes, the dealer gets very tough. When the deck contains a high ratio of high cards, 10-values and Aces, it's the player's turn to multiply his or her winnings.

If you are not a card counter, you may have even confused a favorable deck with "luck." Assume that you play at a six-deck table and that, by the time you begin to play, the majority of the low cards have already been played. You then win five hands in a row and decide that your luck is good. But, in fact, you won because the deck was favorable for the players. Of course, the reverse could also happen. You could sit down at a time when the deck is favorable for the dealer, lose five hands in a row, and decide that you have bad luck.

Card counting is not difficult. It *can* be very difficult if you use a complicated counting system, but exotic counting systems are best left to the experts. What you need is a system that is easy to use and easy to remember—a simple system that will help you win more and avoid losses. I will cover what I feel are the two easiest ways to count cards.

Counting If you watch closely, whether the cards are dealt face up or
10-Values face down, you will see every card that is played when play-

Playing the Games 36

ers bust or when the dealer makes the settlements. All you must do is count the number of 10-value cards that you see. Will it help? Immensely! Is it worth the effort? Absolutely!

There are 52 cards in each deck, of which 16 are 10-values. This means that approximately one of every three cards is a 10-value. If the deck is "even" (the 10-values are spread equally through the deck), one 10-value should be played for about every three cards. When only a few 10-values are dealt on a hand, the next round will be "rich" in 10-values. When a lot of 10-values are dealt on a hand, the next round should be "poor" in 10-values. If the deck is rich, the benefit is to the players. If the deck is poor, the benefit is to the dealer.

Common sense would tell us that if the deck is rich in 10-values, the dealer has the same opportunity of being dealt a good hand as the players, and common sense would be correct. Just because the deck is rich in 10-values, you will not necessarily be dealt a pair of 10-values on the next hand. It might be the dealer who catches that pair of 10-values. So how does counting 10-values, knowing whether the deck is rich or poor, improve our winnings?

Example: The dealer is showing a 10-value. You have 11. The basic strategy says you should double down. However, from counting the 10-values, you know that the deck is very poor in 10-values. Should you still double down? Absolutely not!

Example: The dealer is showing a 10-value. You have a hard holding of 15. The basic strategy says to hit. But you know that the deck is very rich in 10-values. Should you still take a hit? No! You are almost certain to bust. Cross your fingers and hope the dealer doesn't have another 10-value for her hole card.

Example: The dealer shows an Ace and asks if you want to buy insurance. You know that the deck was very rich in 10-values at the start of that round. Should you buy insurance? Of course.

Example: The dealer is showing a 10-value, a Nine, an Eight, or a Seven. You have a miserable 15. You know that the deck is rich in 10-values. Should you hit? Stand? No, you should do neither. This is a perfect example of when you should surrender, if you have that option.

Example: The dealer is showing a Five. You have a holding of eight. You know that the deck is rich in 10-values. Should you hit? No! Instead, you should double down. The dealer's chance of busting is even greater than normal, so take your best shot.

By counting 10-values, you can modify the basic strategies to greatly increase your advantage over the dealer and dramatically increase your odds of winning.

Blackjack   37

Here's an easy way to count 10-values. I have found that, on the average, three cards are used by each player during each round. Some will play with their initial two cards, others will take multiple hits, but the average is usually three per player. That means that you should see, or count, one 10-value for each player, including the dealer, at your table on each round. And, by the way, I don't consider the deck to be rich or poor unless the 10-value count is at least three more or three less than what it should be.

Example: Six players plus the dealer. On the first hand of a new shuffle you count 12 10-values. Is the deck rich or poor for the next round? Figure it out: Six players + the dealer = seven people. Seven 10-values should have been played; one for each player and one for the dealer. Because 12 were actually played, the remaining deck is very poor in 10-values.

Example: You are playing at a table with four other gamblers. For some undetermined reason, you are playing against a shoe of six decks. On the first round of cards you count three 10-values, on the second round you count only two 10-values, and on the third round you count six 10-values. Is the deck rich or poor in 10-values for the next round? Here's how to figure it out. You + four other gamblers + the dealer = a total of six people. So, approximately six 10-values should be played on each round. Three rounds of play should have seen 18 10-values. But how many did you count? Three + two + six = 11. Consequently, the deck at that point is very rich in ten-values. Another benefit to knowing if the deck is rich or poor is that you can bet accordingly. If the deck is rich, to your advantage, you should increase your bet slightly. If the deck is poor, make a minimum wager.

Note: If there is too much fluctuation in your bets, you will stand out to the casino personnel like the lone tree in a barren field. The casino will then either have the dealer reshuffle after every hand, effectively destroying your count, or even ask you to leave.

A good rule of thumb is that your maximum wager should not be more than three times your normal minimum bet. Some people recommend that your maximum bet should not exceed five times your normal wager, but I've found that if you suddenly increase your bet from, say, $10 to $50, you become a closely watched gambler. Even worse, if you bet $10 on one hand, $50 on the next hand, then drop back down to $10 again, it's obvious you're either a counter or sick of mind. If you win that $50 bet, you're a counter. If you lose it, you're sick of mind. So take my advice. If you normally bet $5 on each hand, your largest bet should be $15. If you normally bet $10 on each hand, your largest bet should be $30. Of course there are exceptions to this rule, such as when you are using a progressive betting system. But using a progressive betting system will not brand you as a counter.

Playing the Games   38

If you are counting 10-values and you begin to gain confidence, here's a suggestion. I'll assume you are varying your bets from $5 to $15. Instead of wagering $5 when the deck is even (neither rich nor poor), bet $10. Then, when the deck is poor you can drop down to a $5 wager, when rich go up to $15. The reasons are twofold. First, varying your bets by one unit up or down will not cause anyone to think you are a counter. Second, knowing the richness or poorness of the deck gives you enough additional knowledge to increase to $10, even if the deck is just even. Once you're comfortable with counting 10-values, you're a smarter player, so you can afford to wager a little more.

Counting 10-values is an easy way to help turn the odds in your favor, but it is not an exact science. However, knowing whether the deck is rich or poor gives you that extra bit of information that will add winnings to your gambling stake, or—and that is just as important—help protect you from unnecessary losses.

Just remember this: The deck can only be "rich," "poor," or "even." If it's even, you would continue to use basic strategy. If it is rich or poor, use your common sense. There are only a few minor adjustments that need to be made if the deck is rich or poor, and these have already been covered in the examples.

Counting Aces This will not help as much as counting 10-values, but when the deck is rich in Aces you have an increased opportunity of being dealt a natural blackjack. Also, when the deck is rich in Aces you have more opportunity of being dealt a soft holding, which gives you much more flexibility. And when the deck is rich in Aces, doubling down on a holding of nine or 10 makes for an even greater chance for success.

In addition, if you can manage to count both Aces *and* 10-values, you could be one of the best-informed players in the casino. Try it sometime; it's not that difficult. Or play with a friend. You can count the 10-values, your friend can count the Aces.

One in every 13 cards should be an Ace. Start counting cards after you see an Ace. If more than 13 cards are dealt without another Ace appearing, the deck is rich in Aces. The more cards dealt without an Ace appearing, the richer the deck will be in Aces. Conversely, if Aces appear more often than once in every 13 cards, the deck is poor in Aces.

Every time the deck is rich in 10-values *and* Aces, people are invariably dealt natural blackjacks. It never fails. So, whenever I note that the deck is rich in Aces and 10-values, I make my largest bet. You would be amazed at how many times I've been dealt a natural blackjack with a maximum bet on the table. And don't forget, a natural blackjack is paid off at three to two instead of even money.

Blackjack 39

Aces are powerful cards, even though few in number.

Listen closely the next time you play blackjack. Sometime during your gambling session, one of your fellow gamblers will receive a natural blackjack, moan, and then say something like this: "Damn it, I never have a big bet on the table when I catch a blackjack. Seems like I always get them when I bet small."

Well, no kidding.

But *you*, since you will be watching those precious Aces, will be prepared for those natural blackjacks.

I should now explain two statements I made earlier. First, I indicated that, if at all possible, you should sit at third base. The reason for choosing that position is that by sitting at third base you are able to see, and therefore count, more cards before you need to exercise any options on your hand. This is beneficial even if you're not a card counter, but it is especially beneficial if you have a card-counting system. The more cards you can count, and the more accurate your count, the more you turn the odds in your favor.

Example: At the start of a round of play, you note that the deck is rich in high-value cards. Consequently, you know that the remaining portion of the deck should be favorable for the players. You are dealt a Seven and a Four. The dealer is showing a Queen. Since the remaining deck is composed of a high ratio of high-value cards, you anticipate doubling down. But you are seated at third base, and the five or six players acting before you all take hits. They all receive 10-value cards. Would you still double down? Probably not. By the time it's your turn to exercise your options, the deck is no longer rich in high-value cards.

Your second choice of places to sit should be at first base. The reason? At first base, you are able to exercise your options before all the other players. In the example stated above, had you been seated at first base, you would definitely have doubled down. Had you been at first base, the other players would not have depleted the high ratio of high-value cards remaining in the deck.

Now that I've told you why you should sit at first or third base, let me try to confuse you. Most card counters that I've met prefer first or third base. Most pit bosses know that most card counters prefer third or first base. Consequently people who sit at third or first base tend to be watched more closely by the pit bosses, especially if the players in those two positions are winning consistently or varying their bets. So, while third and first base seats are preferable, don't feel cheated if you can't find one. In fact, there is nothing wrong with sitting in one of the middle seating positions. From the middle of the table it is actually easier to count cards, for the simple reason that you are midway between third and first bases and you therefore can see all

Playing the Games 40

the cards with less difficulty. And now that you may be confused as to where you should sit, let me make one last statement: If you are a card counter, you should try to sit at third or first base. If you are a beginning card counter, if you are not adept at camouflaging your counting, or if you are not an expert, do not sit at third or first base.

I also mentioned earlier that dealers will *burn* one or more cards from the top of the deck or decks before beginning each new deal. Now that we're talking about card counting, I can tell you that the reason the top card (or cards) is burned is to make life more troublesome for card counters. When counting cards, it is imperative to see as many cards as possible. If the dealer burns the top four cards, and all four cards are 10-values, your count will never be entirely accurate. The more cards the casino burns, the more difficult it is to count cards.

I once played at a casino where the dealer burned the top eight cards from a four-deck shoe. I thought she had made a mistake, so I asked her if burning eight cards was a new policy at that casino. Her answer was, "Sometimes." Needless to say, I left that casino after a few hands. But before I exited, I noted that a lady sitting at third base was obviously a card counter. Unfortunately, she was making plays that no person in their right mind would ever make, such as doubling down on a total of seven, and winning. So it became apparent that the dealer had burned eight cards in an attempt to discourage the counter.

To my way of thinking, the players are all in a war against the dealer. No, that doesn't mean we should hate all dealers. To the extent that we players are all trying to win, it makes sense that we should help one another as much as possible. Therefore, if the cards are dealt face down, don't be afraid to let the players on either side of you see your cards. I am a card counter. So when the people around me try to conceal their cards so I can't see them, I sometimes become perturbed. The more cards I can see, the better my count, and the greater my chance of winning. Conversely, I always let the people around me see my cards, in the hope that a small amount of additional knowledge may help them. If I have a holding of 11 and everybody around me has two 10-value cards in their hand, I will certainly think twice before doubling down. Don't hide your cards from the other players!

Money Management By this point, you should know the basic strategies and have an idea on how to count cards. Now let me make a statement: None of that means *anything*, unless you manage your money properly. You can play like a genius and still leave Las Vegas or Atlantic City with horrendous losses if you don't use your money with the utmost care and diligence.

Blackjack 41

My suggestion is this: Don't bother sitting down to play unless you have at least 50 units. A unit could be $2 or $5 or $100, but, whatever it is, you should have 50. If your unit is $2, 50 units would be $100. If your unit is $5 you should have $250. You must have at least 50 units to protect yourself against extended losing streaks, which *do* occur no matter how well you play.

Next, you *must* change tables if you lose five units. There are times when the composition of the deck is such that it favors the dealer for long stretches. This can be true whether you are playing with one deck, two decks, or multiple decks. Again, what some of you may think is "bad" luck can actually be caused by the composition of the cards. If the majority of the high-value cards are situated in the last half of the deck or decks, which is quite possible, then the first half of the deck or decks will greatly favor the dealer.

If you're playing with six decks, there are 312 total cards in the shoe, minus a few burn cards. Approximately half the decks, about 156 cards, will be played before the dealer reshuffles. If you are playing with four other gamblers, you could complete from eight to 13 rounds of play before the deck is reshuffled. Therefore, if the composition of the decks is unfavorable, you could lose from eight to 13 or more units, even if you play each hand perfectly. And it is also possible for the decks to contain the same composition for several hours at a time; that is, the decks could remain unfavorable for the players for long stretches of time. Why play against a dealer who is beating your brains out? I don't care if you need to change tables every five minutes . . . keep changing until you stop losing, keep changing until you find a table where the composition of the decks is more favorable.

Also, if you win as many as 10 units at any table, *do not* lose it back! As soon as you start winning, put your original chips in your pocket and play with your winnings. Once you've won 10 units, do not allow yourself to slip backwards. Leave the table before the casino can recapture its losses.

Last, if you win as many as 25 units, change your unit. If your unit was $2, for example, change it to $5. When you are winning, you must push for all you can. The player most feared by the casinos is the player who gradually increases his or her bets for maximum profits. If you increase your unit and start losing, go back to your original unit. If you win another 15 units, increase your unit again. But one word of caution: If you are a $2 bettor and increasing your unit to $5 or $10 makes you nervous, stay with a lower unit. I know people who play faultlessly with $5 bets, but lose control if they increase to $15 or $25 bets.

Rule Variations Not all casinos use the same rules governing the player and dealer options. What follows is a list of the differences that

Playing the Games **42**

you may find. Remember to ask about the rules *before* you start playing.

- *Doubling down.* In Las Vegas the player can double down on any initial two-card holding. In Reno and Lake Tahoe the player may *only* double down on holdings of 10 or 11, which limits double down opportunities and is subsequently a disadvantage for the player.

- *Splitting.* In Las Vegas, Reno, and Lake Tahoe pairs may be split and resplit; Aces receive only one hit.

- *Surrender.* This is an optional rule in Nevada, so ask everywhere you play.

- *Doubling down after splitting.* Assume that you split a pair of Sixes and then receive a Five on the first Six. In Nevada, at only a handful of casinos, you may then double down on your 11. This is very beneficial to the player, so seek out casinos which offer this option.

- *Dealer options.* In some casinos the dealer *must* stand on any 17. In others the dealer *may* stand on a soft 17 (Ace, Six). In still others, the dealer *must* hit a soft 17. It is to your advantage to play *only* where the dealer must stand on all 17s, whether soft or hard.

- *Dealer blackjacks.* In Atlantic City, all blackjack games are dealt from a shoe of four or six decks. If the dealer shows a 10-value or an Ace, she *cannot* peek at her hole card until *after* all the players have acted on their hands. This is to prevent collusion between dealers and players. If a player splits or doubles down, only to find out that the dealer has a natural blackjack, the player loses *only* the original wager, which is neither an advantage or a disadvantage. Check to see if your casino offers this option.

- *Double exposure.* In some Nevada casinos both the dealer's cards are dealt face up. This, of course, gives the player a tremendous advantage as it eliminates any speculation about the dealer's hole card. If the dealer is showing a total of 20, for example, you would hit your total of 19. But what the casinos give you with the right hand, they take back with the left. Here's what I mean: Though you have the advantage of seeing the dealer's hole card, in this game you are only paid even money if you receive a natural blackjack. And some casinos count all ties or pushes in this game as losses for the player. Only a fool would play against such heavy odds.

  If you haven't tried double-exposure blackjack yet, you might want to try it at a $1 or $2 table, using your "fun" money. And make sure you know *all* the rules before you start making bets.

Casino Games and Slots

The games of roulette, craps, baccarat, keno, and bingo, the Big Six wheel, slot machines, and football betting are analyzed here in articles prepared by *Gambling Times*.

Roulette

Casino roulette uses the same basic rules and procedures in all casinos throughout Nevada and in Atlantic City.

One to six players are seated at the roulette table. Players purchase special roulette chips, each player with his own color, so that the dealer can tell who made a winning bet and pay off that player. The chips generally have a set value of 25¢ or 50¢. A stack of 20 25¢ chips is valued at $5, and a stack of 20 50¢ chips would be worth $10. Usually it takes a minimum of $20 to buy in at the roulette table.

A player may request whatever value he wishes for his chips, above the 25¢ or 50¢ standard amount. The dealer will specify the worth of that particular colored chip by marking a sample chip which is placed upon the rim of the wheel. Players may also bet larger amounts by using $1, $5, and $25 regular casino chips.

It is important to note that roulette chips must be cashed in at the table. They may not be removed from the table when the player leaves.

The betting layout starts with numbers 0 and 00 at the top, then extends from numbers 1 to 36 the length of the table. This area is referred to as the "inside" betting area.

Inside bets consist of the following: Single-number bets, including 0, 00, and 1 to 36 are made by placing your chip in the center of the number you select. If that number wins, you'll receive 35 to 1 for every chip you've bet. Actually, you can pick up a total of 36 chips, which includes your original bet. Additional combinations in the inside betting area are: one chip on a six-number bet (pays 5 to 1); one chip on any four connecting numbers (pays 8 to 1); one chip on any connecting group of three numbers (gets you 11 to 1); one chip placed between two connecting numbers (pays 17 to 1).

The "outside" betting area consists of odd or even bets, which pay even money; red or black bets, which pay even money; and bets on 1 to 18 or 19 to 36, which pay even money. You'll get 2 to 1 odds if you select the winning number within the first, second, or third dozen numbers. The same

---

Reprinted from Gambling Times. *Copyright © 1982 by Gambling Times, Inc., 16760 Stagg St., Van Nuys, CA 91406. Used by permission of the publisher. Write the publisher for its extensive list of gambling books and periodicals, which includes the monthly* WIN *magazine, formerly* Gambling Times.

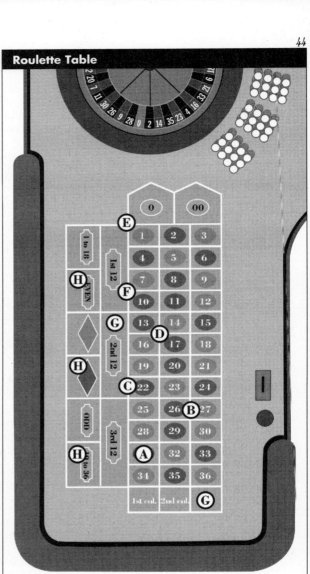

	Bet	Payoff
A	Single number	35 to 1
B	Two numbers	17 to 1
C	Three numbers	11 to 1
D	Four numbers	8 to 1
E	Five numbers	6 to 1
F	Six numbers	5 to 1
G	12 numbers (column)	2 to 1
G	1st 12, 2nd 12, 3rd 12	2 to 1
H	1-18 or 19-36	1 to 1
H	Odd or Even	1 to 1
H	Red or black	1 to 1

Craps 45

2 to 1 odds are given for selecting any of the numbers in the three vertical columns of 12 numbers.

All betting areas are clearly designated in the diagram, a replica of the standard roulette betting layout. For outside bets, the dealer will pay the winning chips alongside your original bet. It is up to you to pick up both your winnings and your original bet after the payoff.

All inside bets are paid, by the dealer, directly to you. The dealer knows you are the winner by the color of your chips. In many instances, more than one colored chip is on a winning number. Again, your original bet is left on the number or combination of numbers, and it's up to you to reclaim that bet. Naturally you can let it ride again on the next roll, or even add other chips from your winnings.

The perfectly balanced roulette wheel consists of 38 identical slots, individually numbered from 0, 00, and 1 to 36. In total, 38 numbers are represented on the betting layout.

Each game begins when the dealer (sometimes called the croupier) spins the wheel in one direction and then rolls the little ivory ball along the inner edge of the wheel in the opposite direction. As the wheel turns, the ball loses momentum. It bounces among the slots and finally falls into one of the numbered slots. That number is the declared winner for that game. About 90 spins or games are played per hour, on average.

When you examine a standard roulette wheel, you will notice that the numbers are not consecutively arranged around the wheel. By design, they alternate between red and black, and opposite each number are the corresponding higher and lower numbers.

The house edge is set at 5.26%, a consequence of the player's receiving odds of 35 to 1 rather than the true odds of 1 in 38, or 37 to 1. All in all, the edge in roulette is comparable to the "rake" in poker and to some bets on the craps table, in baccarat, and in other games and sports betting. The single 0 European wheel has a house edge of just 2.70%; the player has a 1 in 37 chance of winning and still gets 35 to 1 odds.

Some casinos use the "en prison" rule where, when a 0 or 00 occurs, all even-money bets are held (or only half is taken), depending upon the outcome of the next spin.

Craps

In casino craps, the players place their bets and the casino bank "covers" them. In addition to covering every player's bet, the casino bank craps game offers many other types of proposition bets.

Four people actively run the game. The boxman, who sits behind the table in the middle, is the boss. He keeps a constant watch over the game. The two dealers on each side of

Craps Table

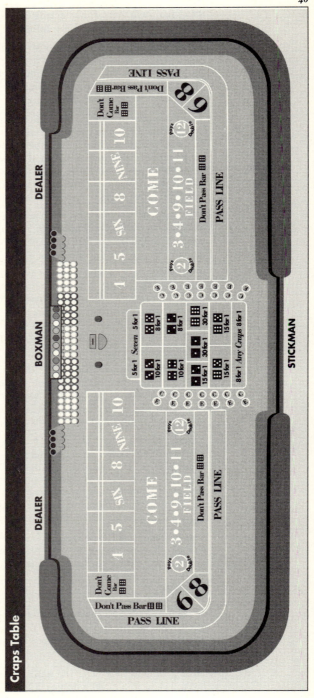

46

Playing the Games   47

him pay off the winners and rake in the losers' chips. Each dealer handles all the players on his side. The table is divided by the center box of proposition bets and also by the stickman, who stands on the players' side of the table.

The stickman controls the action of the dice and the pace of the game. After seeing that all bets are down, the stickman pushes a few sets of dice to the shooter. That player selects a pair of dice and is ready to roll them across the table so that they hit the wall at the opposite end.

If, on the first roll, you make a 7 or 11, you've rolled a "natural" and you win. What you win is the equivalent amount of chips you have bet on the pass line.

If you roll a 2, 3, or 12 on your first throw, that is "craps," and you lose. The dealer picks up your pass line bet. However, the shooter does not relinquish the dice; he continues to roll them until he "sevens out."

If, on the first roll, you shoot a 4, 5, 6, 8, 9, or 10, that is your established "box point." The object then is to keep rolling the dice until you make that number again. You lose, however, if you roll a 7 before making your box point.

These are the bets of craps:

Pass Line. Pays even money, house edge is 1.414%; it's one of the best bets on the table.

Don't Pass. Pays even-money, house edge is 1.402%, slightly better than the pass line odds.

Come and Don't Come. Even-money bets with the same house percentages of 1.414% and 1.402% as the pass line and don't pass bets.

Place Bets. The 4 and 10 pay 9 to 5 (true odds, 10 to 5), house edge is 6.66%. The 5 and 9 pay 7 to 5 (true odds, 7½ to 5), house edge is 4%. The 6 and 8 pay 7 to 6 (true odds, 6 to 5), house edge is 1.51%.

Buy Bets. Player pays 5% vigorish to get true odds on all numbers. Only the 4 and 10 make buy bets worthwhile; they reduce house edge to 4.76%.

The Field. A one-roll bet that pays even money, or 2 to 1 on 2 or 12. House edge is 5.55%.

Big 6 & 8. Player bets in boxes marked as such and receives even money instead of 6 to 5 true odds. House edge is 9.09%.

Hard Ways. This bet can be made on the 4, 6, 8, and 10. Payoff is 9 to 1 on the 6 or 8 (house edge is 9.09%) and 7 to 1 on the 4 or 10 (house edge is 11.11%). *This is a bad bet.*

Any Craps. This is a one-roll bet. If a 2, 3, or 12 hits, you'll get 7 to 1 odds. House edge is 11.11%. *This is a bad bet.*

Seven. This one-roll bet pays odds of 4 to 1; true odds are 5 to 1, giving the house an edge of 16.66%. *This is a bad bet.*

Eleven. This is another one-roll bet. It pays 14 to 1, but true odds are 17 to 1, giving the house an edge of 16.66%. *This is a bad bet.*

Horn Bet. Although the 2, 3, 12, and 11 may be bet sepa-

Playing the Games 48

rately, this area is known as the horn. A player makes a horn bet by handing the bet to the dealer, calling out (for example), "Four-dollar horn bet." This would give the player $1 on each of the four one-roll propositions. Payoff is 30 to 1 on a 2 or 12 (true odds are 35 to 1), 15 to 1 on a 3 or 11 (true odds are 17 to 1). House edge on all four bets is 16.66%. *This is a bad bet.*

Odds. When a point is made (either the shooter's point on the first roll or a come point on a succeeding roll), a player can take the odds. A player will receive 2 to 1 on 4 and 10, 3 to 2 on 5 and 9, and 6 to 5 on 6 and 8. The player lays the same odds when he bets against the point.

Our advice is to play the line and the come, either pass or don't pass. These are the two best areas to bet, offering the best possible odds to the player. If you're betting the pass line, always take your full odds in back of your pass line bet. Some casinos offer double odds; if so, take advantage of this option. One last piece of advice: Increase your bets on wins; do not double up on losses.

Baccarat

The word *baccarat* is derived from the Italian *baccara*, which means "zero." The term refers to the face cards and the Ten, all of which have zero value in the game of baccarat. In Europe baccarat and a similar version called chemin de fer are among the most popular casino games.

Since baccarat's inception in Nevada, the game has assumed a glamorous look. In most casinos baccarat is played in a separate, roped-off area. The intention was to attract the high roller or the more sophisticated, moneyed player. Tuxedo-clad dealers give a further elegance and aloofness to the game.

For all its enchantment, however, baccarat is primarily a simplistic game. There are no decisions or options to be taken, and no degree of skill is required for either player or dealer. Players may sit in any open seat at the table; seating position does not affect the play in any manner. Each seat corresponds to a number on the layout, 1 through 15. Three dealers service the table. The dealer standing between positions 1 and 15 is the caller. He runs the game as cards are dealt from the shoe.

Each player gets a turn to handle the shoe. The player must bet the bank when he has the shoe, but any player may decline the shoe, and it passes along from player to player. Again, there is no advantage or disadvantage in dealing the cards; it's merely a formality and a part of the ambience that players enjoy.

The caller receives the cards from the player with the shoe, places them in the appropriate boxes, and then calls for an-

Baccarat 49

other card, or declares the winner, according to the rigid rules of the game.

Players bet by placing their chips in the numbered box opposite their seat. Bets may be made on the player or on the bank, and both are paid off at even money. In most games, bets range from $20 minimum to $2,000 maximum.

After the winner is announced, the two other dealers at the table pay off the winning bets and collect from the losers. When the bank is the winner, players who won must pay a 5% commission on their winnings. Thus a player who bet $100 on the bank and won would owe the house $5.

Rather than collect this vigorish after each game, a record of what is owed by each player is kept in a numbered box just opposite where the two payoff dealers sit. Players pay this accumulated amount after the finish of a shoe. Each time the shoe is depleted of cards, all eight decks are thoroughly shuffled and replaced in the shoe.

In determining the value of the hands, all cards, Ace through Nine, are valued according to their count, but Tens and face cards count as zero. Thus, if the first two cards dealt are a King and a Four, the count is four.

When any two cards total over a 10 count, 10 must be subtracted. The remaining total is the card count. An Eight and a Six, although totaling 14, would come to four after subtracting 10.

These rules apply in all U.S. casinos, and printed copies of the rules are available wherever baccarat is played. Dealers act according to these rules without consulting players at the table; the rules are automatic.

The highest total any baccarat hand can have is nine. A two-card total of nine is called a natural and cannot lose. An eight is the second best hand and is also called a natural. When player and bank are dealt identical hands, it's a standoff (a tie) and neither bank nor player wins.

No further cards can be drawn to a two-card draw of six or seven.

When holding other two-card totals, player and bank draw another card at the direction of the dealer who does the calling. One can easily determine the rules of the game by consulting the printed chart that accompanies the table diagram.

Baccarat is a matter of letting the dealer do the calling and then declare the outcome. Players are concerned only with how much they will wager on each hand and whether they will bet on the player's side or the banker's. The house edge in baccarat is the lowest of any casino game. With a commission of only 5% on winning bank bets, and nothing taken from winning player bets, the player's disadvantage is only

Baccarat Table

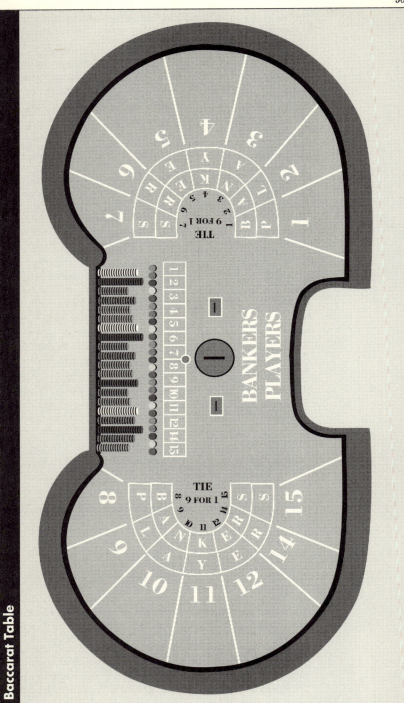

Keno 51

1.37%. In some casinos ties are permitted to be bet on; the payoff is 8 to 1. This is a bad bet for the player, for the house edge is 14.1%.

A number of casinos have installed smaller baccarat tables, usually among the blackjack tables. It's the same game, but passing the shoe and other rituals are missing, and the game is staffed by only one dealer. Yet the layout conforms to the regular baccarat table, and each seat position (1–6) corresponds to a numbered betting box. Limits are usually from a minimum of $2–$5 to a maximum of $500. Minibaccarat is played more quickly, but the same rules apply as in the larger game.

Keno

Keno, based on an ancient game played by Chinese rail workers, is similar to bingo. As in bingo, keno players select numbers that win if they match the numbers called in that game.

Keno is popular throughout Nevada. It's played in practically every large casino around the clock, with a rate of about 200 games in a 24-hour period. That figures out to approximately one game every seven to eight minutes, and that rapid rate of play adds to keno's attraction.

Although the casino advantage is unusually high, the excitement of playing keno lies in the huge payoff possibilities. For as little as $1, players can win as much as $50,000. The full range of cash prizes goes from $1 to $50,000.

Primarily, keno is a fun game: Winning is pure luck, merely a matter of selecting the right numbers against a house percentage that ranges around 25%. There's also a good share of player involvement; as the keno board lights up, players watch anxiously as each of 20 numbers appears.

Keno is played in an area adjacent to the other casino games, and comfortable chairs are provided for those who wish to sit through the games. Some stay and play for hours. Others, passing through the casino, stop to mark a keno ticket and then stand around until the game is called.

Throughout the casino, in restaurants, bars, and cocktail lounges, patrons can sit and play keno. In these places keno runners collect keno tickets and wagers from patrons, take the tickets to the central keno counter, register the tickets, and take the receipts back to the patrons. This is part of the service, and it accounts for a large share of keno business.

Keno boards are strategically placed around the casino, as well as in the dining and bar areas, so that players may watch the board light up with the numbers as each game is called.

Blank keno tickets are stacked in holders, along with marking crayons, throughout the keno area. They are also on

Playing the Games 52

tables in the coffee shop, bars, and cocktail lounges. All keno blanks are exactly the same, and the game is played in the same manner throughout the casinos of Nevada.

A keno blank contains 80 numbers, printed in small squares in consecutive order from 1 to 80. There are 10 numbers to each horizontal line, with four lines on the top half of the ticket and four lines on the bottom half.

Two factors determine the marking of a keno ticket: the number of spots (numbers) selected and the amount of the bet. A popularly priced keno ticket is $1. Our illustration of the payoff chart shows that 15 tickets can be played. For example, if you play a one-spot ticket (you mark one number) and your number is among the 20 numbers called, you'll receive $3 in return for your $1 bet.

The payoffs become larger as you move up the line. Let's use a six-spot ticket as an example. Again it's a $1 bet, but now you select any six numbers from 1 to 80. If three of your numbers are among the 20 numbers called, you'll get back just $1. If four of your numbers come in, you'll receive $4. Five numbers out of your six will get you $88. And if all six of your numbers are called, you will win $1,480.

A $1 bet on a 14-spot ticket will net you the grand sum of $50,000 if all 14 of your numbers are drawn!

Keno payoffs above $1,500 are reportable to the Internal Revenue Service. Anything above that amount requires the winner's signature on a G-2 IRS form.

The best way to mark a keno ticket is to place an *X* in each of the numbered squares you select. You then mark the price of your bet in the upper right-hand corner, and a *6* in the area below. That's how to write a six-spot ticket; the same method applies to writing any other ticket, from a one-spot to a 15-spot.

After marking your ticket, take it to the keno counter. Hand the keno ticket and your $1 wager to the keno writer. He will duplicate your ticket on another keno blank that is numbered with the next game. He will also time-stamp both your original ticket and the duplicate. You receive the duplicate and wait until the next game is called.

After the game is announced as "closed," the random drawing of 20 numbers commences. A total of 80 numbered ping-pong balls are automatically mixed in a large sealed plastic bowl. As the caller presses a button, air forces one ball at a time to be blown up into a narrow transparent tube. (Actually, there are two tubes, one extending out from each side of the bowl.)

Each tube holds exactly 10 balls. As each ball is forced up into the tube, the number is read over a loudspeaker by the caller. At the same time, that number is flashed on the large

Keno Payoffs *(for a bet of $1)*

Numbers Marked	Winning Numbers	Pays $	Numbers Marked	Winning Numbers	Pays $
1	1 number	3			
			11	5 numbers	1
2	2 numbers	12		6 numbers	8
				7 numbers	72
				8 numbers	360
				9 numbers	1,800
3	2 numbers	1		10 numbers	12,000
	3 numbers	42		11 numbers	28,000
4	2 numbers	1	**12**	6 numbers	5
	3 numbers	4		7 numbers	32
	4 numbers	112		8 numbers	240
				9 numbers	600
				10 numbers	1,480
5	3 numbers	2		11 numbers	8,000
	4 numbers	20		12 numbers	36,000
	5 numbers	480			
			13	6 numbers	1
6	3 numbers	1		7 numbers	16
	4 numbers	4		8 numbers	80
	5 numbers	88		9 numbers	720
	6 numbers	1,480		10 numbers	4,000
				11 numbers	8,000
				12 numbers	20,000
7	4 numbers	2		13 numbers	40,000
	5 numbers	24			
	6 numbers	360	**14**	6 numbers	1
	7 numbers	5,000		7 numbers	10
				8 numbers	40
8	5 numbers	9		9 numbers	300
	6 numbers	92		10 numbers	1,000
	7 numbers	1,480		11 numbers	3,200
	8 numbers	18,000		12 numbers	16,000
				13 numbers	24,000
				14 numbers	50,000
9	5 numbers	4			
	6 numbers	44	**15**	7 numbers	8
	7 numbers	300		8 numbers	28
	8 numbers	4,000		9 numbers	132
	9 numbers	20,000		10 numbers	300
				11 numbers	2,600
10	5 numbers	2		12 numbers	8,000
	6 numbers	20		13 numbers	20,000
	7 numbers	132		14 numbers	32,000
	8 numbers	960		15 numbers	50,000
	9 numbers	3,800			
	10 numbers	25,000			

Playing the Games 54

keno board. All of the keno boards throughout the casino are simultaneously lit as numbers are called.

If enough of your selected numbers match those that have been called, you will win the amount shown in the payoff chart. You then take your ticket to the same casino counter, where you will receive your winnings in cash.

We have explained the instructions for writing a basic straight ticket. Other variables in playing keno involve marking more complicated tickets. In each case, it's a matter of combining groups of numbers for at least three or more payoffs. These tickets are known as way, combination, and king tickets.

Once you become familiar with marking straight tickets— and especially after cashing a few winners—you can go on to marking and playing the more complex keno tickets.

Bingo

Bingo, a game of Italian heritage, certainly bears enough similarities to the more ancient Chinese game of keno to qualify them as first cousins. The principal difference is that while keno numbers are selected in advance by the players, with no regard for pattern, bingo wins are contingent upon the successful completion of a horizontal, vertical, or diagonal line of five of the randomly selected and called numbers on prenumbered cards (also referred to as bingo boards). However, bingo is a more diversified form because of the infinite variety of letters, figures, and designs that can be formed upon the cards and designated as winners of special games.

Descendant of a mid-16th-century Italian national lottery, bingo underwent a double transition over the years, first to lotto, a rather tepid home parlor game, and then, coinciding with its commercial adaptation, someone tagged it with a name that had zip: BINGO! From a quietly amusing way to fill an evening, it rocketed into a near-cult recreation.

On April 25, 1965, bingo's immense potential was demonstrated when 10,000 players attended a bingo session at the Empire Pool in London. It is estimated that there are now approximately 35 million devotees of the game in the United States alone. Today the aficionados of this fascinating numbers game are as excited about bingo as any horse player at the track or any blackjack, craps, roulette, or slot machine player in the casino.

Bingo rooms are always separate from the noisier slot and pit areas of the casino itself, with comfortable row seating and convenient racks for holding the players' bingo boards. Free coffee and cocktail service are common. Once relegated to a "poor boy" status by the casino industry—whoever saw a high roller in a bingo room?—it has gained a large and faithful following, is financially self-sustaining,

Bingo

and surely has had a positive financial impact at those casinos that feature it. Strangely enough, this down-to-earth game and the sophisticated European baccarat are the only two completely cloistered games in the casino complex.

Although the mechanics of bingo may seem complicated to the uninitiated reader, it is a simple game to learn. The bingo cards that the customers play with are square, with 24 different numbers between 1 and 75, randomly scattered with no sequence or order. There are five rows across and five rows down, with the center square designated as "free." Above the numbers are the five letters B, I, N, G, O. They have no special significance except to aid the players in scanning their cards when the numbers are called with the particular letter that indicates the correct vertical column. The smallest numbers line up under the B, the highest ones under the O.

On the stage where the drawing is done, 75 differently numbered ping-pong balls are contained in a transparent mixer and blower-equipped box. As each one is randomly blown up into the ball catcher and extracted by the operator, it is placed upon a small cupped dias, where it is plainly visible to all upon the TV monitor screen. The number on the ball is called out, along with the row letter ("Under the N, 34!"), and it is then put into its place on the master board, automatically lighting up the corresponding number on the audience flashboard.

The usual object of the basic game is to complete the five numbers in one row, either horizontally, vertically, or diagonally, with or without making use of the free center square. The first lucky player to do so calls out "BINGO!" After the winning card is checked and verified, that player becomes the lone winner or splits the prize for that game with any others who completed a row at the same time. Splitting is kept at a minimum; the bingo room operators are careful to see that there are no duplicate cards among the hundreds that are available for selection by players at the start of each session. Yet there are still many possibilities for lining up five identical numbers in different ways, which accounts for the ties that sometimes occur.

The most electric recent development in the gaming industry has been the progressive system, which builds up giant jackpots by extracting a small fraction of each bet and channeling it into a special jackpot. This innovation has for some time added an exciting new dimension to slots play, but it has only recently been adapted to bingo. The Bingo Progressive is usually started with a large prize, perhaps $1,000, and $250 is added each day until someone wins the bonanza. This happens on a "cover all" game, which requires the winner to fill an entire card within a specified number of drawn numbers. The number of draws is changed until someone makes the big score. Consolation

Playing the Games 56

prizes are usually awarded in those games that do not have a winner.

Board prices range from $1 to $5. Most establishments have a minimum board buy of $3 (players may take three $1 boards or one $3 board). Boards come in different colors, each color designating the price of the board.

Bingo sessions ordinarily begin at 11 AM, with new sessions at two-hour intervals, the last round of play beginning at 1 AM. The games normally last about an hour, and it is in the open time between sessions that the casino hopes to profit from its bingo players: Many players stay for several sessions and patronize the other casino games, bars, and restaurants during the breaks.

Bingo richly deserves an exalted and prestigious place in the gaming picture. For many years before its advent in the casino world, it served as an effective cleanup hitter in charity fund-raising. It has benefited churches, hospitals, schools, fraternal organizations, and other worthy causes. As a mark of its public image, it has frequently been permitted to operate under tacit approval, without any actual legislative green light. Everyone loves bingo.

Big Six (Wheel of Fortune)

Big Six, or the Wheel of Fortune, is an easy-to-play casino attraction that is reminiscent of the old carnival wheels. The wheel itself is made of wood in an elaborate and colorful design. Approximately six feet in diameter, it's divided into nine sections, each consisting of six identically spaced slots. The 54 slots are separated by metal studs.

Positioned at the top of the wheel is a leather flap, and when the wheel is turning, a tick, tick, tick sound is heard as the strap hits against the naillike metal studs. As the wheel slows down, the strap will settle in one slot, and that particular one of the 54 slots will be declared the winner.

The slots are divided as follows: 23 $1 slots, 15 $2 slots, eight $5 slots, four $10 slots, two $20 slots, and two slots that have joker or casino designs. Each of the slots carries a design of American currency—a $1 bill, for example, in each of the 23 $1 slots spread around the wheel.

A glass-covered table set in front of the wheel is where players place their bets. Pieces of currency, one to match each of the denominations around the wheel, are represented on this betting table layout. Players place their bets on top of their selection. A bet on the $1 bill will pay $1 for an even-money return if the spin of the wheel results in the leather strap stopping in the $1 bill slot.

A bet on the $2 bill pays off at 2 to 1. The $5 winner gets a 5 to 1 return, the $10 winner receives a payoff of 10 to 1, and the lucky player who selects the $20 denomination gets a

Slot Machines 57

20 to 1 payoff when the wheel stops in either of the slots marked with a $20 bill.

If the player selects either the special design or the joker designate, the payoff is 40 to 1. Each of the 40 to 1 selections is an individual bet. In all, there are seven choices for making a bet.

To calculate the percentage in favor of the casino, we multiply each payoff symbol by its dollar value, subtract that from the remaining total number of symbols, and divide by 54. The $1 symbol gives us 23 chances of winning against 31 chances to lose. This leaves eight divided by 54, and the percentage or casino edge is 14.8%.

The 15 $2 slots versus the 39 other chances give the house an edge of 16.7%. The eight $5 symbols, paying 5 to 1 odds, give the house an edge of 11.1%. The four $10 slots paying off at 10 to 1 give the house an advantage of 18.5%. The two $20 slots with odds of 20 to 1 provide the casino an edge of 22.2%. Either the joker or the special design slot works out to a 24% house advantage.

Other combinations of denominations on the wheel will produce different house advantages—and now you know how to calculate the odds.

The attraction to the Wheel of Fortune is the aspect of fun and games. Patrons walking through the casino stop to watch the wheel as it spins and ticks, then stay to play a few dollars to see if their lucky guess produces a winner.

Slot Machines

With individual wins of $250,000 to $1 million, the popularity of the slots is at an all-time high. Even before casino gambling became legal, slot machines were much in evidence. Private social clubs and other seclusive places featured slot machines for the benefit of their members and guests, and these clandestine operations still exist across the country.

When casino gambling became legal throughout the state of Nevada, slot machines were a prominent feature in every licensed establishment. Today slot machines remain the leading gaming attraction to many visitors, and this popularity has led to newer types of slots and higher cash awards.

While it's true that large payoffs are regularly made to lucky slots players, the fact is commensurate with the casino's gross business. There is no gamble on the part of the casino, for the slots are set to provide a predetermined profit that has been worked out on a purely mechanical basis. Each machine retains a certain percentage of the coins played and returns the balance to the players.

Playing the Games   58

Playing three to five coins per pull on one machine is quite ordinary in present-day slots. The chance of hitting a win combination is multiplied, and the amount of the payoff is also commensurate with the number of coins played. It speeds up play, too.

The $1 slots, especially those mounted on a special carousel, generally give the player the best chance of winning. Many casinos advertise the percentage paid, such as "96% guaranteed payout." What this means is that for every $100 played in these slots, $96 will be paid back in various win combinations and in the eventual jackpot. It also means that the house percentage—the profit—is 4%.

Progressive Slots The progressive slots are the ultimate in offerings of super jackpot payoffs. Jackpots of $100,000 to $1 million are occurring with regularity in major casinos, and this is the lure that draws hordes of players—even teams of slot players—to the progressives.

The amount that can be won is registered visibly above the bank of progressive slots. This figure increases by 5% of the amount deposited for each pull. Thus, on a $1 slot, 5¢ would be added to the progressive total for each $1 played.

When playing a progressive slot, you should always put in the maximum number of coins required. Anything less may make your hoped-for jackpot ineligible. Always read the instructions posted on the machine. They're simple to read, understand, and follow.

If you're not sure about the method of playing a particular progressive slot, ask one of the slot attendants or change persons. When you're playing for a super jackpot, you want to make sure that you're following the proper method of play.

When you have a winner for any size jackpot, do not pull the handle again until you've checked with the attendant. In most cases the coins that come tumbling down the chute do not represent the total jackpot payout; the balance of the money will be given to you by the slot attendant.

If your jackpot is for any sizable amount, a casino slot mechanic may come to your machine to verify that it was a legitimate win. This is no reflection on you; it's just a necessary precaution by the casino management.

Always stay by your machine. Do not move away from it if you hit a jackpot. In all probability the jackpot was signaled and an attendant is on the way to your machine.

If a jackpot payoff exceeds $1,500, you will be asked to sign a G-2 IRS form stipulating the amount of your win. That means that your winnings are now a part of the Internal Revenue Service records, just as if you had earned this money. It will be necessary for you to declare this amount on your next income tax return. However, it may be possi-

Football Betting 59

ble to deduct the amount of money you put into the slot machine before winning the jackpot.

Playing the slots is primarily a fun game—it's part of the casino atmosphere, an exciting and easy way to gamble. If you're lucky enough to be at the right machine at the right time, you can hit a super jackpot. Many of those who win big jackpots do so on a very limited number of coins.

Football Betting

Gambling on football has become an enormous international industry. The estimated untaxed money bet on both college and pro football in the United States and Canada is in excess of $20 billion annually!

This engrossing pastime, although stimulating and enjoyable, has one very negative aspect: Approximately 94% of the people who bet on football *lose* money. This occurs because most sports gamblers do not use a set handicapping method or a planned procedure of money management.

For those who need the basics of these critical aspects of football gambling, the following guide will serve as an excellent starting point.

Handicapping Handicapping is the process in which one attempts to predict the winner of a contest (sporting event) by comparing past performance results of the contestants (teams) and analyzing current trends that exist in that medium (sport).

There are probably as many different methods by which one may handicap sports as there are handicappers. It would be difficult to determine which general method performs with the greatest degree of efficiency; all of the approaches have both good and bad points. We will consider the four major methods of handicapping sports.

The emotional method is the most common method used to select teams. The selection is made by the gambler's emotional preference. For example: "Dallas is a better team than Phoenix; Dallas should beat Phoenix; therefore, I will bet on Dallas." Another emotional thought is, "I'm a Viking fan and I want to root for the Vikings; therefore, I will bet on the Vikings." The emotional gambler usually plays the favorites because of the simplicity involved. In many cases he chases a particular team.

The team evaluative method is a comparison of any team's strengths and weaknesses in particular areas such as kicking, rushing, passing, injuries, etc. In recent years the classic example of a team-evaluative handicapper was Jimmy the Greek, who analyzed Sunday pro games on national television.

The psychological team evaluative method is the least common handicapping technique and the most difficult for accuracy. Some typical variables for the method are: "The

Playing the Games 60

team is up for the game" and "The team has let down for the game." A strong play involves a letdown when a team wins an important game either at home or away and then plays a relatively unimportant game away against a weaker team than the one they just beat. The idea is to play the weak team based on the theory that the visitors will be letting down.

The statistical analysis method keeps accurate records on situations where good percentage bets can be made. A simple example is to bet on all the home teams that are the underdogs by 10 or more points in professional football. Yet no individual betting situation can win forever. Be flexible within the framework of the system; individual betting situations fluctuate. Look for consistent winners. Stop playing a losing system and resume playing when the system wins.

Money Management Sports gamblers, no matter how good their handicapping expertise might be, will not win money unless they understand and use good money management. It is the most *critical* aspect of any kind of gambling, and it will by itself separate the winners from the losers.

The first requirement for any money management theory is that the person who is about to gamble must have some money. That will probably sound silly to some readers, yet many people will gamble, week in and week out, without actually having any financial backing.

Assume that a player has a starting bankroll of x. His individual plays (bets) should total between 2% and 5% of x, the determining percentage factor of his play being just how much action he wants.

A conservative player would bet in the 2% to 3% range; the more wide-open style of player might bet around 5% of his bankroll for his plays.

If you can handicap with enough skill to show a profit, stay with an exact percentage of bankroll for each play, and your bets will automatically go up or down as your bankroll does.

Football Bets There are three principal ways in which you can bet on football games.

In a *flat bet* (straight wager) you bet on one team to beat (cover) the point spread in the game it is playing this week. You lay $11 to win $10. In some locations you can exercise the option of buying an extra half-point (plus or minus) by laying $12 to make $10.

In a *parlay* you bet on a multiple of teams, usually two, three, or four teams. All the teams that you select must beat the pointspread. The Parlay Betting Odds chart shows the payoff and the actual odds of winning for each bet.

In a *teaser* you bet, again, on a multiple of teams, but with this wager you receive some amount of additional points to

Parlay Betting Odds

Number of Teams	Payout Odds	True Odds
2	13–5	3–1
3	6–1	7–1
4	10–1	15–1
5	20–1	31–1
6	35–1	63–1
7	50–1	127–1
8	100–1	225–1
9	200–1	511–1
10	400–1	1023–1

Teaser Betting Odds

Number of Teams	6 points	6½ points	7 points
2	even	10–11	1–12
3	9–5	8–5	3–2
4	3–1	5–2	2–1
5	9–2	4–1	7–2
6	7–1	6–1	5–1

the regular handicap (point spread). Also, as in a parlay, all your teams must beat the point spread. While the odds can vary among locations, the most common odds used with teasers are shown in the Teaser Betting Odds chart.

The Point Spread The point spread is designed to make the amount bet on each side of a game even. By determining relative strengths and weaknesses of the teams, and the usual betting patterns, the bookmaker assigns a number of points, which, when the game is ended, are subtracted from the total scored by the favorite.

For example, if the Los Angeles Rams play the New Orleans Saints, and most people feel the Rams are the better team, the point spread would be LA Rams *minus* points; say, –7. If the final score is Rams 23, New Orleans 18, a bet on the Rams would not have covered. This is because the Rams must beat the Saints by seven points for you to tie and eight points for you to win.

Whether you take the favorite at –7 points or the underdog at +7, you must lay 11-to-10 odds; that is, you win $10 when you "cover" and pay $11 if you fail to "cover." Though these odds never change, the point spread does.

The bookmaker is not in business to take sides. His profit comes from the 11-to-10 odds each bettor gives him. Re-

Playing the Games 62

member, the goal of the bookmaker is to keep the action on both sides even. If a large amount is bet on the Rams in our example, the pointspread will be moved up to −8 or −9 to encourage betting on New Orleans.

3 Casinos

You can't win! Yet no matter how many times that's been said, millions of people come to Las Vegas every year, hoping to beat the odds. After all, it does happen now and then, and whenever someone wins a million-dollar jackpot, folks tend to hear about it.

But Steve Wynn didn't spend $630 million to build his new Mirage hotel on the Strip because he expected to make a lot of money by renting rooms. He knew that thousands of people would come to gawk at his new showplace—and drop hundreds of thousands of coins down his slot fountains while they were there.

The casinos make a fortune, more than $3 billion a year, simply by keeping most of the money that comes out of your pocket. With table games they keep around 30% of the money; with the slot machines—the Number One game in Nevada—they hold around 76%.

Slots are the most popular game because they're the easiest to play: Just invest some money and pull the handle; what could be simpler? The game that pays back money most often is craps, which has more rules than any other game. The most enjoyable table game, and the game with the simplest rules, is blackjack, and it's the most popular table game in Nevada.

Casinos appreciate people who drink (you'll notice that drinks are free to gamblers), for the house knows that drinking dulls the senses. Best of all, casinos love gamblers who don't know how to play the game yet will try their luck anyway. They tend to leave lots of money at the table.

So when you want to try a game you aren't already familiar with, take the time to read up on it before you go to the table.

When you have some idea of the basics, you will want to attend the free sessions of gambling lessons that are given at most hotels. Even if you think you know the rules well, these lessons will give you an opportunity to play the game, using practice chips, without spending your money. So if you think you understand craps, try it out this way first and save yourself the potential embarrassment of blowing $50 at the table in five minutes. The courses, which usually last an hour, take you through all the games and let you discover which one is for you.

Further help is provided by the how-to-play guides you'll find in most hotel rooms, and many hotels have in-house TV channels that offer gambling instruction.

Casino Etiquette

Casinos can be confusing places for the first-time visitor. They tend to be large, open rooms with lots of tables, cameras hung from the ceiling watching your movements, and security guards around the floor doing the same. What's missing is some announcement that informs newcomers of the house rules and tells them how to behave. So we'll do that right here.

All players must be 21 years of age, no exception. If you're playing a slot with a kid by your side, the security guard will ask you to leave. But you can walk through the casino with your youngster in tow (figure that one out).

Casino Etiquette

No photographs may be taken in the casinos: Management fears that a gambler may feel uncomfortable having his picture taken and will get up and leave.

The casino of today offers craps, blackjack, and baccarat tables, roulette and Big Six wheels, and keno boards. Large race books with many TV screens show every type of sport imaginable, and there are video slots that have entered the computer age.

The first thing you'll see when you walk in are the slot machines and a long double row of tables. Never walk between the tables to get to the other side of the room; if you do, the security guard will freak out, for the inner sanctum of the tables is reserved for dealers and other casino personnel.

The table games in the rows are blackjack, roulette, and craps. To join a blackjack game, you need only find an empty chair at a table of your choice, one with a minimum bet that meets your budget. Before you sit down, look at the little card on the table that announces the betting minimum. On the Strip most blackjack tables have a minimum $3 bet, while other tables demand minimum bets of $5, $10, $25, or $100. Many downtown casinos have $1 tables. The guide to casinos in this chapter identifies the houses with low minimums.

The five-seat blackjack tables are usually pretty crowded at peak hours, so it might be hard to find places for two or three people together. When this happens, ask for the pit boss and request that a new table be opened for your party. Odds are he'll honor your request. If you're with a friend who chooses not to gamble, he or she will have to stand and watch; the chairs are for players only. (Roulette and craps are primarily standing games.)

You can sit down at a blackjack table at any time, but you can't play until you convert your cash into chips. The dealer will do this for you after a hand has been completed. When you've finished playing, take your chips to the cashier to convert them back into cash.

An old wives' tale holds that dealers aren't allowed to talk to players. Not true; don't hesitate to ask any question you like. If a dealer doesn't answer, or is rude, walk away to another table—or another casino. In the late 1980s the trend among dealers was to be friendlier and more helpful, but there will always be those dealers who prefer to grumble.

At some of the smaller, less busy gambling houses, dealers will take time with new players to point out the right ways and wrong ways of the game. (They have seen everything.) When you're a newcomer to the tables, you'll want to avoid the larger houses, especially at peak hours, because much of the time the personnel will be too busy to give you effective help should you become confused. First-timers will find play much more comfortable in the morning or during the middle of the night, when things are less hectic. The guide to casinos in this chapter points out some of the less crowded gambling houses.

When you plan a tour and intend to gamble, consider the timing of your casino visit. If you arrive at a busy hour, it may be hard to find room for two at a table or room at a table with the minimum bet that's right for you. Your best move is to arrive early—the earlier the better. The activity of Las Vegas starts

Casinos 66

to get under way around 11 AM, builds to 5 PM, remains steady until 8 PM, and then grows busier and peaks between 11 PM and midnight. If you can play at 9 AM, do it. If you can play at 6 AM, do it. At those hours the dealers will be more amicable and less smoke will be blown in your face. (While several houses now have tables for nonsmokers, there isn't a single casino in Vegas entirely for nonsmokers.)

Money Management

The basic rule in betting is to start small and build. Begin with modest bets, increasing their size as your luck and your bankroll improve. Betting $2 blackjack all night is not going to make you a bundle because it pays only even money. You will have to graduate to $10 and $20 bets before a win means something and the payoffs reach the $40 range.

The trick is to know enough to walk away when your luck has turned, which it will do. The goal of the casino is to keep you playing as long as possible, for the odds are always in the house's favor. The longer you play, the more advantageous it is to the casino. Don't give all your money away; set your goals, and when you reach one, take a walk and get something to eat.

Fun Books and Comps Before you begin your casino tour, look for the "fun books" that most casinos offer. These little booklets of coupons return $3 for a $2 bet and offer other bargains. Usually all you have to do to obtain one is to show your hotel room key or an out-of-town driver's license.

Those who come to Las Vegas for the weekend intending to spend $5,000 in the casino might want to look around for the personnel called "casino hosts" or "pit bosses." It's their job to patrol the house and find the people who are playing with big money. If you spend money at a table for a long time, chances are pretty good you'll be approached and asked whether you'd like a free show ticket or a meal.

When you know you will be spending $1,000 at blackjack on a given day, there's no reason to wait for the host to find you. Seek him out and negotiate your freebie right off. He has the power of the pen, and he can assign you many things, from a free hotel room to two tickets to a show to a meal in the "gourmet room." At the very least, he'll give you a line pass for a show, which lets you avoid waiting in line to get in.

But remember, comps cost money. It's a lot less expensive to buy a grilled-cheese sandwich in the casino coffee shop than it is to drop $1,500 at the roulette wheel with the hope of getting a coffee-shop comp.

Tipping Dealers are paid near the minimum wage at the casinos, and they expect to be tipped when you are winning. It's a silly custom; after all, they work for the house, not for you. Yet the theory says that a tip for the dealer keeps good luck in your corner. And if you're new to the game and a dealer is being friendly and helpful, why not slip him or her a chip, particularly if you plan to keep returning to the table? On the other hand, since the dealers change shifts every 20 minutes, you won't have to worry about bad feelings being projected across the table all night when you've forgotten or decided not to be generous.

The Casinos

Our review of the casinos begins at Hacienda Road, the southern end of the Strip, and proceeds north on Las Vegas Boulevard for the entire length of the Strip. Then we cover the downtown casinos on and near Fremont Street. Few people will want to try to visit every casino in town; while each one has its own character and special features, they all deal in the same basic commodity. The descriptions that follow are intended to help you find the casinos that will most appeal to you.

The Strip

The casinos of the Strip tend to be more expensive and more formal than the casinos downtown. There are no dress codes here, but the playing minimums are higher, the decor is ritzier, the dealers wear bow ties, and you sense that management would like to see you dressed up rather than down.

Hacienda Hotel and Casino (3950 Las Vegas Blvd. S, tel. 702/739–8911). The large building at the start of the Strip is a good place to begin a gambling tour: It's usually not very crowded, the tables don't have large minimums (there are plenty of $1 and $2 blackjack tables), and the poker room isn't filled with sharks. Drivers will usually find parking spaces directly in front of the hotel. A waterfall greets you when you pass through the swinging doors, and above the noise of the cascading water you'll hear the sound of coins dropping from slot machines. The Hacienda could also give you your first taste of a Las Vegas wedding: On its grounds is the Little Church of the West, the first Las Vegas wedding chapel. The barnlike structure stood originally on the property of the Frontier Hotel in the 1940s. Then Howard Hughes bought that hotel and decided he didn't want a chapel, so the building was moved to the Hacienda parking lot. The Hacienda throws a free champagne party for casino players every day from 5 PM to 6 PM.

Tropicana Resort and Casino (3801 Las Vegas Blvd. S, tel. 702/739–2222). To hear them tell it, the Trop is not a hotel but an island—the Island of Las Vegas. The Trop's "island" is a large water park, set off by the two Tropicana towers, where the main gambling attraction is swim-up blackjack. Yes, you can actually sit in the pool and play the game, go bust, and return to your breaststroke. And how do you take your money to the table? You stuff it in your swimsuit pocket, and when you reach the table, you put it into the Trop's money dryer. Indoors the casino has a very green, tropical look, with a shopping center off to the right. Stained glass adorns the ceilings, and palm trees are everywhere. Since the Tropicana considers itself a mid-to-upscale hotel, $2 blackjack tables will be hard to find, and you're more likely to play $5 blackjack and $1 slots here. Roulette, baccarat, craps, and blackjack lessons are scheduled every day.

Excalibur (under construction on Las Vegas Blvd. S, opposite the Tropicana Resort and Casino). The folks who own the Circus Circus casino have scheduled the opening of the new 4,000-room, $300 million Excalibur for the spring of 1990. Here the motif is to be that of a European castle, with 100,000 square feet of casino space. Like Circus Circus, Disneyland, and other

Aladdin Hotel and Casino, **6**
Bally's Casino Resort, **9**
Barbary Coast Hotel and Casino, **12**
Bourbon Street Hotel and Casino, **8**
Caesars Palace, **11**
Circus Circus, **28**
Desert Inn Hotel and Casino, **19**
Dunes Hotel and Country Club, **10**
El Rancho Tower Hotel and Casino, **30**
Excalibur, **3**
The Flamingo Hilton and Tower, **13**
Frontier Hotel and Gambling Hall, **20**
Gold Coast Hotel and Casino, **34**
Hacienda Hotel and Casino, **1**
Holiday Casino, **16**
Imperial Palace Hotel and Casino, **15**
Landmark Hotel and Casino, **24**
Las Vegas Hilton, **25**
Little Caesar's Gambling Casino, **5**
Marina Hotel and Casino, **4**
Maxim Hotel and Casino, **7**
The Mirage, **17**
O'Sheas Casino, **14**
Palace Station Hotel and Casino, **33**
Peppermill Casino, **21**
Riviera Hotel, **27**
Sahara Las Vegas Hotel, **31**
Sands Hotel and Casino, **18**
Silver City, **26**
Slots-A-Fun, **29**
Stardust Hotel and Casino, **22**
Tropicana Resort and Casino, **2**
Vegas World Hotel and Casino, **32**
Westward Ho Motel and Casino, **23**

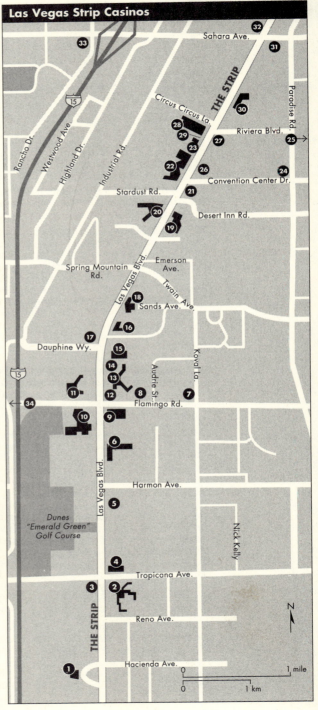

Las Vegas Strip Casinos

68

The Strip 69

great fantasy lands, Excalibur will keep the theme going with a shopping area fashioned after a medieval village and roving performers dressed in period costume. The dungeon will house a miniature golf course, theaters, and video arcades. In planning the building, Circus Circus management visited 20 castles in England, Scotland, and Germany to find the styles they wanted to capture in Vegas. Although a "name the hotel" contest brought many votes for Castle Castle, they chose Excalibur. Expect low minimums on gambling and inexpensive food at the newest castle in town.

Marina Hotel and Casino (3805 Las Vegas Blvd. S, tel. 702/739–1500). The Marina, a small casino across the street from the Tropicana, boasts a low-key atmosphere with low-minimum twenty-one, low-pressure poker, and low-priced slots. The weekly $21 twenty-one tournament has a top jackpot of $2,000. The Marina is a Las Vegas casino with a nautical theme. But this is the desert, and you'll be hard-pressed to find water amid all that sand.

Little Caesar's Gambling Casino (3665 Las Vegas Blvd. S, tel. 702/734–2827). Whenever the national media carry a story about Nevada sports betting, the managers of Little Caesar's are almost always quoted. That's because this little hole-in-the-wall is recognized as the haven of sports bettors. Unlike the grand sports books at the major casinos, with their plush seating and rows upon rows of large TV screens, Little Caesar's is a stand-up sort of place with no video at all. It's a smoky sports hangout inhabited by guys who wear hats and smoke stogies. They feel comfortable here, perhaps because of its location in a minimall with free parking directly in front. Gamblers can pull in and out without having to deal with the giant casino parking lots. It was at Little Caesar's that the Vegas World casino owner Bob Stupak's $1 million 1989 Super Bowl bet was accepted. (Stupak won and walked away with $2 million.) In addition to sports betting, Caesar's has two $1 twenty-one tables and 50¢ roulette.

Aladdin Hotel and Casino (3667 Las Vegas Blvd. S, tel. 702/736–0111). Here's another great Vegas image: a gold building in the middle of the desert, with a neon genie's lamp on the roof that glows all night long. If only you could rub it, maybe your wish would come true! In 1987 the Aladdin was purchased for $55 million by Ginsu Yasuda, a Korean-born Japanese resident who liked to shoot craps in Las Vegas. He moved the family here, took over the penthouse, and sunk more millions into the hotel on a remodeling spree. The *Arabian Nights* theme remains, with Islamic arches and the decor of a harem. New attractions are the red and gold carpets, a major paint job, and a neon sign that reads YOUR WISH IS OUR COMMAND. Cocktail waitresses patrol the casino floor dressed in genie outfits with pantaloons, their belly buttons showing, and white wigs flowing from their natural hair. Gamblers will find minimums in the middle range, with plenty of $2 tables and 25¢ slots as well as tables with higher minimums. Tables for nonsmokers are available.

Maxim Hotel and Casino (160 E. Flamingo Rd., tel. 702/731–4300). The near-in location of the Maxim makes it a nice alternative to the Strip's busier casinos and a favorite with local residents. The dark green casino has some $2 tables and lots of slots. Cab drivers say that the Maxim has some of the more liberal slot comps in town, that casino personnel spot slot players

Casinos   70

and offer them free meals and shows in return for their hours on the machines.

Bourbon Street Hotel and Casino (120 E. Flamingo Rd., tel. 702/737–7200). New Orleans is the theme here, and in order to compete with its larger neighbors, the Bourbon Street keeps food prices and table-game minimums low. The 99¢ breakfasts are served all day, and there are plenty of $2 tables. When the crowds at the Flamingo and Bally's get you down, you'll find the neighboring Bourbon Street a lot more relaxed.

Bally's Casino Resort (3645 Las Vegas Blvd. S, tel. 702/739–4111). Bally's, one of the largest hotels in the world, boasts a 50,000-square-foot casino that is one of the largest in Las Vegas. It's so big, Bally's says, that you could play the Super Bowl in it—provided the ball didn't crash into the lavish chandeliers and the cheerleaders could be kept from running into the more than 1,000 slot machines. Even without football, Bally's is usually packed—and it's an expensive place to play. There are no $2 tables, and on Friday and Saturday nights the $3 tables have $5 minimums unless they are deserted. One night I asked the pit boss where the $3 tables were, and he transformed his $5 sign into a $3 sign since business was slow. But that was unusual; Bally's is one of the busiest hotels in Vegas because it's across the street from the Flamingo Hilton, the Dunes, and Caesars Palace and because of the large convention trade Bally's accommodates. Yet the casino is so roomy that when the crowds get to you, you can simply move to another section of the floor. Management once advertised "Bally's is Slots!" and you'll find a lot of slots here, from 25¢ to $100 machines, including progressive, blackjack, and keno slots. Keep an eye out for the male cocktail waiter; he may be the only one of his gender in this field. Bally's also offers a large shopping arcade, a comedy club, two showrooms, and a curious statue out front of a woman squeezing (and squirting water from) her breasts. Craps, baccarat, blackjack, and roulette lessons are given daily.

Dunes Hotel and Country Club (3650 Las Vegas Blvd. S. tel. 702/737–4110). Usually parked on the sidewalk in front of the Dunes is a brand-new van or truck with a sign that reads WIN THIS CAR. Indoors, when three cherries turn up on a slot machine, instead of coins dropping, bells will ring, lights will flash; the grand prize could be the new vehicle. The minimums at the Dunes are lower than at Bally's—there are many $2 tables and 25¢ slots—and the casino is often crowded with regulars looking for bargains. If you like neon, you'll love the Xaanadu slot area, which is completely covered in blue, red, and green neon lighting and mirrors; it's like stepping onto the set of a "Star Trek" episode. The machines are mostly 25¢ video poker. The dominant color in the main casino is dark red, and the Arabian theme has remained through the years. At one time the Dunes was considered a "classy joint," and while the scope of its appeal may be different today, the inside of the building, with its soft, dark woods and large chandeliers, hasn't changed much. Out front, the Dunes has one of the largest and best neon signs in town: Red stripes run up and down two large columns, then spell out DUNES in yellow flashes at intervals. It makes a striking backdrop for a photo.

Caesars Palace (3570 Las Vegas Blvd. S, tel. 702/731–7110). At the center of Caesars is the Roman casino, the original room

The Strip 71

built by the founder, Jay Sarno, in 1966. A former owner of a string of Palo Alto cabana motor hotels, Sarno believed that Vegas hotel operators were not playing off the fantasy imagery enough and that the casinos were too square—literally: He saw the oval as a magic shape that was conducive to relaxation, and consequently both the building's exterior and the casino at Caesars are rounded. Caesars was originally called Cabana Palace, then Desert Palace. When Sarno finally opted for Caesars, he refused to allow an apostrophe in the name, insisting that Caesars belonged to everyone. It may be everyone's casino, but Caesars is no place to gamble for those who are just starting out. The Palace is a haven for *serious* gamblers, those folks who come to town with hundreds of thousands of dollars in their pockets, and the dealers here are trained to handle the situation. Ordinarily, spectators love to watch these players do their thing at the twenty-one and craps tables, but the Caesars security guards don't like this and will ask you to move on if you stop to watch. It's considered kosher, however, to watch the baccarat players in their room, where you could see lots of pink and brown casino chips. Their denomination is $10,000, and they exist only at Caesars (the other casinos stop with $1,000 chips). At Caesars the *serious* baccarat players take part in million-dollar Saturday-night games. The slots run the gamut from the traditional nickel, quarter, dollar, and $5 machines to $25, $100, and even $500 denominations. The Million Dollar Baby $1 slots ($3 investment) are the only million-dollar jackpot slots in town that will pay you all your winnings in one year; the other million-dollar jackpots pay off over much longer periods.

Barbary Coast Hotel and Casino (3595 Las Vegas Blvd. S, tel. 702/737–7111). The Barbary Coast is aimed at tourists who don't care to spend a lot of money, so the table minimums are lower and the dealers friendlier than at many neighboring hotels. The casino is modeled after a San Francisco Barbary Coast establishment of the 1880s, with Victorian chandeliers and lamps, dealers who wear red garters on their sleeves, and Klondike Annie cocktail waitresses who wear garters on their legs. Want to send a message from the Coast? An operating Western Union office here will wire it. The casino is usually pretty crowded, but not on the same scale as its neighbors, Bally's, the Flamingo Hilton, and Caesars. Photo fans should remember that they can capture a bit of the interior action by placing a subject before the doorless front entrance, on the platform that leads into the casino, and taking a few quick shots.

The Flamingo Hilton and Tower (3555 Las Vegas Blvd. S, tel. 702/733–3111). History lovers, this is where modern Vegas began. In 1946 Bugsy Siegel was preparing to transport Miami luxury into the desert in the form of a gambling hall where his Hollywood buddies could gamble legally, where the lure of big-time entertainment would bring the beautiful people to play, and where the ordinary Joe would follow because he wanted to be around them. Here's what Siegel told Las Vegas in a newspaper ad on the day the Flamingo opened, December 26, 1946: "Las Vegas will be proud of the Flamingo. It will become one of the world's greatest playgrounds. The Flamingo is for the people of Las Vegas as well as for visitors from anywhere. Come as you are and enjoy yourself." On the grounds, a sign in the shape of a pink flamingo still announces THE FABULOUS FLAMINGO. TO

Casinos 72

CASINO, DINING ROOM, LOBBY AND POOL. The Flamingo hasn't officially been "Fabulous" since the Hilton organization took over in 1969, and there are now six dining rooms instead of one. (The other visible reminder of the Siegel era is a little plaque by the pool that identifies BUGSY'S ROSE GARDEN.) The action inside the casino is usually intense; this is one of the busiest houses in town. Because of the throngs of people, it can take quite some time to move from one end of the casino to the other or to find the room to maneuver between the slots. Consequently, the Flamingo was undergoing remodeling and new construction during much of 1989. A casino annex—O'Sheas, with an Irish theme—opened in a portion of what had been the parking lot, and the main casino was being expanded. Table minimums at the Flamingo are on the high side (there are more $5 tables than $3 tables). The neon rainbows above the slot machines point out the Hilton Pot of Gold slots, which pay off a million bucks (at a cost of $3 per arm pull), and the Hilton has had several million-dollar winners. Hilton trivia lovers please note: Barron Hilton's son David, who could have worked at any Hilton of his choosing, came to Nevada, where he is senior vice-president of casino operations for the Flamingo.

O'Sheas Casino (3555 Las Vegas Blvd. S, tel. 702/733–3111). The crowds at the Flamingo casino were so thick that the Hilton organization decided to tear out some windows and build a small addition to it. That wasn't enough, so they tore down a neon sign and a small motor hotel unit and used the space, along with a former parking area, to put up a new building. The two-story gambling house is called O'Sheas, Irish good luck is its theme, and it opened in June 1989. The third floor of the structure is used for parking.

Imperial Palace Hotel and Casino (3535 Las Vegas Blvd. S, tel. 702/731–3311). You keep reading about the weirdness of Las Vegas, but you won't believe it. Well, how about a blue pagoda-style building with an oriental theme—a house of dragons? As you sit in the casino pulling the arm of a one-armed bandit, you look up at the ceiling, where this great, ugly dragon with big teeth is sticking his long red tongue out at you. Now, is that a sight to make you want to drop more quarters down the chute of the slot? The Imperial Palace seems like a home to which many rooms have been added on without a thought to how the additions might affect the master plan. To the right of the central casino is an escalator that will take you upstairs to a "gaming school" and showroom. Farther toward the back, an elevator in the middle of the casino takes you up to the restaurants. Walk straight on, and you'll come to the stairways leading to the parking garage and the museum of vintage cars on the third floor. Don't look for signs to help you find your way around; there aren't any. To add to the general confusion, the hotel's booming business with tour groups makes the Imperial Palace seem packed at any time of the day, and you'll be bumping into people right and left. There are few $3 tables; $5 minimums are more the norm. The gaming school has free lessons on all the games Monday through Thursday.

Holiday Casino (3475 Las Vegas Blvd. S, tel. 702/732–2411). Welcome to the Big Easy. You can't miss the Holiday—with its statues of a New Orleans Dixieland band playing atop a steamboat in an actual lagoon. Instead of the green of most Holiday Inns, this Vegas version is emphatically red. Strips of red neon

The Strip

hang above the slots, red wallpaper covers the walls, and the dealers adorn their white shirts with red string ties and red garters. The Holiday is a good place for beginning gamblers and players on a budget. In keeping with the "good old days" theme, dealers here tend to be friendlier than those at some neighboring casinos. The Holiday has lower table minimums (there are some $2 tables), cheap slots, and tables for nonsmokers. The best deal may be the bingo parlor on the third floor. If you don't want the trouble of adding up the numbers in blackjack or learning the rules of craps but you do want to play, what better game than bingo? All you need to do is cover the spaces with those red markers as the numbers are called. Cards can cost as little as 20¢, drinks are free, and winners get cash prizes in the $200–$500 range.

The Mirage (3400 Las Vegas Blvd. S, tel. 800/639–3403). Across the boulevard from the Holiday and the Imperial Palace, Steve Wynn's expensive new showplace, The Mirage, on its opening day in November 1989, was the site of a $4.6 million Megabucks jackpot payoff, the largest in Las Vegas history. When the Golden Nugget chief announced plans to build yet another casino on the Strip, his competitors said the man was nuts—and began making their own plans to expand. Circus Circus announced the Excalibur; the Sahara, Imperial Palace, Flamingo Hilton, Riviera, and Holiday Casino began adding hundreds of rooms in anticipation of the throngs of people the new tropical-theme Mirage would attract. Wynn's plans for The Mirage included tigers, palm trees, pools, lagoons, islands, grottoes, and sea animals. To draw nighttime visitors, he signed the hottest act in town, the magicians Siegfried and Roy, to a five-year, $55.5 million contract. For the high roller who seeks seclusion in gambling, Wynn set aside a plush private room where the minimum bet is $1,000. The Mirage has acres of open parking and palm trees, two giant towers with gold windows, and an oval dome in front.

Sands Hotel and Casino (3355 Las Vegas Blvd. S, tel. 702/733–5000). The large oval building on the Strip contains more than 750 rooms and is rich in history. Back in the swinging 1960s the Sands was headquarters for Frank Sinatra, Sammy Davis Jr., Dean Martin, Peter Lawford, and Joey Bishop. It was here at the Sands that they made that quintessential Vegas film, *Ocean's 11*, about a bunch of guys who try to heist a Vegas casino. You can still live the 1950s and 1960s Sands experience in the gardens and pool area, which haven't changed much since the day they made the classic publicity photo of the floating crap game in the Sands pool. Indoors, the casino has changed a lot. The world-famous Copa Room no longer features headliners; at this writing, the San Francisco revue *Beach Blanket Babylon* was in its second year. You'll see lots of bright neon throughout the Sands casino, more than in any other house in town. Yellow, red, blue, green, and pink neon overhangs various sections of the casino (yellow for the quarter slots, red for the dollar slots, etc.). The Sands has a few blackjack tables for nonsmokers and more $2 blackjack tables than most casinos of its size.

Desert Inn Hotel and Casino (3145 Las Vegas Blvd. S, tel. 702/733–4444). One of the first casinos in town, the Desert Inn was built in 1952 by the Cleveland Boys, a group of former bootleggers who had run an illegal gambling joint in Covington,

Casinos 74

Kentucky, until they saw that Bugsy Siegel could do it legally and came to Nevada to go legit. The Boys attracted wealthy Eastern gamblers by running a house with no limits when the limit at the Flamingo was $100. The Cleveland Boys—Moe Dalitz, Morris Kleinman, Lou and Bernie Rothkopf—managed the place, but the onetime San Diego bellhop Wilbur Clark was the front man—thus it was Wilbur Clark's Desert Inn. The old sign still stands at the corner of Paradise and Desert Inn roads, but Clark's name has been rubbed out, leaving a hole where it once shone above DESERT INN. After selling TWA in 1966, Howard Hughes came to the Desert Inn for an extended stay. Asked to leave after a few months to make room for gamblers, he refused and bought the place instead (and went on to buy the Frontier, the Landmark, and the now defunct Silver Slipper). Want to see what Hughes called home? It was the entire ninth floor; just press "9" in the elevator, ride up, and look around. You can also rent the "Howard Hughes suite" for $250 a night. There are no known photos of the reclusive Hughes in Vegas because virtually no one outside his close-knit group of servants saw him; Hughes left the Desert Inn for the Bahamas in 1970, and the hotel changed hands again in 1986. The Desert Inn has always been a medium-size, lavish, upscale casino with a Southwest theme, and it's one of the most comfortable places in town. Unlike some of the bigger gambling houses, the Desert Inn seems well managed, well laid-out, and well controlled. Good lighting lets you enjoy the Arizona-New Mexico Southwest decor, which gives welcome relief from the dark walls and TV cameras that hang from the ceiling. Because its clientele are the wealthy, the Desert Inn's games cost more to play. While there are a few $3 tables, most are at least $5, but nickel and quarter slots are plentiful. Poker lessons are scheduled daily.

Frontier Hotel and Gambling Hall (3120 Las Vegas Blvd. S, tel. 702/734–0110). Across the street from the Desert Inn, the Frontier is the last remnant of the beginnings of the Las Vegas Strip. The first Strip resort, El Rancho, was built in 1941 and burned down in 1960; the Last Frontier followed in 1942, to be succeeded by the New Frontier in 1956 and the present Frontier in 1967. While the Frontier of today stands on the same property, it bears no resemblance to the old place, but you'll find mementos of it on the second-floor walls of the executive offices. Those who like places with a "good old days" feeling, that make no pretense of serving the upper crust of society, will love the Frontier. When Margaret Elardi bought the property in 1988, she took it drastically downscale. Siegfried and Roy and Wayne Newton used to be advertised on the Frontier's large marquee; now the star is single-deck blackjack. Diamond Jim's Gourmet Room steakhouse was replaced with a Mexican restaurant where tortillas are made in an open area overlooking the slots—and their aroma carries to the players. The casino has nickel to $1 slots and lots of $2 and $3 tables, and the crowds are larger than they used to be. Beginning poker lessons are given every day but Sunday.

Peppermill Casino (3047 Las Vegas Blvd. S, tel. 702/732–2211). Between the Desert Inn and the Riviera is a small shopping center with tacky gift shops and, in the middle, a little casino called the Peppermill. Its name will be familiar to most visitors because they will have seen the Peppermill "fun books" all over town. The little coupon booklets offer 25¢ ice cream cones and strawberry daiquiris, 14¢ nachos, 39¢ bacon-and-eggs break-

The Strip 75

fasts, and a free pull of a special slot machine. (Remember, food fans, you get what you pay for.) Most of the Peppermill twenty-one tables have $1 minimum bets.

Stardust Hotel and Casino (3000 Las Vegas Blvd. S, tel. 702/732–6111). The Stardust has one of the best neon shows on the Strip: Pink and blue neon tubing runs down the front of the hotel, leading to a 183-foot multiprogrammed sign that erupts in bursts of neon stars. On its debut in 1958, the sign was the largest and brightest in Vegas, its glow visible from 3 miles away. The vision for the Stardust came from the mobster Tony Cornero, who had run gambling ships off the southern California coast in the 1930s and 1940s and dreamed of building the biggest, classiest casino in town. But he never lived to see his dream realized; one morning, while shooting craps at the Desert Inn, he had a heart attack and died with the dice in his hands. Today the Stardust is owned by the Boyd Group, the operators of middle-market hotels (Sam's Town, the Fremont, the California) that emphasize cheap slots, low table minimums, and good deals on food. The Stardust is my favorite among the Strip casinos because of its layout. No matter how crowded the Strip becomes, the Stardust always seems to have room for you to move around; it never feels overly crowded or claustrophobic. Others have complained that the Stardust is *too* large, that it's a long walk from the sports book up front to the video poker room out back. But the walk is no worse than at any other casino, and with the greater room between the machines and tables here, you will bump into fewer people. Strips of pink and blue neon near the ceilings give a pleasant, colorful glow to the tables and the slots. On the tables you'll notice that the felt is blue instead of the usual green. As you stand and pull the arms of the slot machines, you can look out through the glass doors and watch the real world pass by on the Strip. Another nice touch is the collection of overstuffed red plush chairs in the slot area that allow you to take a comfortable break from the play (an unusual courtesy in Vegas). The Stardust calls itself a grind joint, meaning it attracts gamblers who don't intend to spend a lot of money. It has plenty of $2 blackjack tables, nickel slots, and roulette with 50¢ chips (minimum bet $2). Blackjack, craps, and roulette lessons are given daily.

Westward Ho Motel and Casino (2900 Las Vegas Blvd. S, tel. 702/731–2900). The Ho has something few Strip casinos can offer: parking *right out front!* It also has plenty of $2 blackjack tables and chances to play slots for new cars or boats. One more thing makes the Ho interesting: Male dealers wear four-in-hand ties rather than the bow or string ties you'll see in virtually every other gaming house. The bias against the four-in-hand lies in the fact that dealers can stick money in them; with a bow tie there's little room for shenanigans.

Landmark Hotel and Casino (364 Convention Center Dr., tel. 702/733–1110). Paris has the Eiffel Tower, Seattle the Space Needle, and New York the Empire State Building; what Las Vegas needs, Howard Hughes decided in 1969, is a landmark of its own. And so there came to be this unusual 31-story round tower that overlooks the Las Vegas Convention Center and the Las Vegas Hilton. What could be stranger than playing games in a round casino? While only the hotel section of the Sands is round, the Landmark's casino is entirely in the round, and you must walk in circles to get where you want to be. Landmark

Casinos 76

players are low rollers, so the table minimums are on the low side, and there are lots of slots here.

Las Vegas Hilton (3000 W. Paradise Rd., tel. 702/732–5111). What began in 1969 as Kirk Kerkorian's International Hotel became, just a few years later, the Hilton organization's first foray into gambling. Today the Hilton gaming properties in Vegas and Reno account for 60% of the corporation's annual profits. In the beginning the International had a different theme for every floor (French, Italian, etc.) and a variety of international restaurants. Barbra Streisand opened the hotel with a four-week gig and was followed by Elvis Presley, who made the International his official Vegas residence for the 1970s. This is where the Elvis we have come to know and love through impersonators—the King in the white jumpsuit and giant belt buckle, handing out hankerchiefs to the screaming ladies in the front row and opening shows with "C. C. Rider"—developed. For many years the Hilton has had the largest showroom in Vegas (1,500 seats), the biggest pool (until the new pool opens at The Mirage), and the most rooms (3,174). Either the new Excalibur or the expanded Riviera will soon capture the last honor, but in the meantime the Hilton has shown it knows how to use its size. Here the casino is clearly in the middle of the floor, surrounded by slot areas, a keno lounge, and a race and sports book, all very well laid out so that you can stand in the lobby and see where everything is. The Hilton's clientele are high rollers and $1 slot players, and the casino tends to have high minimums. You may find a few $3 blackjack tables, but most begin at $5, especially during a busy convention. Because the Hilton is next door to the Las Vegas Convention Center, many delegates stay here, and they pack the casino at all hours. Craps, blackjack, and roulette lessons are given daily.

Silver City (3001 Las Vegas Blvd. S, tel. 702/732–4152). Another gambling house in the style of the Wild West, with free popcorn, 50¢ hot dogs, $1 blackjack, and pictures of cowboys on the walls, Silver City has a much more relaxed atmosphere than that of its next-door neighbor, the large Riviera. And you can park in the lot directly in front of the casino.

Riviera Hotel (2901 Las Vegas Blvd. S, tel. 702/734–5110). When the Riviera opened in 1957, it was the tallest building in town, a nine-story T-shape structure reminiscent of lavish French seaside resorts. Throughout its history the hotel had appealed to the social upper crust until, in the 1980s, a new owner changed its focus and went after the bettors of today, Dick and Dottie Slots. The owner shocked the Vegas old guard by putting a Burger King and a video arcade in the middle of the casino. With the higher profits that have resulted from the new policy, the Riviera has embarked on a construction program that will make it the largest hotel in Vegas, with 4,000 rooms by 1993. So far the remodeling has consisted of tacking on additions with no apparent thought as to how the final product will look. Walk through the side entrance, beneath the marquee for the "Splash" show, and you're in a slot room. Keep on strolling, and you'll pass a shopping arcade (men's and women's clothing, toys, gifts, T-shirts), then room registration, then another T-shirt shop. The next attraction is the casino, one of the smallest in Vegas, with about 30 table games. Walking on will take you to another slot room, the one with the Burger King. So far you've been following pretty much a

The Strip

77

straight line; veering off to the right or left will take you to restaurants, a wedding chapel, a race and sports book, and many more slot rooms. Perhaps the completion of the casino's expansion plans will in time bring order to the general confusion that prevailed in 1989. The Riviera's betting minimums start at $3, with more $5 tables than $3 tables. Blackjack, craps, roulette, poker, keno, and sports betting lessons are offered daily. Finally, here's a casino trivia question: What hotel is owned in part by the most successful family recording act in history? Yes, it's the Riviera; the Jackson family owns 5% of it.

Circus Circus (2880 Las Vegas Blvd. S, tel. 702/734–0410). Only in Las Vegas would you find a 125-foot sign picturing a clown sucking a lollipop, with a statue of a nude dancer at his side. And only in Las Vegas could you find Circus Circus, the tent-shape casino with a huge hotel (the fourth largest in Vegas in 1989) in its backyard. Under the Circus Circus tent the clowns, trapeze stars, high-wire artists, unicyclists, and aerial dancers perform daily, every 20 minutes from 11 AM to midnight). Jay Sarno, who built Caesars Palace, believed he could follow it up with a casino that had a totally different philosophy. He was certain that a low-roller haven could prosper on the Strip, and was he ever right! While Caesars is still the most profitable casino in town, Circus Circus isn't far behind. (Caesars makes its bucks more easily, from a small number of wealthy individuals, while the larger numbers of Circus Circus bettors tend to be much thriftier gamblers.) In addition to the circus acts, an observation gallery is lined with food, game, and carnival concessions. The midway features such games as dime toss, milk can, bushel basket, and Fascination, along with clown-face painting, a video arcade, funhouse mirrors, and corn dogs and pizza. Seats for watching the circus acts are on the midway. Many parents park their kids here while they go off to pull the handles of the slots downstairs. Though the Midway can be a convenient place to leave the kids, you'll find that on weekends it's like Times Square on New Year's Eve—packed solid. It always seems more crowded here than at any other casino in town. Once inside the big pink top of Circus Circus, you'll walk and walk and walk, seeing dealers in pink shirts and cocktail waitresses wearing yellow toga outfits that look like rejects from Caesars Palace. The two Circus Circus attractions you won't want to miss are the slot merry-go-round— 20 slots sit on a revolving stage and players ride in circles as they operate the machines—and the merry-go-round bar on the midway, with actual carousel horses, booths with pink tables where folks sit and drink, and a bartender who does not revolve. Some of the kitschiest gift shops in Vegas are at Circus Circus; you can buy Elvis decanters, $80 slot replicas, Vegas bells, toothpick holders, thimbles, clowns that go round, and gag signs (PLEASE DON'T PEE IN OUR POOL. WE DON'T SWIM IN YOUR TOILET or SOME MORNINGS I WAKE UP GROUCHY. OTHER MORNINGS I LET HIM SLEEP). Don't look for $100 blackjack games here; there aren't any. And you'll have a hard time finding tables with minimums under $3. Because the slots pay the bills, you'll see lots more slot machines than table games. Blackjack, craps, and roulette lessons are given every morning.

Slots-A-Fun (2880 Las Vegas Blvd. S, tel. 702/734–0410). As you leave Circus Circus, you'll be handed a sheet of coupons for free popcorn, 50¢ hot dogs, 99¢ shrimp cocktails, free pulls of a slot machine, and a free gift (usually a key chain) at Slots-A-

Casinos 78

Fun, the Circus Circus annex. This is another noisy, smoky casino with lots of slots and a few $2 and $3 blackjack tables.

El Rancho Tower Hotel and Casino (2755 Las Vegas Blvd. S, tel. 702/796–2222). The present-day El Rancho is not the El Rancho Vegas that was the first major Strip resort and that burned down in 1960. (It stood on the desert land opposite the Sahara Las Vegas that remains vacant except for the billboards.) The El Rancho of today, however, has its own history. In 1948 the fourth major Strip casino (after the old El Rancho Vegas, the Last Frontier, and the Flamingo) was the Thunderbird. In 1977 the Thunderbird became the Silverbird, and in 1982 a new management renamed it El Rancho. (The original Thunderbird building still stands by the pool.) El Rancho has much to offer those who seek low-pressure, low-cost gambling. The motif, again, is the Old West; El Rancho doesn't do it as well as some other casinos, but the atmosphere is not overbearing. The attraction is that when the neighboring Circus Circus and the Riviera are packed and the table minimums start at $5, you can walk across the street to El Rancho and find a more sedate atmosphere and lots of 5¢ slots, $1 roulette, and even a few $2 blackjack tables. And when you want a break from the cards and the keno boards, you can pick up a bowling ball and roll it down one of El Rancho's 52 lanes.

Sahara Las Vegas Hotel (2535 Las Vegas Blvd. S, tel. 702/737–2111). The largest freestanding neon sign in Vegas, 18 feet high by 10 feet wide, announces S-A-H-A-R-A, the place where Shecky Green, Louis Prima and Keely Smith, and Don Rickles were lounge regulars in the 1950s. Following a decade in which the Casbah Lounge was a shadow of its former self, it was refurbished and opened up in 1989 to give the Sahara a new, lively feeling. Most Vegas lounges are covered, dark rooms where you go to drink and dance; in the Sahara casino, you can hear and see the musicians playing in the Casbah, creating a musical presence that surpasses the sounds of coins dropping from slots and pit bosses clicking for drinks. When the Sahara opened for business in 1952 with statues of camels in the parking lot, it suggested a trip to the desert. Today the oasis theme remains, and in 1988 the entire Sahara was spruced up with new carpets, lighting fixtures, painted walls, and pink neon for the ceiling. The Sahara is one of the roomiest casinos in town, with slots on one side and table games on the other. A second section of table games on the north side of the casino takes on the overflow when the principal section becomes too crowded. A middle-market hotel, the Sahara appeals to weekend slot and table game players, and minimums are in the middle range, with a few $2 tables. Baccarat lessons are offered daily.

Beyond the Strip

Vegas World Hotel and Casino (2000 Las Vegas Blvd. S, tel. 702/382–2000). This could be the strangest casino in town. The Vegas World facade is decorated with the painting of a spaceman tied to a roulette wheel and lost in space. Indoors, a mannequin of an astronaut is suspended above the casino, floating alongside the spaceships and meteors that adorn the walls, which are black with white dots to suggest stars. Vegas World is Bob Stupak's place, and he won't let you forget it; his name and his picture are everywhere. A gambler who regularly shows up at poker tournaments, the author of a self-published book on winning at craps (autographed copies for sale in the

Downtown 79

gift shop), and the biggest sports-book winner in Vegas history ($1 million on the Super Bowl in 1989), Stupak is a former Vegas mayoral candidate (he lost by a few thousand votes). The casino's Big Six wheel is the largest in the world, nearly 25 feet across, so large the operator can't spin it manually and must use a machine to set it in motion. Stupak displays $1 million in cash behind a large glass window in the casino and offers a million-dollar slot jackpot to the player who lines up four 7s on the center line of a special million-dollar slot ($3 investment). Since the million-dollar slots were installed in 1984, no one has won. Vegas World's location—beyond the Strip and short of downtown—is one of the least desirable, sort of in the middle of Wedding Chapel Row. Stupak knows that, and he makes an effort to lure customers. The casino has low table minimums and lots of slots. Coupons available around town (check the visitors centers) offer $50 in playing money free—$20 for keno, blackjack, and craps; $30 for slots. The ads promise "no gimmicks," but you must pay a $2 registration fee to get the $50 playing money, which is doled out in small increments every 45 minutes over a two-and-a-half-hour period. The objective, of course, is to keep you in the casino as long as possible, spending and losing your own money in addition to the free bucks. Another package offers $1,000 worth of casino action and a hotel room for two nights, for one or two persons, for $396: You get $600 worth of chips (any denomination, $1 and up), $400 in tokens for the dollar slots, two free pulls of the million-dollar slots, a pair of dice, a deck of used casino cards, and a photo of you at Vegas World. The chips can be used at any of the table games (twenty-one, craps, roulette), but they travel only one way: If you bet $2 on an even-money game and win, instead of getting $4 back, you get only $2. The Vegas World chips go to the dealer no matter what happens, and the profits go to you. (You're ahead all along because the casino has fronted you the money with which to play.) The slot tokens are good on 20 special machines that have been adapted to accept the tokens, worth $5 each, so you get 80 pulls on the slots. For more information about this package, tel. 800/634–6301. *Playboy* has called it the best deal in Vegas.

Palace Station Hotel and Casino (2411 W. Sahara Ave., tel. 702/ 367–2411). Palace Station was originally the Bingo Palace, and it has the best bingo room in town, but today the theme is railroads. Palace Station looks and feels like a big, smoky railroad station, with restaurants for cars, and the hotel for a depot. This is a friendly, low-minimum casino whose only fault is that it's so popular with local gamblers that it can become too crowded for comfort's sake.

Gold Coast Hotel and Casino (4000 W. Flamingo Rd., tel. 702/ 367–7111). Whenever you're at the airport and you see people losing money in the slots, think of the Gold Coast: This casino west of the Strip and west of Interstate 15 was built on airport slot losses. A popular casino with local gamblers, the Gold Coast shows up regularly in the *Las Vegas Review-Journal*'s reader polls for having some of the loosest slots in town. Like the Palace Station, the Gold Coast also has low minimums, a friendly atmosphere, and considerable crowds at times.

Downtown

Fremont Street is the place to come for low table minimums and food bargains. The downtown casinos have more $1 tables than

Casinos 80

anywhere else in Las Vegas; beginning gamblers and those who just don't care to shell out $5 and $10 a hand will be comfortable here. The dealers wear string ties, the decor is usually reminiscent of the 1800s or early 1900s, and a come-as-you-are atmosphere prevails.

Union Plaza Hotel (1 Main St., tel. 702/386–2110). Back in the 1920s, when cowboys rode their horses on Fremont Street and miners came to town to gamble and buy grub, Main Street was anchored by a railroad station. Today that station is the Union Plaza Hotel (the UP), one of the largest casinos downtown, with a train station in the hotel. (Riders who leave the train are dropped off in the casino.) The UP has low minimums ($1 and $2 tables) and a rack of eight 1¢ slots, where the jackpots can reach $30,000. The casino's theme is "live it up" (up, as in UP).

California Hotel and Casino (12 E. Ogden Ave., tel. 702/385–1222). The California is a hotel that hasn't gotten its geography together. You might come here expecting a Gold Rush theme, but instead you'll find that the motif is Hawaiian. All the dealers wear Hawaiian shirts. Aggressive marketing on the part of tour operators in the 49th state brings a lot of Hawaiian tourists to the California. The casino has lots of $2 tables, 5¢ slots, and room in which to move around.

Las Vegas Club Hotel and Casino (18 E. Fremont St., tel. 702/385–1664). A lobby wall devoted to sports hall of fame memorabilia announces the sports motif of the Las Vegas Club. The dealers wear baseball shirts, and the house rules for twenty-one purport to be the most liberal in town. You can double down on two, three, or four cards at any time; you can split and resplit aces and split and resplit any pair as often as you want; six cards totaling 21 or less wins automatically; and you may surrender your original hand (first two cards) for half the amount of your bet. Plenty of tables have a $2 minimum.

Binion's Horseshoe Hotel and Casino (128 E. Fremont St., tel. 702/382–1600). The Horseshoe is where serious gamblers come to play, the only house in town where you'll see a line of people waiting to get to a twenty-one table. This is the home of the annual World Series of Poker event in April; it is also the only place in Las Vegas where you can have your picture taken with $1 million in cash. (The Horseshoe will provide a complimentary Polaroid of you standing in front of the money, which you can't get your hands on.) The unlabeled six-foot statue of a man wearing a cowboy hat and sitting on a horse by the parking garage represents the Horseshoe's founder, Benny Binion. A former bootlegger, Binion came to Vegas from Texas in the 1950s, set up a respectable shop (though he served time on a tax-evasion charge in the 1950s), and built a house for pure gambling. No entertainment, no fancy hotel rooms, just gambling. He even shied at calling it gaming, as many of the corporations in town do: "That's like calling a whorehouse a brothel." Binion died in 1989, and the Horseshoe is run by his sons, Jack and Ted. In 1988 they bought their neighbor, the Mint, knocked a wall down, and the Horseshoe became an entire city block long. A visit finds that it still seems like two different establishments. On one side is the rustic, smoky, Wild West atmosphere of the original three-story Horseshoe; on the other side, once the Mint and now officially the East Horseshoe, is a modern red casino. You'll find more $1 tables on the East Horseshoe side.

Binion's Horseshoe Hotel and Casino, **4**
California Hotel and Casino, **2**
El Cortez Hotel, **11**
Fitzgerald's Hotel and Casino, **8**
Four Queens Hotel and Casino, **6**
Fremont Hotel and Casino, **7**
Gold Spike Hotel and Casino, **10**
Golden Nugget Hotel and Casino, **5**
Lady Luck Casino and Hotel, **9**
Las Vegas Club Hotel and Casino, **3**
Sam's Town Hotel and Casino, **12**
Union Plaza Hotel, **1**

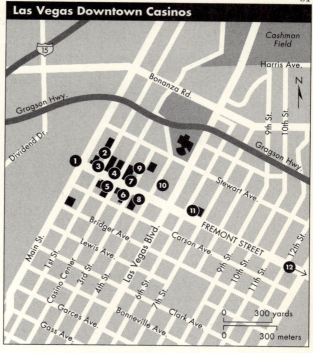

Golden Nugget Hotel and Casino (129 E. Fremont St., tel. 702/385-7111). The Golden Nugget is the only major casino in Vegas that has no neon. It's an ironic situation, because a common subject in postcards and photographs of Vegas since the 1950s has been the enormous old yellow Golden Nugget neon sign. But when Steve Wynn acquired the Nugget in the mid-1970s, he decided the old sign was ugly and tore it down. Originally, the Nugget was a gambling hall in turn-of-the-century style, with only a casino. Wynn's plan was to create a Dynasty of the Desert, adding lots of hotel rooms and attracting wealthier gamblers with whom plain folks would come to rub shoulders. The entire face of the Nugget has been redone in white marble, accented with white canopies and gold leaf, and surrounded by palm trees and a white granite sidewalk. Inside are gold-plated elevators, pay phones, slot machines, and the "world's largest" gold nugget. Weighing 63 pounds and valued at $1 million, it was discovered in Australia and now resides behind plate glass in the Golden Nugget lobby. In the casino the dealers dress in 1880s Western garb, wearing vests and sleeve garters. The Nugget today, no longer exclusively for the wealthy, has become a luxurious grind joint: The 5¢ slots and $1 tables wouldn't have been found here in the old days. Even if you don't care to play at the Nugget, you'll want to stroll through to see how radically different it is from every other downtown casino.

Four Queens Hotel and Casino (202 E. Fremont St., tel. 702/385-4011). When you walk along Fremont Street and come upon four painted playing cards in the pavement—four queens,

Casinos 82

in fact—you will be standing at the entrance to the Four Queens. You'll also notice the yellow neon sign that stretches for two sides of a city block. The Queens has a New Orleans decor, with milk-glass French chandeliers and—get this—pink felt tables: pink roulette, pink twenty-one, and pink craps. The Queens Machine has been certified by Guinness as the world's largest slot: It's the size of a motor home, eight feet long and seven feet high, and six people can play at one time. The players sit in chairs and invest dollar coins from their consoles, then a woman wearing a long, red, Elizabethan-style dress pulls her handle. The goal is to get at least three of the eight reels (queen faces, cherries, lemons) to match hers. When all eight come up with queens, it's a $300,000 jackpot. If more than one person is playing when the jackpot comes up, the pot is split among the players. All other wins are paid out to individual players. Craps lessons are scheduled on Tuesday through Friday afternoons; poker lessons daily.

Fremont Hotel and Casino (200 E. Fremont St., tel. 702/385–3232). The Newton Brothers, Wayne and Jerry, made their Las Vegas debuts in the Fremont's Carnival Room Lounge and played here for five years until the lounge closed in 1966. (Wayne moved to the Strip, where he has been playing ever since; Jerry played guitar in Wayne's band for a while, then returned to Phoenix.) Today the spruced-up Fremont has one of downtown's few bingo rooms ($3 minimum) and table minimums that tend to be $2 and $3. The Fremont sign—bright, bright red with a green, green trim—makes a wonderful backdrop for a photo. When you shoot someone with that sign in the background, remember to use a flash.

Fitzgerald's Hotel and Casino (301 E. Fremont St., tel. 702/382–6111). This was the Sundance Hotel & Casino until a group of Reno businessmen who run a Fitzgerald's up north bought it, painted it green, and renamed it. The tallest building (34 stories) in Nevada, the Fitz calls itself the Luck Capital of Las Vegas. Its theme is the luck of the Irish, and leprechauns and four-leaf clovers are rampant. Since this is downtown, come-ons are rampant as well. Fitzgerald's boasts that its slots offer a 101% payback. Study the claim more closely, and you'll learn that it's the slots in the Blarney Castle area that are loose. Keep on reading, and you'll find that four of the 48 slots in the castle area—they won't tell you which ones—average a 97% payback, while 28 of the 48 average a 96% payback. You are free to take the house at its word; my own experience was that an investment of $10 in two machines earned a return of $2. Those who appreciate good-luck charms may want to touch the lucky horseshoe from the Triple Crown winner Secretariat (in the Blarney Castle), drop a coin in the wishing fountain, or take a stroll on the Fitz's "lucky" wishing steps. The Fitz's video poker slots pay back on 10s or better (most casinos pay only on jacks or better), and some slots offer wild-card joker poker. Better than having the odd table for nonsmokers, the Fitz has an entire area of the second floor reserved for nonsmoking slot players. Twenty-one, craps, roulette, and Red Dog instruction is available daily.

Lady Luck Casino and Hotel (206 N. 3rd St., tel. 702/384–4680). The Lady Luck, at 3rd and Ogden streets, across from the Gold Spike, is a bit off the beaten track, but management will make it worth your while to stop in. A free photo, a free shrimp cock-

Downtown 83

tail, a free long-distance phone call, and five keno games for $1 are yours when you show your out-of-state driver's license to the folks at the welcome center. Expect a long line of people waiting for their shrimp cocktails and free phone calls, too. In the casino are a few $1 blackjack tables and tables for nonsmokers. Expansion is under way here; a new hotel tower was built in 1989.

Gold Spike Hotel and Casino (400 E. Ogden Ave., tel. 702/384–8444). The Gold Spike, one block north of Fremont Street, is the best deal downtown, period. It's a small gambling hall, the sort of place that you'd imagine the cowboys of the old days used to inhabit. At the tables there's no question of whether or not they have $1 blackjack—every table is a $1 table. The Spike features 5¢ video keno and poker machines, live 40¢ keno, 10¢ roulette, and plenty of penny slots. A royal flush on the 1¢, 5¢, or 25¢ video poker machines pays off with a free meal for two in the Gold Spike coffee shop.

El Cortez Hotel (600 E. Fremont St., tel. 702/385–5200). The oldest standing casino in Las Vegas, El Cortez opened for business on Fremont Street in 1941, when cowboys still rode up and down the street. While the venerable sign out front proclaims GAMBLING/COFFEE SHOP/FLOOR SHOW, there are no more floor shows at El Cortez. (The last floor show in Vegas is believed to have been Donn Arden's dancers, at the Desert Inn in 1951.) It's just an old casino, one without a lot of charm but with low table minimums and good deals on food. The majority of the blackjack tables have $1 or $2 minimums.

Sam's Town Hotel and Casino (5111 W. Boulder Hwy., tel. 702/456–7777). About five miles from the Strip, on the route to the Hoover Dam, stands this monument to the way Vegas used to be. Sam's Town isn't a casino, it's a gambling hall; it doesn't have bars, it has saloons. Everything is oversize here, the food is cheap, and the emphasis is on having a good time and capturing the feeling of being a cowboy in the Old West. Sam's Town is nickel slots, $1 tables, and crowds of locals, and the Boulder Highway route to Hoover Dam is much more picturesque than the freeway. The California Hotel in downtown Vegas offers free shuttle service to Sam's Town. If you're driving, head out Tropicana Avenue or Flamingo Road (toward the mountains), and you can be at Sam's Town in about 15 minutes.

4 Exploring Las Vegas

The heart of Las Vegas is the Strip, the 3½-mile stretch of Las Vegas Boulevard South that runs north from Hacienda Avenue, plus the downtown area north of the Strip, whose center is Fremont Street east of Las Vegas Boulevard North. Our exploration of the city visits the Strip and downtown in two tours.

Tour 1 proceeds the length of the Strip, starting just south of Hacienda Avenue and taking in all the major hotels and casinos, three shopping malls, a museum, a water park, and other attractions. You could begin this tour, or any part of it, at any time of day, but the earlier in the morning you set out, the smaller the crowds you'll have to contend with.

Tour 2 takes you downtown to Fremont Street and the honkytonk capital of Las Vegas, with its bright lights, hawkers, and con games, and to nearby sights. The best time to see downtown is in the evening or at night; a few of the nearby attractions are better seen in the daytime, perhaps in an afternoon.

It's easy to get around Las Vegas by car, even for those who are terrible with directions. Las Vegas Boulevard (the Strip) is the major thoroughfare. Many of the east-west streets that cross it are named for major hotels: Tropicana Avenue, Flamingo Road, Desert Inn Road, Sahara Avenue.

For those who come from Los Angeles or other major metropolitan areas, the traffic lights in Vegas may seem slow to change. In making a left turn, you can expect a wait for the left-turn signal to turn green; when it does, there should be time enough for about 10 cars to go through. To drive the length of the Strip might take only five minutes on a Tuesday morning, but it could take 20 minutes on a Friday or a Saturday night.

Walking, too, can take longer than you expect. The hotels—large structures often separated from one another by open spaces—generally turn out to be farther off than they appear, and a stroll "next door" may take 15 minutes.

One could forgo transportation and take the full 3½-mile stroll along the sidewalks of the Strip, but most folks would find this uncomfortable; the constant dry heat of this city in the desert tends to leave the walker hot, thirsty, and tired.

Highlights for First-Time Visitors

Caesars Palace and the statues (Tour 1: The Strip)
Circus Circus (Tour 1: The Strip)
Liberace Museum (*see* Museums in Sightseeing Checklists, below)
Downtown Las Vegas at night (Tour 2: Downtown)
Sam's Town (*see* Casinos in Chapter 3)
At least one Vegas show (*see* Chapter 9)

Tour 1: The Strip

Numbers in the margin correspond with the numbered points of interest on the Las Vegas Strip map. The casinos pointed out on this tour were described in detail in Chapter 3.

At the southern end of Las Vegas Boulevard, two blocks south of Hacienda Avenue, the **WELCOME TO LAS VEGAS sign,** a familiar part of the landscape since the early 1950s, makes a fitting start

Bonanza, **15**
Caesars Palace, **5**
Candlelight Wedding Chapel, **11**
Circus Circus, **13**
Fashion Show Mall, **7**
"Free Aspirin and Tender Sympathy" sign, **3**
Guardian Angel Cathedral, **8**
Imperial Palace Automobile Museum, **6**
Las Vegas Convention Center, **10**
Las Vegas Museum of Natural History, **4**
Paul-Son School of Gaming, **16**
Peppermill Shopping Center, **9**
Trader Ann's Trading Post, **12**
Visitors Center, **2**
"Welcome to Las Vegas" sign, **1**
Wet 'N Wild water park, **14**

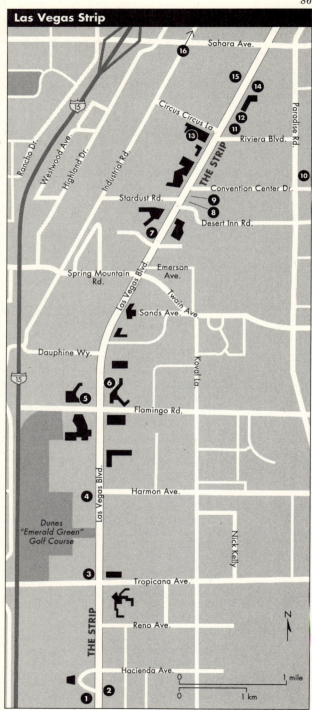

Tour 1: The Strip

for a Las Vegas tour and a great photo backdrop, especially at the beginning of a home video record of your trip. The sign is on an island in the middle of the street; when traffic allows, you can double-park in front of it, step out and take your picture.

Heading north on the boulevard, you'll see the Las Vegas **Visitors Center** on your right. Here you can pick up brochures and book hotel rooms and tours. Also look for the casinos' coupon promotions (good for free shrimp cocktails, 25¢ blackjack, etc.). A service charge is added to hotel bookings and to prepaid show tickets, but you can get into most shows easily without prepayment or a surcharge. You may also be pressured into signing up for a tour, but you don't necessarily have to do that right away. *4000 Las Vegas Blvd. S, tel. 702/731–3333. Open daily 9–9.*

Next door to the Visitors Center are the big blue gates of the **Las Vegas Air Charter Terminal** at the southwest corner of McCarran International Airport. The traffic here is that of the charter flights and the fixed base operators, those who fly their own planes into town.

The **Tropicana Resort and Casino**—featuring the "Island of Las Vegas," an oversize swimming pool with rocks and exotic animals—sprawls at the southeast corner of Tropicana Avenue and Las Vegas Boulevard. On the opposite (west) side of the Strip, expected to open in 1990, is the new, castlelike **Excalibur,** with its Old England theme. The small **Marina Hotel and Casino** is north of the Tropicana, on the north side of Tropicana Avenue.

A photo that frequently accompanied magazine articles on Las Vegas in the 1950s showed a Strip gas station with a FREE ASPIRIN AND TENDER SYMPATHY **sign.** The sign still stands today, with an invitation on the other side: ASK US ANYTHING. You'll find the sign on the west side of the Strip, one block north of Tropicana Avenue, at the front of the Kenneth L. Lehman Strip Union 76 gas station (3758 Las Vegas Blvd. S, tel. 702/736–0513).

About a block farther up the boulevard, on the east side, the large gold hotel with a magic lamp shining atop is—what else?—the **Aladdin Hotel and Casino.** In a small shopping center that adjoins the hotel you'll find **Little Caesar's Gambling Casino,** one of the most popular sports books in town, an old-fashioned, smoke-filled room with no TV projection system or deli sandwiches, just wise guys and hot dogs.

Opposite Little Caesar's, on the west side of the Strip, is a very different collection of relics. The **Las Vegas Museum of Natural History** has exhibits of prehistoric fossils, including 14 dinosaur skeletons and a skull and foot of *Tyrannosaurus rex*. Three animated dinosaurs make roaring sounds as their heads move up and down and their tails stir. Additional displays depict 300 species of present-day animal life. *3700 Las Vegas Blvd. S, tel. 702/798–7975 or 702/739–7280. Admission $5 adults, $4 senior citizens and military personnel, $2.50 children. Open daily 9–9.*

Just north of the museum is the Four Corners area of the Strip, named for the four large casino hotels at the four corners of the intersection of Las Vegas Boulevard and Flamingo Road. The **Dunes Hotel and Country Club** is at the southwest corner, **Cae-**

Exploring Las Vegas 88

sars Palace has the northwest corner, **Bally's Casino Resort** occupies the southeast corner, and the **Flamingo Hilton and Tower** had the northeast corner property until the small **Barbary Coast Hotel and Casino** interposed itself between the Flamingo Hilton and Flamingo Road.

⑤ **Caesars Palace** (3570 Las Vegas Blvd. S, tel. 702/731–7110) is the must-see casino of Las Vegas. The folks here have done the best job of transforming Bugsy Siegel's fantasy vision of Vegas into a reality: Walking into Caesars is like entering another world. After passing the big fountains, you move into the Roman gardens with a marble statue of Apollo, the Greek god of sunlight, prophecy, music, and truth. A large guard bearing a shield and other ancient garb invites you to enter the $2.5 million dome of the World of Caesar. A moving sidewalk carries you on into a darkened rotunda with a miniature re-creation of ancient Rome that employs holography, fiber optics, and laser-powered audio effects. Next you find yourself inside a lush green casino, where two actors playing Caesar and Cleopatra sit on a pedestal next to the $100 slot machines and sign autographs. You are now in the Olympic casino with the less expensive games, the 25¢ slots and $3 blackjack tables. Walk on for a while and you'll end up in the shopping area, underneath a giant replica of Michelangelo's *David*. Walk on farther still and you'll run into Cleopatra again, this time smiling down at you from the bow of her ship, Cleopatra's Barge, where music acts perform nightly for customers' listening and dancing. Yes, folks really dance on the ship, which rocks on real water, and the cocktail waitresses, called goddesses, wear Roman togas.

East of the Four Corners, beyond the Barbary Coast on the north side of Flamingo Road, are two casinos popular with local residents: The **Bourbon Street Hotel and Casino** and the **Maxim Hotel and Casino** offer lower table minimums and smaller crowds than you'll find in the Strip casinos. The Flamingo Hilton's solution to the crowd-control problem in 1989 was to build another casino next door—**O'Sheas Casino,** with a Luck of the Irish theme. The next attraction north on the Strip, the **Imperial Palace Hotel and Casino,** has an Oriental motif and a collection of old cars in its parking facility.

⑥ The **Imperial Palace Automobile Museum** is a collection of more than 200 vintage cars on display on the first level of the hotel's parking garage. Among the cars, trucks, and motorcycles on view is a 1939 Mercedes touring sedan once owned by Adolf Hitler, said to be worth more than $600,000. *3535 Las Vegas Blvd. S, tel. 702/731–3311. Admission: $3.75 adults, $2 children 5–11 and senior citizens. Open daily 9:30 AM–11:30 PM.*

The **Holiday Casino** is north of the Imperial Palace; opposite them, on the west side of the boulevard, is Las Vegas's newest spectacle: **The Mirage,** opened in the late fall of 1989, has a towering waterfall, lagoons, tropical plants, and white tigers prowling a glassed-in area of the grounds.

Back on the east side of the Strip, beyond the Holiday Casino, the **Sands Hotel and Casino** was the locale in 1960 for the film *Ocean's 11,* with Frank Sinatra, Dean Martin, Sammy Davis Jr., Peter Lawford, and Joey Bishop.

⑦ The large building at the northwest corner of Spring Mountain Road and Las Vegas Boulevard is the **Fashion Show Mall,** a Strip shopping mall that has more than 140 specialty shops and

Tour 1: The Strip

boutiques. You can't lay a bet here, but you can buy gaming tables, playing cards, and other gambling paraphernalia, as well as clothing, shoes, books, and fast food. *3200 Las Vegas Blvd. S, tel. 702/369–8382. Open weekdays 10–9, Sat. 10–6, Sun. noon–5.*

The **Frontier Hotel and Gambling Hall,** north of the mall, was the second resort to open on the Strip (as the Last Frontier); its forte is low-priced gaming. Opposite the Frontier, on the east side of the boulevard, the **Desert Inn Hotel and Casino** is where the reclusive millionaire Howard Hughes resided on the ninth floor; from Thanksgiving 1966 until December 1970, he never left his room.

8 The busiest church in town, **Guardian Angel Cathedral** (302 E. Desert Inn Rd., tel. 702/735–5241), just east of the Strip, has standing room only on Saturday, as visitors pray for luck and drop casino chips in the collection cups.

9 Those who find the Fashion Show Mall high-priced may appreciate the other extreme, the **Peppermill Shopping Center** ("Friendliest Shops in Vegas") on the east side of the Strip, north of Desert Inn Road. It's a minimall with a host of gift shops offering Las Vegas pens, pencils, salt shakers, ashtrays, dice clocks, and T-shirts (JIM AND SUE MARRIED IN LAS VEGAS); a Western shop with cheap cowboy shirts; a Frederick's of Hollywood outlet; a children's clothing store; and the Peppermill Casino. *3047 Las Vegas Blvd. S. Open daily 9 AM–1 AM.*

Back on the west side of Las Vegas Boulevard, the **Stardust Hotel and Casino,** with one of the most impressive neon signs in Vegas, and the **Westward Ho Motel and Casino** north of it, a large motel with a small casino, are separated by the only McDonald's in America with a flashing neon sign. Inside, the window seats provide a good view of the lights and the traffic of the Strip.

Opposite the Stardust, Convention Center Drive leads east from Las Vegas Boulevard to Paradise Road and the Las Vegas Convention Center. The **Landmark Hotel and Casino,** on Convention Center Drive at Paradise Road, is the large building in the shape of a spaceship, built by Howard Hughes, who thought it could be his Eiffel Tower. Just to the north, on the east side of Paradise Road, stands what was for many years the country's largest hotel, the **Las Vegas Hilton,** with 3,147 rooms. While other hotels have succeeded to the title, the hotel and casino here are still among the largest in town.

10 The great dome of the sprawling **Las Vegas Convention Center** (Convention Center Dr., tel. 702/733–2323) was raised in the 1950s in an effort to draw more folks to Las Vegas midweek, and it worked. Nearly 2 million of the 16 million annual visitors to Las Vegas are now convention delegates. Two of America's largest conventions are held here in January: the Consumer Electronics Show (100,000 people) and COMDEX (computer dealers; 90,000 people). Convention business is so important to Vegas that a $35 million expansion of the center is scheduled to begin in 1990; the rotunda—site of appearances by President John F. Kennedy and the Beatles—will be demolished and the center greatly enlarged.

Continuing up the east side of Las Vegas Boulevard, north of Convention Center Drive, you'll find **Silver City,** a Circus Cir-

Exploring Las Vegas 90

cus enterprise with lower minimum betting and smaller crowds than the parent casino. Beyond it, the **Riviera Hotel** has a Burger King inside and the "Splash" water show.

⑪ Next door to the Riviera, on the north, the **Candlelight Wedding Chapel** (2855 Las Vegas Blvd. S, tel. 702/735–4179) is the busiest chapel in town. On a Saturday at the Candlelight you'll see lines of folks waiting to be married at the only chapel with a Strip address. There's no reason you can't look on; just walk in and take a seat in a pew. Some ceremonies take place outside the chapel, in the gazebo.

Adjacent to the chapel are another shopping minimall and **⑫** **Trader Ann's Trading Post.** The gift items are less tacky here than at the Peppermill, there's a parking lot out front, and you can select from among I LOST MY ASS IN LAS VEGAS T-shirts, Elvis decanters, American Indian jewelry, moccasins, and photos of Marilyn Monroe. *2845 Las Vegas Blvd. S, tel. 702/732–1983. Open daily 9 AM–1 AM.*

⑬ **Circus Circus** (2880 Las Vegas Blvd. S, tel. 702/734–0410) has to be the busiest casino in town. It may be a madhouse inside, and it may require an effort to deal with the traffic in getting here, but if you have kids, you will probably want to visit. Downstairs are a mammoth casino, gift shops, a buffet, and a wedding chapel. Upstairs is a midway with carnival games, funhouse mirrors, and free circus acts daily, 11 AM–midnight. Kids seem to prefer Circus Circus to any other Vegas casino experience. The smaller casino out front, Slots A Fun, has a tacky gift shop and—what else?—lotsa slots.

The last two casinos, before the Strip comes to an end at Sahara Avenue, are **El Rancho Tower Hotel and Casino** and the **Sahara Las Vegas Hotel,** both on the east side of Las Vegas Boulevard.

⑭ Between them, the 26-acre **Wet 'N Wild water park** provides opportunities for family-oriented recreation in a 500,000-gallon wave pool, three water flumes, a water roller coaster, slides, cascading fountains, and lagoons. Showers, changing rooms, and lockers are available, and inner tubes and rafts are for rent. Shops and concession stands sell souvenirs and food. *2601 Las Vegas Blvd. S, tel. 702/737–3819. Admission: $13.95 adults, $10.95 children 3–14. Open May–Oct., daily 10–8.*

Those who are determined to visit only one gift shop in Vegas **⑮** will want to make it **Bonanza,** World's Largest Gift Shop, on the west side of the Strip opposite the Sahara. No, it may not really be the world's largest, but it is the biggest and best in town, with an impressive selection of wood novelties, John Wayne plaques, Injun headdresses, jackalopes, T-shirts, place mats, slides, Wayne Newton blow-up dolls, film, fudge, moccasins, and aspirin. *2400 Las Vegas Blvd. S, tel. 702/384–0005. Open daily 9 AM–midnight.*

At Sahara Avenue you've come to the end of the Strip, yet there's one more casino here you'll have to see: **Vegas World Hotel and Casino,** on the west side of Las Vegas Boulevard just north of the avenue, is the place with the Lost in Space theme—a spaceman drifts outside the building, and strange planets float in the casino airspace.

If by now you're beginning to think about chucking your present job, moving to Vegas, and going to work as a dealer, the **⑯** **Paul-Son School of Gaming** (2133 Industrial Rd., tel. 702/598–

Tour 2: Downtown 91

1669) will teach you the ins and outs of the profession. It has four-week and five-week courses on dealing blackjack, baccarat, roulette, and craps, and it places graduates in jobs afterward. The courses cost about $375–$400. You'll find the school a few blocks north of Sahara Avenue on Industrial Road, which runs parallel to Las Vegas Boulevard and is about ½ mile west of it. The school is run by Geno Munari, a former executive at the Imperial Palace and Bourbon Street casinos, who writes a syndicated column on gambling.

Tour 2: Downtown

Numbers in the margin correspond with the numbered points of interest on the Las Vegas Downtown map. The casinos pointed out on this tour were described in detail in Chapter 3.

Two miles from the northern end of the Strip at Sahara Avenue, Las Vegas Boulevard meets Fremont Street in downtown Vegas. The best collection of neon signs in town is here, but it can be appreciated only after the sun has gone down. Because the downtown hotels are almost on top of each other, you're hit with a blast of bright lights when you first turn the corner onto Fremont Street at night. Las Vegas gambling began on Fremont in the 1930s, and the original honky-tonk atmosphere remains. The oversize neon cowboy (Vegas Vic) and cowgirl (Sassy Sally) stand ready to greet visitors at one end of Fremont Street, while barkers along the street offer come-ons.

Here's how a sample come-on works: A woman offers you free coins with which to play the slots. You accept a roll from her and take it to the visitor center. There you are told you have won the game, and you're asked what your favorite jackpot is. You answer, 7–7–7. You are handed a sheet of paper that says 7–7–7 and are told to take it to a slot girl at a casino. The slot girl congratulates you, telling you the casino will pay you double if you get 7–7–7 on a slot, and you should begin inserting your dollar coins in the slots—three of them at a time. And have a lucky day! Because all the downtown come-ons end this way, most people just keep walking when they are approached.

Fremont Street runs east from Main Street, five blocks west of Las Vegas Boulevard, where the **Union Plaza Hotel** houses the train station and a casino. The heart of downtown Vegas, called Glitter Gulch, is the four-block stretch of Fremont Street that begins at the Union Plaza. Directly in front of the UP, on the south side of Fremont Street, the neon cowgirl with sexy blue neon legs who sits atop a hotel building is **Sassy Sally** (Golden Gate, 1 Fremont St.), one of two landmark Vegas images in this block.

On the opposite side of the street, the **Las Vegas Club Hotel and Casino** has a sports theme and, like many downtown casinos, relatively low table minimums. Atop the old gambling hall next door stands **Vegas Vic** (Pioneer, 50 Fremont St.), the neon cowboy who waves his arms back and forth—the complement to Sassy Sally across the street.

At 1st Street you might walk a block north to Ogden Avenue to inspect the **California Hotel and Casino** (that's the one with the Hawaiian decor). The 100 block on Fremont Street finds the

Cashman Field, **4**
Las Vegas High School, **5**
Ripley's Believe It or Not Museum, **3**
Sassy Sally, **1**
Vegas Vic, **2**

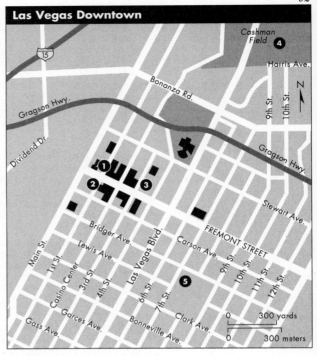

block-long **Binion's Horseshoe Hotel and Casino** on the north facing the **Golden Nugget Hotel and Casino** on the south. Binion's hosts the annual World Series of Poker and often has people waiting in line for a place at a blackjack table; its old-time ambience—hardwood walls and dealers wearing string ties—is so convincing that you get the feeling that Binion's has always been here. The white-marble walls and the gold-plated slots, pay telephones, and elevator of the upscale Golden Nugget make this casino radically different in appearance from all the other downtown gambling halls. (The ornate neon sign of the old Golden Nugget, a favorite subject of Vegas postcards, is no more.)

In the next block east on Fremont Street, the **Fremont Hotel and Casino** on the north, with a photogenic neon sign outside and a bingo room inside, faces the **Four Queens Hotel and Casino** on the south. The felt on the Four Queens gaming tables is red instead of green, and this is the home of the largest Ripley museum anywhere.

3 The Vegas edition of **Ripley's Believe It or Not Museum,** like the others, displays weird artifacts from the collection of Robert Ripley, whose *Believe It or Not* newspaper cartoon panels were widely read—often with disbelief—in the 1940s. Among the treasures here are shrunken heads, log cabins made from pennies, and a replica of a Hindu man who remained on a bed of nails for 18 years. *Four Queens Hotel and Casino, 202 E. Fremont St., tel. 702/385–4011. Admission: $4.95 adults, $3.95 senior citizens, $2.95 children 5–12. Open Sun.–Thurs. 9 AM–midnight, Fri.–Sat. 9 AM–1 AM.*

Las Vegas for Free 93

A turn to the north on 3rd Street and a one-block walk to Ogden Avenue will take you to the **Lady Luck Casino and Hotel,** where free shrimp cocktails, photos, and long-distance phone calls draw the traffic (and long lines). In the next block east on Ogden Avenue, the **Gold Spike Hotel and Casino** offers the best gambling deal in town: Every twenty-one table has a $1 minimum bet, and most of the video poker machines are 5¢ slots.

In the 300 block on Fremont Street, across 3rd Street from the Four Queens, the 34-story **Fitzgerald's Hotel and Casino**— formerly the Sundance—is the tallest building in Nevada, and it's another casino with a Luck of the Irish motif.

For a look at the "other" convention center in Las Vegas, which doubles as a sports facility, drive one mile north from Fremont Street on Las Vegas Boulevard. **Cashman Field** (850 Las Vegas Blvd. N, tel. 702/386–7100) has a 100,000-square-foot exhibit hall, 17,000 square feet of meeting space, and a 2,000-seat auditorium that was used as the courtroom for the trial of Wayne Newton's libel suit against NBC News.

Our last casino stop on Fremont Street, one block east of Las Vegas Boulevard between 6th and 7th streets, is the city's oldest standing casino, **El Cortez Hotel,** which opened for business in 1941. Contrary to the sign out front, there are no more floor shows here.

A two-block stroll south on 7th Street to Bridger Avenue will take you miles from the honky-tonk of downtown and bring you to the everyday life of **Las Vegas High School** (315 S. 7th St.), the oldest permanent school building in Las Vegas. Built in 1930 for $350,000, the structure is a state historical landmark, the only example of 1930s art deco architecture in the city. Many Nevada officials are Las Vegas High graduates.

Las Vegas for Free

Circus acts at Circus Circus (Tour 1: The Strip).

Clark County Library. One of the best libraries in town, Clark County is on the south side of Flamingo Road, a little more than 2 miles east of the Strip. It's a modern general library with current reference materials. *1401 E. Flamingo Rd., tel. 702/733–7810. Open Mon.–Thurs. 9–9, Fri.–Sat. 9–5, Sun. 1–5.*

James R. Dickinson Library. The special-collections department of this library of the University of Nevada, Las Vegas, has the best gathering of materials about Las Vegas and gambling that you'll find anywhere. *4505 Maryland Pkwy., tel. 702/739–3285. Open Mon.–Fri. 8 AM–midnight, Sat. 8–7, Sun. 1–5.*

Las Vegas Museum of Natural History. Desert animals, Native American jewelry, and photos of early Las Vegas can be seen at this museum of the University of Nevada. *4505 Maryland Pkwy. at University Rd., tel. 702/739–3381. Admission: $5 adults, $2.50 children. Open daily 9–9.*

Popcorn at the Slots A Fun Casino (Tour 1: The Strip).

Shrimp cocktails at the Lady Luck Casino and Hotel (Tour 2: Downtown).

Exploring Las Vegas   94

What to See and Do with Children

Even though children are not welcome in casinos (state law requires that bettors be over 21), there are plenty of things for families to do together in Las Vegas.

Circus Circus's performances, midway, and video game room (Tour 1: The Strip).

Discovery: The Children's Museum (833 Las Vegas Blvd. N, tel. 702/382–3445). The museum's hands-on exhibits are aimed at stimulating young people's curiosity and interest in the arts and sciences. In recent years Discovery was housed at the Nevada State Museum while awaiting the completion of its own new facility. The new Discovery was scheduled to open in spring 1990 in the vicinity of Cashman Field.

Imperial Palace Automobile Museum (Tour 1: The Strip).

Las Vegas Museum of Natural History (Tour 1: The Strip).

Omnimax Theater. The large-screen 70mm movies shown in the round at the Caesars Palace cinema are the kind you'll see at major expositions and at the Smithsonian in Washington, D.C. Their subjects typically include such topics as rafting the Grand Canyon, surfing in Hawaii, and space exploration. *Caesars Palace, 3570 Las Vegas Blvd. S, tel. 702/731–7110. Admission: $4 adults, $3 children under 13. Shows daily, on the hour, 11 AM–midnight.*

Ripley's Believe It or Not Museum (Tour 2: Downtown).

Scandia Family Fun Center. The center has three 18-hole miniature-golf courses, a video arcade, baseball batting, and the Li'l Indy Raceway for miniature-car racing. *2900 Sirius Ave., tel. 702/364–0070. Admission free; fee to play each game. Open Mon.–Thurs. 10 AM–11 PM, Fri.–Sat. 10 AM–1 AM.*

Video arcades will be found at Bally's Casino Resort, Caesars Palace, Circus Circus, and the Riviera Hotel (Tour 1: The Strip).

Wet 'N Wild water park (Tour 1: The Strip).

Youth Hotel. Guests of the Las Vegas Hilton and the Flamingo Hilton can leave their kids aged 3 to 18 in the Las Vegas Hilton dormitories, where counselors supervise sports activities and arts and crafts. Children can also spend the night (midnight–8 AM). *Las Vegas Hilton, 3000 W. Paradise Rd., tel. 702/732–5111.*

Off the Beaten Track

Young Electric Sign Company (YESCO; 5119 Cameron St., tel. 702/876–8080). The headquarters of the company that makes virtually every neon sign in town is less than 2 miles west of the Strip. Its backyard is a bizarre yet picturesque "graveyard" of old neon signs lying around on the ground. You probably won't get permission to rummage through them, but you can drive by and around the parking lot and get a pretty good glimpse of a real neon jungle. YESCO is off Tropicana Avenue, nearly 2 miles west of Las Vegas Boulevard.

Sightseeing Checklists

These lists of Las Vegas's principal attractions include those that were covered in the preceding tours and others that are described here for the first time.

Historical Buildings and Sites

The Fabulous Flamingo, the original four-story motor hotel that Bugsy Siegel built in 1946, on the grounds of The Flamingo Hilton and Tower (Tour 1: The Strip).

Las Vegas High School (Tour 2: Downtown).

Old Mormon Fort. Southern Nevada's oldest historical site was built by the Mormons in 1855 as an agricultural mission to give refuge to travelers along the Salt Lake–Los Angeles trail, many of whom were bound for the California gold fields. Left to the Indians after the gold rush, the adobe fort was later revitalized by a miner and his partners. In 1895 it was turned into a resort, and the city's first swimming pool was constructed by damming Las Vegas Creek. Today the restored fort contains more than half the original bricks; antiques and relics help to recreate a turn-of-the-century Mormon living room. *Corner of Washington Ave. and Las Vegas Blvd. N, at Cashman Field (enter through parking lot B), tel. 702/386–6510. Admission: $1 adults, 50¢ children. Open Labor Day–Memorial Day, Mon. and Sat. 10–4, Sun. 1–4; Memorial Day–Labor Day, Mon. and Sat. 8–3, Sun. noon–3.*

The Thunderbird of 1948, on the grounds of El Rancho (Tour 1: The Strip).

Churches, Temples, Wedding Chapels

Las Vegas is one of the most religious communities in America. The Mormon leader Brigham Young was a founder, and when he left because of the heat, many of his followers stayed behind. There are more churches per capita in Las Vegas—a.k.a. Sin City—than anywhere else, for local residents tend to be avid church goers and visitors come to pray for better luck.

Churches **First Baptist Church** (300 S. 9th St. at Bridger Ave., tel. 702/382–6177).

First Southern Baptist Church (700 E. St. Louis Ave., tel. 702/732–3100).

Guardian Angel Cathedral (302 E. Desert Inn Rd., tel. 702/382–9909) is the busiest church in town, largely because of its location on the Strip. Donations are made in casino chips more often than in cash, and once a week a priest takes them to Caesars Palace to cash them in. Unlike other churches in Vegas, Guardian Angel's attendance on Sunday is more than 75% tourists. The 4 PM mass on Saturday is so crowded, usually with 300 standees, that visitors are asked to attend the 5:15 mass or one of the five Sunday masses instead.

Joan of Arc (315 S. Casino Center Blvd., tel. 702/382–9939).

Temples **Las Vegas Nevada Temple of the Church of Jesus Christ of the Latter-day Saints** (827 Temple View Dr., tel. 702/438–7488) sits atop 12 acres on Sunrise Mountain, overlooking the Las Vegas

Exploring Las Vegas   *96*

Valley. It is open to "worthy" members of the religion who have been "recommended," and the recommended can come from any Mormon church, so those who have their passes will be admitted. Members of the general public are invited to enjoy the view and grounds. While Las Vegas has no Young Street or Brigham Street, members of the Church of the Latter-day Saints, known as Mormons, constitute the largest religious group in Vegas. Yet until they opened this temple in 1989, church members drove two hours to attend services in St. George, Utah, the site of the nearest temple. (Mormon teaching is that one can be married for "life" in a chapel but must be married in a temple to be married for "eternity.")

Temple Beth Sholom (1600 E. Oakley Blvd., tel. 702/384–5070).

Wedding Chapels   When the governor signed the "wide open" gambling bill in 1931, Nevada also got liberal divorce and marriage laws as part of the strategy to attract tourists. A divorce could be obtained after six months of residency; a wedding could be arranged without a blood test once you had a license and a minister willing to perform the ceremony. The rules are the same today, and weddings are big business in Nevada, with 65% of them taking place in Las Vegas. New Year's Eve and Valentine's Day are the most popular wedding dates.

Celebrities (Bruce Willis, Bette Midler, Joan Collins, Lisa Bonet) have found it expedient to pop into a chapel in the middle of the night and have a quick ceremony. It's also a popular formula for folks from around the country; drive along the Strip on a Saturday afternoon, and you'll be amazed at the long lines waiting in front of the chapels. Critics complain that the 15-minute weddings have all the charm of a fast-food hamburger; proponents note that on a day when families can drive a couple crazy with guilt and obligations, the bride- and groom-to-be can hop in a car, come to Vegas, and enjoy the experience by themselves.

Candlelight Wedding Chapel (2855 Las Vegas Blvd. S, tel. 702/735–4179), **Little Church of the West** (3960 Las Vegas Blvd. S, tel. 702/739–7971), and **Little White Chapel** (1301 Las Vegas Blvd. S, tel. 702/382–5943 or 800/545–8111) are the three most popular wedding chapels. All operate in basically the same way: You make an appointment, you show up, you pay a fee for a wedding (usually $50), and everything else (photos, music, flowers, videos) is extra. So is the suggested "donation" of $25 for the minister. Most chapels accept credit cards but ask that the donation be paid in cash. Wedding ceremonies can also be performed in your hotel room, in a car, in a hot-air balloon, or wherever you suggest, provided you'll pay for it.

Marriage Licenses   **Clark County Marriage License Bureau** is the place to obtain a marriage license, which costs $27. Both applicants must apply in person; those age 16 to 18 need the consent of their parents or legal guardians. Blood tests are not required, and there is no waiting period. *200 S. 3rd St., tel. 702/455–3156 or 702/455–4415 (after 5 PM, weekends, and holidays). Open Mon.–Thurs. 8 AM–midnight, Fri. 8 AM–Sun. midnight.*

Throughout Vegas you'll see signs offering "free wedding information" services; what you'll get from them is what you've just read here—plus a sales pitch for whatever chapel is paying that service a commission. If you have questions about Vegas weddings, call the chapels; they'll answer them all.

Sightseeing Checklists   97

Museums and Galleries

Clark County Southern Heritage Museum. Exhibits on settler life, early gambling, and nuclear testing are included in a chronological history of southern Nevada. Other attractions are a fully restored bungalow home from the 1920s, built by a pioneer Las Vegas merchant; a replica of a 19th-century frontier print shop; and buildings, structures, and machinery dating from the turn of the century. The gift shop offers Native American artifacts. *1830 S. Boulder Hwy., Henderson, tel. 702/455–7955. Admission: $1 adults, 50¢ children 6–15 and senior citizens. Open 9–4:30.*

Guinness World of Records Museum (2780 Las Vegas Blvd. S). This new museum of world records was scheduled to open late in 1989.

Imperial Palace Automobile Museum (Tour 1: The Strip).

Las Vegas Art Museum. Constructed in 1935 from railroad ties, the art museum has both a permanent collection and changing exhibitions of the work of local and national artists. *3333 W. Washington Blvd., tel. 702/647–4300. Admission free. Open Tues.–Sat. 10–3, Sun. noon–3.*

Las Vegas Museum of Natural History (Tour 1: The Strip).

Liberace Museum. Clothing, other belongings, photographs, and mannequins of the late entertainer make this museum the kitschiest place in town. In addition to Lee's collection of pianos (one of them was played by Chopin; another, a concert grand, was owned by George Gershwin), you can see his Czar Nicholas uniform and a blue velvet cape styled after the coronation robes of King George V. Be sure to check out the gift shop—where else can you find Liberace soap, ashtrays, and other novelties? The museum is run by Mr. Showmanship's sister-in-law, Dora Liberace. *1775 E. Tropicana Ave., tel. 702/798–5595. Admission: $6.50 adults, $4.50 senior citizens, $2 children under 12. Open Mon.–Sat. 10–5, Sun. 1–5.*

Nevada State Museum and Historical Society. Regional history from the time of the Spanish exploration and the building of Las Vegas after World War II are the big subjects in this museum of the history, archaeology, and anthropology of southern Nevada. Outdoors, the park and ponds that surround the lakeside museum in Lorenzi Park show plants and animals native to the region. *700 E. Twin Lakes Dr., tel. 702/486–5205. Admission: $1 adults. Open Mon.–Tue. 11:30–4:30, Wed.–Sun. 8:30–4:30.*

Ripley's Believe It or Not Museum (Tour 2: Downtown).

Parks

Las Vegas families, too, have youngsters who like swings and teeter-totters, and there are more than 100 parks in the Las Vegas area.

Jaycee Park (2100 Eastern Ave.) is a small park situated behind the Chamber of Commerce on Sahara Avenue, 2 miles east of the Strip. On Sahara Avenue, turn north on Eastern Avenue and go one block to reach the entrance of the park.

Lorenzi Park (3300 W. Washington Ave.) is a little more than 2 miles west of downtown and the railroad tracks. From down-

Exploring Las Vegas 98

town, head west on Bonanza Avenue to reach the back entrance of the park at Twin Lakes Drive. The park houses a museum and a historical society.

Paradise Valley County Park (4770 Harrison Dr.) is 3 miles east of the Strip and a block north of Tropicana Avenue.

Sunset Park (Corner of Sunset Rd. and Eastern Ave.) is the largest park in Vegas at 325 acres. Almost 3 miles east of the Strip and 2 miles south of Tropicana Avenue, it's on a lake where fishing is allowed.

Zoo

At **Southern Nevada Zoological Park,** five minutes from downtown, the hot desert air helps keep a Bengal tiger, an Asian spotted leopard, and African green monkeys happy. Among other attractions are a large collection of exotic birds, a rare-and endangered-species breeding program, and a petting zoo with smaller animals. *1775 N. Rancho Dr., tel. 702/648–5955. Admission: $5 adults, $2 children under 17 and senior citizens. Open daily 9–5.*

Photographing Las Vegas

Among the top 10 tourist destinations in the United States, Las Vegas is the only one whose major attractions discourage photography. At Disney World, the Grand Canyon, Washington, D.C., or anywhere in California, your camera is as welcome as your kids. But walk into a Vegas casino with a camera hanging from your neck, and the security guard will give you stares. Start to pull off the lens cap, and the guard will tell you sternly, "No pictures in the casino."

"But I'm just taking a photo of my wife."

"No pictures in the casino. No exceptions."

Imagine a tourist visiting the Space Needle in Seattle or the Empire State Building in New York City, pulling out a camera, and hearing an official say, "No pictures."

The Nevada Gaming Control Board has issued hundreds of rules for Nevada casinos to follow, but picture taking isn't mentioned in any of them. The rule is one that the casinos themselves have instituted: no pictures, no exceptions.

The practice goes back to the 1940s and 1950s, when the "boys" ran Vegas. In New York and Los Angeles they had always refused to allow themselves to be photographed, and in their new casinos they kept their old habits and phobias. Remember the scene at Don Corleone's daughter's wedding in *The Godfather*, when a photo is taken of one of the dons and he orders that the film be exposed and the camera broken?

The reasoning in Vegas went like this: If a guy is sitting at a twenty-one table with a woman at his side who is not legally his, and a photograph is taken, the guy might feel very uncomfortable and decide to leave the premises. Another player simply might not want other people to think that he could be dropping thousands of dollars in a casino. Forget that hundreds of onlookers coming and going might see him in the act; it's the photo that could be incriminating.

The irony here is that, outside the casinos, Las Vegas is a great city to photograph, and for the most part all you have to do is point and shoot. Its very name is synonymous with the word *neon*. At nighttime Vegas is brighter than any other city in America, all because a man from Salt Lake City named Thomas Young convinced a casino owner that a bright sign would attract business. Young cut his deal with the Boulder Club downtown in 1946, and when the sign brought results, everyone else in town wanted one. A major neon sign today can cost $1 million and will have little neon in it. More in demand are the flickering lights of the electronic message centers, whose moving video screens announce food bargains, casino attractions, and showroom acts.

Cameras and Film

An ordinary point-and-shoot camera will do fine, but if you have 35mm camera equipment and a wide-angle lens, your pictures will look even better. With so much to take in when shooting Vegas, the wide-angle (28mm or 35mm) really pays off by fitting as much as possible into the picture. When you're shooting video, you'll probably want to leave your lens set at

Exploring Las Vegas 100

the widest point of view and zoom in only for the occasional close-up.

If you're shooting color print film (as most of us do), get the 100 ISO film; it's cheaper, and it offers the best color reproduction. I recomend Fuji film, which has sharper and more vibrant colors than Kodak's print film. In Vegas you won't have much need for high-speed film (400 or 1000 ISO) because most of your subjects will be outdoors, under the bright desert sun.

Those who want the best possible color will go for slide film. Fuji 50 produces hues so rich you won't believe it; the bright colors of Vegas will look surreal.

When you shoot neon signs at nighttime, and when you shoot slides, the low-ISO films are a must. High-speed films dilute the colors and give you a bland photo. Signs will photograph best when you mount your camera on a tripod and make exposures of up to half a second.

You can still get decent color prints of signs by using 100 ISO print film; the important thing to remember is not to shoot them at night. The best time is immediately after the sun has gone down, when the sky is still blue and a desert haze has fallen, leaving strands of reds and yellows in the sky. At that time the neon signs have been turned on, giving you full-strength "signage" against a blue sky, which will be far more photogenic than a black sky. Take a look at any hotel's promotional brochures, and you'll notice that every one of the marquee pictures has been shot this way.

Shooting immediately after sunset is the best time for people pictures, too, because the light adds a nice warm tone to the skin. If you're shooting with a flash, you can easily light the person posed in front of the sign and not have to worry about the sign being overexposed.

All of the above applies to video as well. Just after sunset you'll get the flickering of the signs against a blue rather than a black sky—and a much more pleasing picture. But keep in mind that these signs are very large; you'll need steady camera work on your part to get everything into the frame. Rest the camcorder on your shoulder, not on your hand, take a deep breath, and move your body up and down to pan across the sign.

Subjects

Go downtown for the best neon photos; there's simply more neon here than anywhere else. If you're looking for a portrait of your loved one with neon in the background, downtown is where you will want to shoot. At the corner of Fremont and Third, place your subject on the street during a red light, and you've got either the Fremont and the Horseshoe, or the Vegas Vic and Sassy Sally signs as backdrops. You also might want to get a shot of your subject with one of the great downtown barkers, the ladies dressed in dollar bills pasted to their yellow suits.

Many of the neon signs on the Strip (Dunes, Circus Circus, Sahara) are so large that they are quite difficult to photograph. The manageable ones are those of the Stardust and the Flamingo Hilton. Downtown's greatest shots are the Horseshoe, the Four Queens, and the Vegas Vic and Sassy Sally signs.

Photographing Las Vegas

Las Vegas may be the kitsch capital of the world, and your video or photo album should get lots of laughs if you include any of these subjects:

The statue of a nude dancer and the 125-foot Lucky the (Neon) Clown at Circus Circus.

The pink elephant in front of the Mirage Motel, below the Tropicana on the Strip.

The discarded neon signs that sometimes sit in hotel parking lots.

The tuxedoed dealers on the sign advertising the Strip Dealers School on Las Vegas Boulevard and Sahara.

The marquees promoting free shrimp cocktails and one-deck blackjack.

Overhead shots of the Strip are pretty easy to get. Most hotels have hallways with picture windows overlooking the Strip; all you need to do is to take an elevator to the floor of your choice, aim your camera out the window, and shoot. Outside town you'll find handsome desert scenery, Hoover Dam, and Lake Mead.

And you *can* take photos of the interior of a casino. You will have to work at it, but it can be done. On the Strip, begin with the Barbary Coast, which has no doors. Place your companion in front of the large staircase that leads into the casino, shoot quickly, and you've got your photo. You could do much the same thing at many of the casinos downtown, such as the Fremont and the Horseshoe, which also do not have doors. Just stand your subject directly in front of the entrance and shoot, and the odds are you'll have a slot machine or a Big Six wheel in the background.

This technique may work even better for video because you won't have to take the time to set up a shot but can film quickly. You will probably have finished before a security guard realizes what's going on.

One casino that will let you shoot pictures inside is Caesars, but only in a few select locales. You are allowed to photograph the Cleopatra actress, the replica of Michelangelo's *David*, and as much as you like of the outdoor fountains.

How about a photo of your subject out in the desert with all the big hotels of Vegas in the background? It's easy: Drive south on the Strip toward the Hacienda. About a block before you get there, on your right, you'll see a dirt road with no sign. Turn down it, heading west. At the end of the road, pull over, and you'll have a perfect view of the middle of nowhere—and a big city rising out of the sand. This photo should also be taken just after sundown, with the light still on the sand and the colorful signs in the background. It's a good location for both still and video photography.

Excursions from Las Vegas

What the city of Las Vegas may lack in the variety of its attractions for the visitor is offset by a number of man-made and natural scenic wonders a short drive away. The price categories of hotels and restaurants mentioned in the excursion tours are those used in the Reno and Lake Tahoe chapter.

Excursion 1: Hoover Dam and Lake Mead

Numbers in the margin correspond with points of interest on the Lake Mead National Recreation Area map.

Boulder City, the enormous Hoover Dam, and Lake Mead to the north of it are the objectives of the first day trip most new visitors to Vegas want to take.

On leaving Las Vegas, follow Boulder Highway (U.S. 93/95) through desert terrain and small-town settings for 23 miles to reach **Boulder City.** In the early 1930s this town was developed to deter construction workers on the Hoover Dam project from spending their hard-earned dollars on wine, women, song, and the Las Vegas scene. To this day, that model city is the only community in Nevada where gambling is illegal. Originally, 4,000 workers lived here; when the dam was completed, the city served as a center for the management and maintenance of the site. Boulder is a pleasant small town with a movie theater, numerous gift shops, and a small hotel. The **Boulder City Chamber of Commerce** (tel. 702/293–2034) is a good source of local information.

Continue east on U.S. 93 about 11 miles to reach the site of **Hoover Dam.** When Congress authorized the funding of the $175 million dam in 1928, workers flocked to the area; when the dam was completed in 1935, many of them stuck around. The dam was created for two purposes: flood control and the generation of electricity. One of the seven man-made wonders of the world, the dam is 727 feet high (the equivalent of a 70-story building) and 660 feet thick (greater than the length of two football fields). Construction of the dam required 4.4 million cubic yards of concrete—enough to build a two-lane highway from San Francisco to New York. Originally called Hoover Dam, after President Herbert Hoover, the structure was rechristened Boulder Dam during President Franklin Roosevelt's time and then given its original name again by Congress in 1947. More than 600,000 people a year take the Bureau of Reclamation's 35-minute guided tour of the dam, which takes visitors deep inside the structure for a look at its inner workings. Tours leave every few minutes from the exhibit building at the top of the dam. *Hwy. 93 east of Boulder City, tel. 702/293–8367. Admission: $1 adults, 50¢ senior citizens. Tours daily 8–6:30.*

For the approach to **Lake Mead,** return west on U.S. 93 about 6 miles to the intersection with Lakeshore Drive. Here the **Alan Bible Visitor Center** (tel. 702/293–8906) can provide information on the history of the lake and on the accommodations available along its shore. Lake Mead, whose surface covers 229 square miles and whose irregular shoreline extends for 550 miles, was formed when the Hoover Dam was built to hold back the Colorado River. Come here for fishing, waterskiing, swimming, boating, and sailboarding; the **National Parks Service**

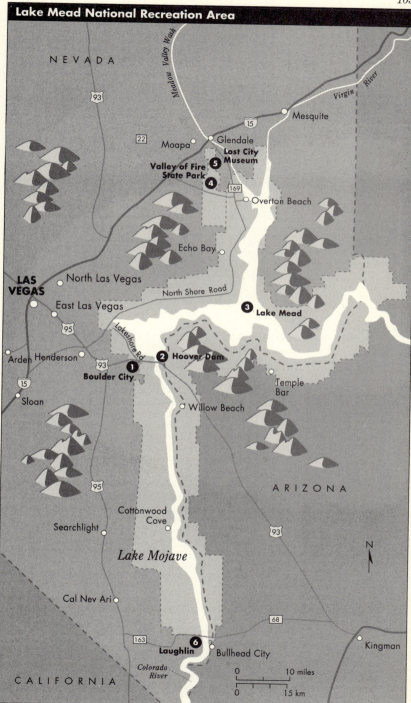

Exploring Las Vegas 104

(tel. 702/293–4041) can give you details on the recreational facilities available at Lake Mead.

A five-minute drive along the shore will bring you to the first marina, **Lake Mead Marina** (tel. 702/293–3484). Here you'll find boat rentals, the beach, camping facilities, a gift shop, and a restaurant. A drive of about an hour will take you along one side of the lake, where you'll find five more marinas. When you reach the upper arm of the lake, about a mile past Overton Beach, look for the sign announcing the Valley of Fire. Turn left here and go about 6 miles to reach the **Valley of Fire Visitor Center** (tel. 702/397–2088).

Excursion 2: Valley of Fire

4 The 56,000-acre **Valley of Fire State Park,** dedicated in 1935, was Nevada's first park, situated less than 2 miles west of the upper arm of Lake Mead and 55 miles northeast of Las Vegas. The Valley of Fire takes its name from its distinctive coloration, which ranges from lavender to tangerine to bright red, giving the valley an otherworldly appearance. Here are incredible rock formations that have been weathered into unusual shapes suggest elephants, domes, beehives. Mysterious signs and symbols, called petroglyphs (carvings etched into the rock) and pictographs (pictures drawn or painted on the rock's surface), are believed to be the work of the Basketmaker and Anasazi Pueblo people who lived along the nearby Muddy River between 300 BC and AD 1150.

The visitor center has exhibits, films, lectures, slide shows, and information about the 50 campsites within the park. While the park is open all year, it is in the heart of the desert, and you would probably find it uncomfortable to visit during the summer. *Hwy. 169, Overton, 89040, tel. 702/397–2088. Open daily 8:30–4:30.*

5 To visit the **Lost City Museum,** head east from the Valley of Fire on South Highway 169 for about 8 miles. Turn left at the "T" and continue for another 8 miles to the museum. Here you'll find on display early Pueblo Indian artifacts, Paiute basketry, weapons, and a restored Basketmaker pit house. *721 S. Hwy. 169, tel. 702/397–2193. Admission: $1 adults. Open daily 8:30–4:30.*

Excursion 3: Laughlin, Nevada

Those who can't get gambling out of their blood and would like to have a sense of what the Western town of Las Vegas was like in earlier times might opt for the two-hour drive through the **6** desert to **Laughlin,** Nevada. From Las Vegas, take Boulder Highway (U.S. 95/93) east and follow U.S. 95 south almost to the California border, where you'll find Highway 163 to take you east in the direction of Laughlin.

Laughlin is a classic stateline city, separated from Arizona by the Colorado River. Nevada's newest community, Laughlin is fast becoming a major resort area, with 5,000 rooms now and 2,000 more by the summer of 1990, when a new Flamingo Hilton is scheduled to open. The city generally attracts older, primarily retired travelers who spend at least part of the winter in Arizona. Like Las Vegas, Laughlin draws folks who like to gamble—especially those who prefer low-pressure, low-minimum tables, cheap food, low-cost rooms, and slots galore.

Excursions from Las Vegas   105

Laughlin casinos are less crowded than those of Vegas, and this gives the dealers greater opportunity to be friendly and the bettors a more relaxed playing time. A turn to the south off Highway 163 onto Casino Drive will take you to the gambling halls: **Riverside Resort** (1650 S. Casino Dr., tel. 702/298–2535 or 800/227–3849), **Regency Casino** (1950 S. Casino Dr., tel. 702/298–2439), **Edgewater** (2020 S. Casino Dr., tel. 702/298–2453), **Colorado Belle** (2202 S. Casino Dr., tel. 702/298–4000), **Golden Nugget** (2300 S. Casino Dr., tel. 702/298–2512 or 800/237–1739), **Pioneer Hotel** (2200 S. Casino Dr., tel. 702/298–2442 or 800/634–3469), **Ramada Express** (2121 S. Casino Dr., tel. 702/298–4200 or 800/272–6232), and **Sam's Town Gold River** (2700 S. Casino Dr., tel. 702/298–2242 or 800/835–7903).

The **Laughlin Chamber of Commerce** (tel. 702/298–2214 or 800/227–5245) can provide further information on the area.

Those who elect to cross over into Bullhead City, Arizona, should follow the directions from Casino Drive to the bridge leading into Arizona.

Excursion 4: Red Rock Canyon and Old Nevada

For a 13-mile drive through the red rock formations and unusual high-desert scenery of southern Nevada, head west from Las Vegas on Charleston Boulevard for the Red Rock Canyon scenic loop (about 16 miles). The **BLM Visitor Center** here has exhibits of plant, animal, and desert life. *Charleston Blvd., tel. 702/363–1921. Open daily 9–4. Loop open daily 8–8.*

Leave the loop by exiting south onto Highway 159 (Charleston Boulevard) and go 3 miles to Highway 160 and Spring Mountain, a state park and working ranch. A drive of 1 mile farther will bring you to the Old Nevada amusement area and the Bonnie Springs Ranch. **Old Nevada Ranch,** built in 1843, was the site of the filming of some episodes of "Bonanza." The Old West theme is played to its fullest here, with hangings and gunfights staged in the street, silent movies, an opera house, museums, and a cemetery. *Hwy. 160, tel. 702/875–4191. Admission: $5.50 adults, $4.50 senior citizens, $3.50 children. Open daily 10:30–6.*

After shopping for gifts or souvenirs at Old Nevada, most folks mosey on next door to the Bonnie Springs Ranch, which had its start in 1843 as a stopover for the wagon trains traveling the Old Spanish Trail to California. Today the Springs offers a duck pond, a petting zoo where kids can feed baby lambs or stroke a buffalo, and a small railroad that runs on weekends. Equestrians can make use of the large stable of horses, and the guided trail rides through the desert encounter cacti and Yucca and Joshua trees. The **Bonnie Springs Motel** here has rooms for overnight stays. *1 Gun Fighter La., tel. 702/875–4400. 50 rooms. Facilities: swimming pools, some rooms with Jacuzzi, theme rooms. AE, MC, V.*

Excursion 5: Mt. Charleston, Kyle and Lee Canyons

For a mountains retreat, head northwest from Vegas on Highway 95 about 45 miles to Mt. Charleston, the fifth highest mountain in the state. At Highway 157, turn off to Kyle Canyon. In the wintertime this area is a local skiing haven; in the summer it's a welcome respite from the 115-degree desert sun

Exploring Las Vegas 106

as well as a place to hike, picnic, and camp. For camping information, contact the **U.S. Forest Service** (tel. 702/388–6255).

For overnight accommodations, try the **Mount Charleston Inn.** *2 Kyle Canyon Rd., tel. 702/872–5500. 60 rooms, 3 suites. Facilities: restaurant, lounge, gift shop. AE, CB, DC, MC, V. Expensive–Very Expensive.*

The **Mount Charleston Restaurant and Lounge,** part of the inn, offers hot food in typical mountainside fashion, with a wood fireplace and picture windows looking onto the mountains. The restaurant also has a full assortment of video and regular slots. *2 Kyle Canyon Rd., tel. 702/386–6899. Dress: informal. Reservations not necessary. AE, DC, MC, V. Expensive.*

On leaving Mount Charleston, return to Highway 157 and drive about ½ mile to exit 156. Turn left to Lee Canyon, where the wintertime skiing lasts from November to early March and the 9,000-foot elevation offers a peaceful view all year round.

Excursion 6: St. George, Zion National Park, Bryce Canyon

From the neon jungle of Las Vegas it's a journey of 116 miles north on Interstate 15 to the small, picturesque town of St. George, Utah. In getting there you'll pass through Littlefield, Arizona, cross the Utah border, and see the landscape become increasingly red in color; in St. George you'll find an assortment of low-priced motels, bed-and-breakfast inns, an old movie theater and a new Twinplex, souvenir shops, a variety of restaurants (American, Chinese, Mexican), Mormon historical sites, and red rocks.

On a wintertime visit you might encounter snow here, and in the summer you can expect to find temperatures cooler than those in Las Vegas. An evening in St. George can be spent exploring the Victorian-style streets, climbing the red rock cliffs, or looking out over the town.

Yet the red rocks of St. George are only a preview of the miles of rich redness to be seen at Zion National Park, about 30 miles to the northeast. Follow I–15 to the first Hurricane exit, which will take you through the small town of that name. Driving up the mountain, you'll see signs directing you into the 6-mile park drive among mammoth red rocks.

The Mormons believed they had found God's country when they discovered Zion National Park. In addition to giving the area its name, they christened the park's major rock formations: *Great White Throne, Angel's Landing, Cathedral Mount, Three Patriarchs,* and *Pulpit.* The elevation ranges from 3,600 feet to 8,700 feet—higher than the North Rim of the Grand Canyon. Many of the park trails are wheelchair accessible; others are narrow climbs with sheer drops that would be difficult treks for small children.

Accommodations in the park are available May–October at the **Zion Canyon Lodge TW Services Inc.** (Box 400, Cedar City, UT 84720, tel. 801/586–7686) and at the nearby **Best Western Driftwood Lodge** (Rte. 9, Utah Hwy. 9, Springdale, UT 84767, tel. 801/772–3262 or 800/528–1234).

To reach Bryce Canyon National Park and what may seem like the prehistoric world of the Flintstones, continue east on High-

Excursions from Las Vegas 107

way 9 to Highway 89 and turn north. You'll drive about 40 miles to Route 12 and turn east, and another 17 miles will bring you into the park.

Most of the activity at Bryce occurs below the trail entrances, at the foot of the canyons. Bryce offers driving tours and hiking trails, and visitors in the wintertime can explore the trails on snowshoes or cross-country skis. The rock formations are red, but the rocks have been sculpted into various shapes by the waters and weathers of several million years. The visitors center at **Bryce Canyon** (tel. 801/834–5322) will answer any questions you may have about the park.

Although there is a 110-room lodge at Bryce, open from mid-May to October, many visitors like to stay at **Ruby's Inn,** 2 miles from the main entrance. Ruby's, open all year, has basic motel rooms and rates that drop significantly beginning in October. *Best Western Ruby's Inn, Hwy. 63, Bryce, UT 84764, tel. 801/ 834–5341 or 800/528–1234. 166 rooms. Facilities: indoor pool, restaurant, general store, campground. AE, CB, DC, MC, V. Inexpensive–Moderate.*

Other accommodations near Bryce are few. Some motel rooms can be found in Panguitch, 25 miles to the north on Highway 89, and in Tropic, 7 miles to the east on Route 12.

5 Shopping

Where you shop in Las Vegas will depend more on how much you want to spend than on what you're looking for. Joe and Joanna Tourist, who are happy to spend lots of money in high-priced gift shops, can remain on the Strip and find whatever they want, from expensive furs to the cheesiest dice clock. Those who enjoy paying a lot of money for products that cost much less anywhere else will be happy in the casino shopping malls. Anyone who wants to shop for more practical items (sneakers, sweaters, sporting goods) at reasonable prices will have to look elsewhere, beyond the Strip and the casinos.

Major Shopping Districts and Malls

The Strip The Strip is a giant shopping mall in and of itself. Here you will find rows and rows of gift shops with T-shirts, newspapers, toys, and items that say LAS VEGAS on them, as well as a large indoor mall (the Fashion Show) and shopping arcades at every major casino resort.

Many of the hotels on the Strip have exclusive shops that sell expensive furs, dresses, swimsuits, and men's clothing. For example, the Caesars Palace shopping area, dubbed the Appian Way, features tony shops such as Gucci, Ted Lapidus, and Ciro. It is said that if you own one or two slot machines in the proper location, you can make a very good living in Las Vegas; four machines, and you are rich; 10 or more, and you will never have to worry about money again. Perhaps the same can be said for owning a store in a casino hotel. One browse through these shops and you'll see why. My personal favorite among the offerings is the $400 yellow, purple, or green men's jackets at Mort Wallin in the Bally's shopping arcade.

In the same vein as the casino gift shops is the **Fashion Show Mall** (3200 Las Vegas Blvd. S, tel. 702/369–0704), the largest mall in town. Centrally located on Las Vegas Boulevard, across the street from the Desert Inn and next to the Frontier, it's hard to miss. And realizing that, the proprietors have set their prices to welcome you. Yet it's a very well kept mall, and not all the stores are overpriced. The two-story building contains 140 shops, including Neiman Marcus, Saks Fifth Avenue, Bullock's, Goldwaters, and Dillards. There are also designer boutiques, Abercrombie & Fitch, and Lillie Rubin (she's the designer who makes clothes for Mary Hart of TV's "Entertainment Tonight"). One unusual mall inhabitant, the American Museum of Historical Documents, offers framed autographed letters of Abraham Lincoln, Marilyn Monroe, and other famous people. The mall's fun food court has selections that run the gamut from hot dogs on a stick to Herbie Burgers. If you're in a panic about last-minute gifts, you'll find plenty of places to buy expensive Vegas souvenirs. You'll also find Waldenbooks here, the only bookstore on the Strip.

The other side of the Strip couldn't be more different. Inside the casinos the gifts are elegant and expensive; outside, it's Tacky City. The endless gift shops along Las Vegas Boulevard all sell wooden Jesus plaques, Taos moccasins, blow-up Wayne Newton dolls, dice clocks, used casino cards, key chains, T-shirts, and bath towels. Some stores are so schlocky you'll be embarrassed you stepped inside. **Bonanza "World's Largest Gift Shop"** (2460 Las Vegas Blvd. S, tel. 702/385–7359), across the street from the Sahara Hotel, is the best of the bunch. It

Las Vegas Shopping

Ace Loan, **31**
Adams Western, **28**
B. Dalton, **14, 27**
Bonanza "World's Largest Gift Shop", **20**
Boulevard Mall, **14**
C & R Clothiers, **14**
Casino Clothiers of Nevada, **23**
Clothestime, **1**
Contempo Casuals, **16, 27**
Dealers Room Casino Clothiers, **14**
Ethel M Chocolates, **34**
Fashion Show Mall, **16**
Foot Locker, **14, 16, 27**
Furs by Le Nobel of Athens, **3**
Gambler's Book Store, **30**
Gamblers General Store, **29**
Harris and Frank Clothing, **14, 16**
The Hock Shop, **33**
House of Antiques and Slots, **26**
K Mart, **24**
Kinney, **14, 16**
The Limited, **14, 16**
Lucky, **7**
Major Video, **12**
Marshall-Rousso, **2, 3, 4, 17, 18, 19**
The Meadows, **27**
Miller Stockman, **16, 27**
Paul-Son Dice and Card, **25**
Princess Furs, **5**
Record Surplus, **21**
Sam's Town, **35**
Stoney's Loan and Jewelry, **32**
Target, **6**
Tiffany Furs, **22**
Tower Records, **8**
Toys 'R Us, **10**
Union Premiums, **9**
Vans of California, **15**
Video Park, **11**
Waldenbooks, **16, 27**
Waldenbooks and More, **13**
Ziedler and Ziedler Ltd., **16**

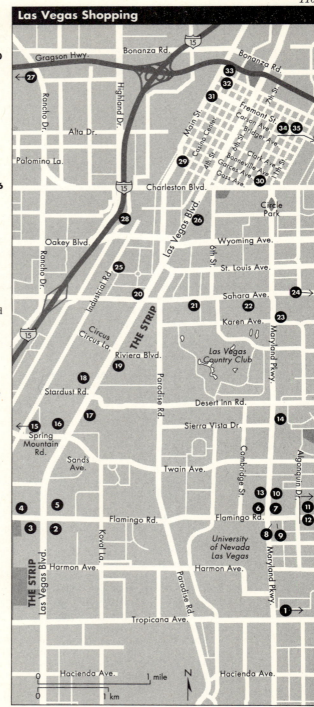

Shopping 111

may not in fact be the world's largest, but it is the largest in Vegas, and while it has some of the same junk that the others have, it sells some nice things as well. It's so huge that you won't feel trapped, as you might in some of the smaller shops. And it's open until midnight.

Maryland Parkway The major shopping district for Las Vegas is on Maryland Parkway, 1 mile east of the Strip and parallel to Las Vegas Boulevard. A shopper's paradise, Maryland Parkway has scores of fast-food spots and every type of store that caters to mall goers. A drive along Maryland Parkway will undoubtedly bring you to the store of your choice. **The Boulevard Mall** (3528 Maryland Parkway, at Desert Inn Rd., tel. 702/735–8268), popular with local residents, usually has lower prices; the million-square-foot complex boasts 75 stores.

The Meadows The other major Vegas mall, **The Meadows** (4300 Meadows Ln., tel. 702/878–3331), is located in a residential district west of the downtown. The largest enclosed mall in Nevada, the Meadows has 144 specialty stores in addition to the Broadway, Dillards, Sears, and J. C. Penney's department stores.

Specialty Stores

Books **Waldenbooks and More** (3783 Maryland Pkwy. S, tel. 702/369–1996) is appropriately named, carrying all kinds of books, magazines, tapes, games, and cards. Other bookstores in the malls include **B. Dalton** (The Boulevard Mall, tel. 702/735–0008, and The Meadows Mall, tel. 702/878–4405) and **Waldenbooks** (Fashion Show Mall, tel. 702/733–1049, and The Meadows Mall, tel. 702/870–4914).

Casino Clothes If you've caught the gambling spirit and want to go home in a white shirt and a big red bow tie, two stores will be happy to sell you dealer's duds: **Dealers Room Casino Clothiers** (3661 Maryland Pkwy. S, tel. 702/732–3932) and **Casino Clothiers of Nevada** (900 Karen Ave., tel. 702/732–0449).

Chocolates **Ethel M Chocolates** (2 Cactus Garden Dr., about 15 minutes from the Strip, tel. 702/458–8864). The Mars family runs an operation in Nevada that isn't allowed elsewhere in the country: They're permitted to make chocolates containing liqueurs. This is the family—headed by Ethel in the early days—that brought us Snickers, Milky Way, Mars bars, Three Musketeers, and M&Ms. This fancy chocolate factory hosts more than a thousand people daily, who come to watch the candy-making. All the tours end in the gift shop, where visitors are encouraged to buy souvenirs.

Clothing for Men The men's stores in Vegas are primarily representatives of national chains, among them **C&R Clothiers** (3507 Maryland Pkwy. S, tel. 702/733–7093), **Harris and Frank Clothing** (3570 Maryland Pkwy. S, tel. 702/735–1102, and 3200 Las Vegas Blvd. S, tel. 702/737–7545), and **Ziedler and Ziedler Ltd.** (3200 Las Vegas Blvd. S, tel. 702/369–8878).

Clothing for Women **Marshall-Rousso** (at Bally's Las Vegas, Caesars Palace, Desert Inn, Dunes, Riviera Hotel, and Stardust) is one of the most expensive women's stores in town. Most of the popular mall chains are here in Vegas, too: **The Limited** (Fashion Show Mall, 3200 Las Vegas Blvd. S, tel. 702/737–7522, and Boulevard Mall, 3528 Maryland Pkwy. S, tel. 702/369–0221), **Clothestime** (4906 E.

Shopping 112

Tropicana Ave., tel. 702/451–1900), and **Contempo Casuals** (Meadows Mall, 4300 Meadows Ln., tel. 702/870–9857, and Fashion Show Mall, 3200 Las Vegas Blvd. S, tel. 702/735–9075).

Discount Stores When you need an inexpensive tie, shirt, or swimsuit and you can't get to the mall, you might want to hop a cab to **Target** (4001 Maryland Pkwy. S, tel. 702/732–2118), which is about eight blocks from the Strip, down Flamingo Road. Anything you may have forgotten to pack can probably be replaced inexpensively at **K Mart** (2975 E. Sahara Ave., tel. 702/457–1037).

Film Don't buy your film on the Strip or at the gift shops if you can help it; their prices are markups of the retail prices at **Union Premiums** (1325 E. Flamingo Rd., tel. 702/737–1717). This is also a good place to shop for camera, video, and audio equipment.

Food **Lucky** (1300 E. Flamingo Rd., in the Mission Shopping Center, tel. 702/733–2947). You might laugh, but just try finding an apple, an orange, a banana, or a box of Special K on the Strip. Lucky is the closest food store, and it's open 24 hours.

Furs Stop by **Furs by Le Nobel of Athens** (Dunes Hotel, tel. 702/734–9722), if only to see the photographs of Anna Nateece, a self-described "designer of the stars," pictured here with her customers Liberace, Mike Tyson, Queen Frederica of Greece, and others. If you can't get here and are desperate for fur, you can visit **Tiffany Furs** (953 E. Sahara Ave., tel. 702/735–0186) or **Princess Furs** (3555 Las Vegas Blvd. S, tel. 702/369–5500).

Gambling Memorabilia Now is the time to stock up on gambling books, cards, dice, green felt, and anything else of a gaming nature you might require.

Gambler's Book Store (630 S. 11th St., tel. 702/382–7555) has the best collection of current and out-of-print books about twenty-one, craps, poker, roulette, and all the other games; novels about gambling and crime figures; and anything else that relates to gambling and Las Vegas.

Gamblers General Store (800 S. Main St., tel. 702/382–9903) offers more of the same: poker chips, green felt, and books on gambling and sports betting. It's eight blocks down the street from the Union Plaza Hotel.

House of Antiques and Slots (1243 Las Vegas Blvd. S, tel. 702/382–1520). If taking home a classic slot machine would make your trip to Vegas complete, you might want to stop in here, down the street from the Little White Chapel (where Joan Collins was wed). But be warned: Old slots can be very expensive, with prices in the $2,000–$5,000 range, and in-home slots are legal in only 40 states. The proprietors will let you know if they are legal where you live.

Paul-Son Dice and Card (2121 Industrial Rd., tel. 702/384–2425). Want to take home some authentic casino dice and chips? This downtown store is a major supplier to the casinos.

Pawn Shops Las Vegas is a great place to pick up cheap guitars, watches, and cameras because local residents who can't pay their gambling debts—or get the urge to drop more money at the casinos—frequently turn to pawn shops for a little extra cash. All are located in the heart of downtown: **Ace Loan Company** (26 E. Fremont St., tel. 702/384–5771), **Stoney's Loan and Jewelry**

Shopping

(126 N. 1st St., tel. 702/384–2686), and **The Hock Shop Ltd.** (206 N. 1st St., tel. 702/384–3042).

Records   **The Record Surplus** (547 E. Sahara Ave., tel. 702/796–8001) is the only place in town where you'll be able to find classic records made in Las Vegas by such stars as Don Rickles, Tom Jones, Godfrey Cambridge, and Jan Peerce.
Tower Records (4110 Maryland Pkwy. S, tel. 702/731–0800) has the city's largest collection of new CDs, records, audio tapes, and videocassettes, and it's open until midnight every day.

Shoes   **Foot Locker** (Boulevard Mall, tel. 702/737–8646; Fashion Show Mall, tel. 702/737–5623; and the Meadows Mall, tel. 702/878–8226). The specialty here is athletic footwear.
Kinney (3200 Las Vegas Blvd. S, tel. 702/737–0976, and 3454 S. Maryland Pkwy., tel. 702/735–3930). This chain store stocks a large selection of contemporary shoes.
Vans of California (5020 Spring Mountain Rd., tel. 702/871–2564). Look here for hard-to-get large sizes, high-tops, slip-ons, and low tie-ups.

Toys   **Toys 'R Us** (4000 Maryland Pkwy. S, tel. 702/732–3733). You'll find this a larger, better-run store than most others in the chain. Discount toys are the name of the game here.

Video   Las Vegas may very well be the VCR capital of the world, largely because so many residents work nights and don't want to miss prime-time television. The Vegas Video stores, most of which are open 24 hours, are large and well stocked.
Major Video (3870 E. Flamingo Rd., tel. 702/456–9560, and 3441 W. Sahara Ave., tel. 702/364–1242), the principal chain in town, has a super-large stock of all kinds of movies.
Video Park (3300 E. Flamingo Rd., tel. 702/367–0074) bills itself as "the world's largest video store!" and whether it is or not, it's not to be missed. When the Video Software Dealers Association meets in Vegas every year, most delegates make a trip to Video Park just for the experience. Each video genre is displayed in its own theatrical setting. To reach the horror section, for example, you have to step over a coffin complete with mannequin and sound effects. The music-video titles are placed within a 40-foot-long, 15-foot-high yellow submarine that you must climb into in order to look around.

Western Goods   Las Vegas loves its Western roots, and the city has some of the best Western shops around. The best one of all is **Sam's Town Western Emporium** (5111 Boulder Hwy., tel. 702/454–8017), a large shopping village with boots, hats, clothing, jewelry, belt buckles, string ties, a bakery, and a barber shop. It's adjacent to Sam's Town Hotel and Casino.
Miller Stockman (3200 Las Vegas Blvd. S, tel. 702/737–7326, and 4300 Meadows Ln., tel. 702/870–2951), a higher-priced Western shop that lacks the atmosphere and old-time feel of Sam's Town, is located in both the Fashion Show Mall and the Meadows Mall.
Adams Western Store (1415 Western Ave., tel. 702/384–6077) is the sort of traditional Western shop you might expect to find in Montana or Wyoming; the emphasis is on equestrian supplies and "wearing apparel." It's also the oldest Western shop in town, circa 1951, and it'll probably be the toughest for you to get to. It's off Sahara Avenue, near the freeway, on a back street named Western.

6 Sports and Fitness

The playful spirit of Las Vegas, epitomized in its casinos, is also very much alive in its sports. Vegas's 13 championship golf courses host several prestigious tournaments that include a $1 million stop on the PGA tour, and many boxing superstars—Muhammad Ali, Larry Holmes, Sugar Ray Leonard, Thomas Hearns, Marvin Hagler, and Mike Tyson—have faced each other in a Vegas ring.

Participant Sports and Fitness

Biking You can rent bikes at **Sunglass City** (515 Fremont St., tel. 702/388–0622) and **Bikes USA** (1539 N. Eastern Ave., tel. 702/642–2453). Don't expect to find many scenic biking trails, but for a unique view of the city you can cycle up the Strip or up Flamingo Road. To avoid the exhaust fumes from the many cars, you might ride through the University of Nevada campus or along the side streets downtown—and you'll want to take along plenty of water to combat the heat.

Boating Boats may be rented at **Jet Ski Fun** (639 N. Pueblo Blvd., Henderson, tel. 702/564–6551), **Lake Mead Resort and Marina** (322 Lakeshore Rd., Boulder City, tel. 702/293–3484), and **Ski Boat Rentals of Southern Nevada** (600 W. Sunset Rd., Las Vegas, tel. 702/564–6464). All are on the shores of Lake Mead, 30 miles from town, where the fishing is excellent.

Bowling Many casinos offer 24-hour bowling facilities. The 106-lane **Showboat** (2800 Fremont St., tel. 702/385–9153) is the world's largest bowling alley. Several other good bowling spots are the 56-lane **Sam's Town** (5111 Boulder Hwy., tel. 702/456–7777), the 52-lane **El Rancho** (2755 Las Vegas Blvd. S, tel. 702/796–2222), and the 72-lane **Gold Coast** (4000 W. Flamingo Rd., tel. 702/367–4700).

Golf With an average of 315 days of sunshine a year, Las Vegas's top sports recreation is golf. A number of 18-hole courses are at the resorts—**Desert Inn** (3145 Las Vegas Blvd. S, tel. 702/733–4288), **The Dunes** (3650 Las Vegas Blvd. S, tel. 702/737–4747), **The Tropicana** (3801 Las Vegas Blvd. S, tel. 702/739–2579)—and at the **Las Vegas Municipal Golf Course** (4349 Vegas Dr., tel. 702/646–3003). Watch out for the golf hustlers who hang around the resort courses looking for an easy mark.

Health Clubs The **Sports Club–Las Vegas** (3025 Industrial Rd., tel. 702/733–8999), behind the Stardust Hotel, has 12 racquetball courts, two tennis courts, a basketball court, a volleyball court, exercise equipment, outdoor jogging tracks, and aerobics classes; the fee is $17.50 a visit. The three facilities of the **Las Vegas Athletic Club** (1070 E. Sahara Ave., tel. 702/733–1919; 3315 E. Spring Mountain Rd., tel. 702/362–3720; and 5090 S. Maryland Pkwy., tel. 702/795–2582) offer racquetball courts, saunas, Jacuzzis, Nautilus and free weights, indoor and outdoor swimming pools, and aerobics classes. Most hotels have health-club facilities.

Hiking Hiking enthusiasts should explore the trails of Mt. Charleston, which are much cooler than the desert trails (*see* Excursions from Las Vegas in Chapter 4).

Horseback Riding **Bonnie Springs Ranch in Old Nevada** (1 Gun Fighter La., tel. 702/875–4191), 18 miles from the Strip, offers a one-hour guided ride for $13. **Mt. Charleston Stables** (Kyle Canyon Rd., tel. 702/872–7009), 25 miles from Las Vegas and next door to

Sports and Fitness 117

the Mt. Charleston Hotel, has horses for hire at rates that start at $15 for one hour.

Jogging **The Desert Inn** and **Caesars Palace** have jogging trails behind their hotels. The **University of Nevada–Las Vegas** (4505 S. Maryland Pkwy., tel. 702/739–3011) has a regulation track (Bill Cosby's favorite hangout when in town) from which you can see the Strip in the distance as you run. The most pleasant time to hit the streets of Vegas, especially in the April or September heat, is in the early morning or the late afternoon.

Racquetball **Caesars Palace** (3570 Las Vegas Blvd. S, tel. 702/731–7110), the **Las Vegas Athletic Club** (1070 E. Sahara Ave., tel. 702/733–1919, and 3315 E. Spring Mountain Rd., tel. 702/362–3720), and the **Sports Club–Las Vegas** (3025 Industrial Rd., tel. 702/733–8999) have racquetball courts.

Skiing **Lee Canyon** (State Hwy. 156, Mt. Charleston, tel. 702/646–0008), southern Nevada's skiing headquarters, is equipped with a 3,000-foot double chair lift and chalet. To get here, drive north on Highway 95 to the Lee Canyon Exit (Highway 156), and drive up the hill. You'll know you're only 47 miles from Las Vegas when you see the slope names: Blackjack, High Roller, Keno, The Strip, Bimbo 1 and 2, Slot Alley.

Swimming Every hotel and most motels have large pools that are open from April to October—but only until 6 PM daily, even on days when there's light in the sky until 9 PM. Hotel managements maintain that they can't afford to hire lifeguards to work through the night; in fact, they can't afford to have you lounging in the water when you could be spending your time and your money in the casino. Two **public pools** (430 E. Bonanza Rd., tel. 702/386–6309, and 1100 E. St. Louis Ave., tel. 702/386–6395) are open Memorial Day through Labor Day. For lake swimming, take the 30-mile drive to Lake Mead.

Tennis Las Vegas has an abundance of tennis courts, and many of them stay open through the evening. **Bally's Casino Resort** (3645 Las Vegas Blvd. S, tel. 702/739–4598) and **The Desert Inn** (3145 Las Vegas Blvd. S, tel. 702/731–7110) have 10 courts each, and **The Tropicana** (3801 Las Vegas Blvd. S, tel. 702/739–2222) has eight courts. The **University of Nevada–Las Vegas** (4505 S. Maryland Pkwy., tel. 702/739–3150) has a dozen lighted tennis courts.

Spectator Sports

Auto Racing In April **Binion's Horseshoe Hotel and Casino** (128 E. Fremont St., tel. 702/382–1600) hosts the **Nissan Mint 400,** a weekend desert auto race that attracts more than 400 drivers to Las Vegas. Former "Mint 400 girls" include Vanna White and Lynda Carter.

Baseball The Las Vegas Stars of the triple-A Pacific Coast League play at **Cashman Field** (850 Las Vegas Blvd. N, tel. 702/386–7200), north of downtown, where professional baseball made its Las Vegas debut in 1983. Winners of the league championship in 1986 and 1988, the Stars have become a successful baseball franchise and a thriving farm club for the San Diego Padres.

Basketball The hottest ticket in town during the school year are the basketball games of the Runnin' Rebels at the **University of Nevada–Las Vegas** (4505 S. Maryland Pkwy., tel. 702/739–3267).

Sports and Fitness 118

Bowling Las Vegas is home to the **Showboat Invitational Bowling Tournament** (Showboat Hotel, 2800 Fremont St., tel. 702/385–9123) the Professional Bowling Association's oldest competition, which airs on ESPN cable.

Boxing The major big-time sports event in Vegas is the prizefight. A title match draws the moneyed folk, sports stars, and celebrities from all fields—and brings out the high roller in everyone. Spectators willingly fork over $500 a seat to watch two guys pummel each other, then hang around the casinos laying down chips for the rest of the evening, sometimes for the rest of the week.

Championship boxing came to Vegas in 1960, when Benny Paret took the welterweight title from Don Jordan at the Las Vegas Convention Center. Since then most of boxing's superstars have fought in Las Vegas. To learn about upcoming boxing events, look for the fight odds posted on the wall in the race and sports book of any casino. For the most comprehensive fight listings, check **Caesars Palace** (3570 Las Vegas Blvd. S, tel. 702/731–7110), **Little Caesars Gambling Casino** (3665 Las Vegas Blvd. S, tel. 702/734–2827), or the **Stardust Hotel and Casino** (3000 Las Vegas Blvd. S, tel. 702/732–6111).

Golf October brings the annual **Las Vegas Invitational golf tournament,** with top PGA golfers competing for high stakes at the Desert Inn and Las Vegas Country Club. (This used to be a spring event.) For more information, contact **Las Vegas Events** (2030 E. Flamingo Rd. 89109, tel. 702/736–4199).

Rodeo When the **National Finals of Rodeo** (tel. 702/731–2115) comes to town in December, the casinos showcase country stars and the fans sport Western gear. The NFR, said to be the Super Bowl of professional rodeo, offers more than $2 million in prize money.

7 Dining

Elliot Krane, the restaurant editor of the Las Vegas Review-Journal, *made the selection of highly recommended restaurants.*

The restaurants of Las Vegas number more than 750. A major hotel and casino will have four or five eating places (the Las Vegas Hilton has 11), and the hotel marquees that used to announce revues and celebrity performers now proclaim food bargains: PRIME RIB $4.95! SHRIMP COCKTAIL 49¢! Yes, there are dining bargains here, for the hotels keep the prices of meals, liquor, and rooms low in order to draw you inside and steer you toward the casino. What the hotel loses in its restaurants it expects to more than make up in the gambling hall.

Hotel menus serve every pocketbook, offering a daily variety that extends from $2 buffets to $50 "gourmet" meals to 49¢ breakfasts in the wee hours. The buffets at breakfast (around $4), lunch ($6), and dinner ($8) are cafeteria-style, all-you-can-eat affairs where the food is plain and generally filling. And who can resist such old favorites as chipped beef, macaroni and cheese, stewed prunes, and canned fruit? Some hotels try harder; many items at the Golden Nugget buffet, for example, are prepared to order.

Gourmet dining has its place in Las Vegas because hotels recognize that the high roller, the player who may drop $40,000 or $50,000 in a weekend without blinking, expects treatment that acknowledges his status. No coffee shop or bargain buffet for him; he looks for the exclusivity of the intimate, dimly lighted gourmet room where the diners wear jacket and tie, the chef has been trained in Europe, and the service is attentive and professional—and the high roller is happy to pay for it. Everyone else benefits because the price of a first-class meal in Vegas is still much lower than it is in New York or San Francisco.

Those who want to spend as little money as possible on food should save their hunger for the hours between 11 PM and 6 AM. That's when many hotels drop their prices drastically, in still another attempt to lure you to the gaming tables and keep you playing while you're tired and likely to make poor decisions (such as not leaving the table when you should). These are the hours of the $2 steak dinner and the famous 49¢ breakfast of eggs, bacon, and toast. Keep in mind, too, that you can get a free shrimp cocktail at the Lady Luck casino at any time of the day and free popcorn at the Slots-A-Fun casino.

Perhaps the soundest restaurant advice for Vegas is to stay with the middle of the price range. Some of the best food in town is served in the hotel coffee shops, where the atmosphere is relaxed, the food is cooked to order, and, regrettably, the lines are usually quite long. You'll also find long lines at most hotel restaurants when a convention is in town, and there frequently is one. Delegates generally eat at the most convenient place—a restaurant in or close by their hotel.

Outside the hotels, the many proper restaurants of the city offer a variety of cuisines and the opportunity to get away from games of chance for a while. The food may be a bit more expensive here, but there will often be shorter waits for a table, and you'll have a greater sense of "dining out."

Restaurants, both in and out of hotels, are considered here according to cuisine. A tip of 15% is common practice in Las Vegas restaurants, and in some circumstances you might want to slip the maître d' $5 or $10 for a special table. Except where noted, reservations are unnecessary and casual dress is the norm.

Dining 121

Highly recommended restaurants in each price category are indicated by a star ★.

Category	Cost*
Very Expensive	over $50
Expensive	$20–$50
Moderate	$10–$20
Inexpensive	under $10

Average cost of a three-course dinner, per person, excluding drinks, service, and (7%) sales tax.

The following credit card abbreviations are used: AE, American Express; CB, Carte Blanche; D, Discover Card; DC, Diners Club; MC, MasterCard; and V, Visa.

American

★ **The Flamingo Room.** If you like pink surroundings, ice sculptures, and a view of pretty swimming pools, the Flamingo Room may be just the place for you. Pink neon adorns the room, and diners sit in plush blue booths with pink tablecloths. Specialties are the mixed grill (lamb chops, beef medallion, pork tenderloin, bacon, broiled tomato, potato, and vegetable) and the medley (sautéed beef medallion with béarnaise sauce, pork tenderloin with *picante* sauce, chicken scaloppine with mushrooms, potato, and vegetable). At lunch the salad bar costs a dollar less, and sandwiches and burgers are available. It's a comfortable place for viewing the original Flamingo Hotel, still standing on the other side of the pool, and reflecting on the nature of Las Vegas in the old days. *The Flamingo Hilton and Tower, 3555 Las Vegas Blvd. S, tel. 702/733–3111. Reservations advised. AE, CB, D, DC, MC, V. Moderate–Expensive.*

Center Stage. The Stage's second-story view of downtown Fremont Street takes in Vegas Vic and Sassy Sally, and this is one of the rare chances you'll have to see them from behind. The restaurant is set in a dark green oval glass bubble with large windows that let in lots of red and yellow from the big neon light show outside. Steak, chicken, and veal are the principal entrées; all dinners come with soup or salad, potato, vegetable, and beverage. *Union Plaza Hotel, 1 Main St., tel. 702/386–2513. Reservations advised. AE, CB, D, DC, MC, V. Dinner only. Moderate.*

The Skye Room. Traditional American fare and the best view of downtown Vegas, from 15 floors high in the Horseshoe Hotel, formerly the Mint Hotel, are reason enough for climbing to this vantage point for dinner. The menu offers prime rib, steak, chops, and chicken, all served with potato and salad. *Binion's Horseshoe Hotel and Casino, 128 Fremont St., tel. 702/382–1600. Reservations advised. AE, CB, D, DC, MC, V. Dinner only. Moderate.*

Cafe Michelle. Here's a café with a European ambience that makes a welcome change of pace when the casino experience has gotten to you. Situated in a small shopping mall, between a Lucky Foods and a Sav-On Drugs, the cafe has red-and-white checked tablecloths indoors and the traditional Cinzano umbrellas above the tables in the plaza outdoors. Chops, chicken,

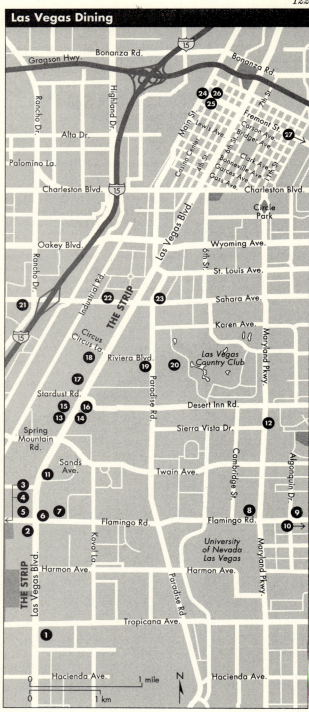

Alpine Village Inn, **19**
Andiamo, **20**
The Bacchanal, **5**
Battista's Hole in the Wall Italian Restaurant, **7**
Binion's Coffee Shop, **26**
Cafe Michelle, **8**
Cafe Roma, **5**
Capozzoli's, **12**
Center Stage, **24**
Chin's, **13**
Circus Circus, **18**
Dome of the Sea, **2**
Elaine's, **25**
Empress Court, **5**
The Feast, **21**
The Flame, **16**
The Flamingo Room, **6**
Food Fantasy, **6**
The Golden Nugget Hotel, **25**
The Golden Steer, **22**
Ho Wan, **14**
The Island Buffet, **1**
Joe's Bayou, **11**
Le Montrachet, **20**
Lillie Langtry's, **25**
Margarita's Mexican Cantina, **15**
Mary's Diner, **27**
Oh No! Tokyo, **4**
Palace Court, **5**
Pamplemousse Restaurant, **23**
Primavera, **5**
Ralph's Diner, **17**
Santa Fe, **3**
The Silver Dragon, **9**
The Skye Room, **26**
The Steak House, **18**
The Sultan's Table, **2**
The Tillerman, **10**
Uptown Buffet, **27**
William B's Steakhouse, **17**
Willy and Jose's Cantina, **27**

Dining

and salads are the fare, with sandwiches and salads at lunchtime. *1350 E. Flamingo Rd. in the Mission Shopping Center, tel. 702/735–8686. AE, MC, V. Inexpensive–Moderate.*

Buffets

All buffets listed below fall in the Inexpensive category.

Circus Circus (2880 Las Vegas Blvd. S, tel. 702/734–0410) has the most widely attended buffet on the Strip, with more than 10,000 people served every day. Among the 40 or more trays of eats you'll find set out are ravioli, ambrosia, sliced apples, O'Brien potatoes, chipped beef, macaroni and cheese, and chicken-fried steak. The official designation for this kind of preparation is "steam cooking"; some may see it as warm food with little flavor. Since this is Circus Circus, the food is served on pink plates in a pink-and-white room with circus tents, giraffes, and elephants painted on the wallpaper. A long line of people is usually waiting to get in.

The Golden Nugget Hotel (129 E. Fremont St., tel. 702/385–7111) has the best buffet in town, and you won't find Velveeta cheese, chipped beef, or the other staples of buffets elsewhere. At the Golden Nugget buffet the eggs are cooked to order, the cheese and cold cuts are appealing, and the salad bar, raisin bread, and muffins are freshly prepared. This buffet costs about twice as much as any of the others, but it's worth it.

The Island Buffet (Tropicana Resort and Casino, 3801 Las Vegas Blvd. S, tel. 702/739–2222), the **Uptown Buffet** (Sam's Town Hotel and Casino, 5111 W. Boulder Hwy., tel. 702/456–7777), and **The Feast** (Palace Station Hotel and Casino, 2411 W. Sahara Ave., tel. 702/367–2411) are other good buffets in town.

Cajun

Joe's Bayou. Among the Cajun, Creole, and other Southern cooking at Joe's are Louisiana chicken gumbo, Natchez prime rib, shrimp Creole, St. Louis steak, and Memphis barbecue (with slow preparation over mesquite). All dinners include plantation greens, cornbread, and salad. The setting is a nautical one; the statue of a sea captain greets diners up front, and a collection of oars, ship's clocks, and nets hangs from the ceiling in a quiet, dark atmosphere. *Holiday Inn, 3473 Las Vegas Blvd. S, tel. 702/369–5000. Reservations advised. AE, CB, D, DC, MC, V. Dinner only. Moderate.*

Chinese

★ **Empress Court.** "We don't serve chop suey here," the tuxedoed maître d' exclaims, "no moo shu or cashew-nut chicken either, just traditional, authentic Cantonese cuisine." Welcome to the newest addition to the Caesars Palace family of restaurants, a $4 million rest stop for the wealthy Asian gamblers who drop millions in the Caesars casinos. The theme is water and the animal life that inhabits it. A two-story staircase has a koi pond at its center; etchings of fish decorate the glass panels in the main dining room; patterns of blue fish swim in the carpeting; and a large aquarium of exotic fish occupies the middle of the room. The food is exotic: braised shark's fin with crabmeat, imperial Peking duck, and double-broiled bird's nest. For the truly adventurous, a set menu for two, The Emperor, includes

Dining 124

Cantonese roast duck salad in sesame sauce, velvet chicken soup with mushrooms, prime sirloin strips with rainbow vegetables, Szechuan chicken with hot pepper sauce and sea fried rice, and ginger ice cream and cookies. *Caesars Palace, 3570 Las Vegas Blvd. S, tel. 702/731–7731. AE, CB, D, DC, MC, V. Reservations advised. Jacket and tie required. Dinner only. Very Expensive.*

Ho Wan. Those who are hungry for familiar Chinese food— cashew-nut chicken, moo shu, and chop suey—will find it in an elegant setting at Ho Wan. It's a dark room near the Desert Inn casino, decorated in a luxurious mix of modern and antique Oriental decor. The booths are red, the lights turned low, and white-gloved waiters serve meals on oversize plates. The food is warmed at your table. Formerly a second-floor restaurant, Ho Wan moved to the ground floor when the Monte Carlo Room, an Italian restaurant, moved out. Among the house specialties are Ho Wan prawns (prawns, steamed mushrooms, snow peas, carrots, baby corn, bamboo shoots, water chestnuts) and sautéed almond chicken (with water chestnuts, diced celery, sliced mushrooms, carrots, green peas, bamboo shoots). *Ho wan* is Chinese for "good fortune." *Desert Inn, 3145 Las Vegas Blvd. S, tel. 702/731–7731. Reservations advised. AE, CB, D, DC, MC, V. Dinner only. Very Expensive.*

Lillie Langtry's. You might well expect a steak house with this name, but no, it's a Chinese restaurant in a Victorian mock-up of 1890s San Francisco, with tapestries, crystal chandeliers, and paintings that suggest the Gold Rush era. Lillie's is a multilevel, wood-paneled room with high-back, brocade-covered chairs and a stained-glass dome. The menu offers ginger beef (with green onions and oyster sauce) and lemon chicken. The Golden Nugget's house magician, Michael Skinner, works the room while diners attend to their plates. *The Golden Nugget, 129 Fremont St., tel. 702/385–7111. Reservations advised. AE, CB, D, DC, MC, V. Dinner only. Very Expensive.*

★ **Chin's.** An upscale Chinese restaurant with a bright, contemporary decor, Chin's forgoes the Old West and Old China themes and the familiar Chinese menu favorites as well. The specialties here are the likes of strawberry chicken and pepper orange roughy. The restaurant is on the Strip, in the front of the Fashion Show shopping mall. *3200 Las Vegas Blvd. S, tel. 702/733–8899. Reservations advised. AE, CB, D, DC, MC, V. Expensive.*

The Silver Dragon. On Flamingo Road, 2 miles east of the Strip (and two blocks east of the Maryland Parkway) stands this Las Vegas landmark, a replica of a Peking palace. If you seek a less crowded restaurant than many of those on the Strip, or if you have a yen for sweet-and-sour at an early hour, the Silver Dragon, open until 5 AM, has traditional Chinese fare and moderate prices as well. *1510 E. Flamingo Rd., tel. 702/737–1234. AE, MC, V. Moderate.*

Coffee Shops

★ **Cafe Roma.** Less expensive than the other restaurants of Caesars Palace, Cafe Roma continues the Roman theme in a two-tiered restaurant with large columns and gold walls. The American menu is available 24 hours, the Chinese menu after 5 PM. Portions are large, the atmosphere pleasant, with a view overlooking the bustling casino. Here you'll find one of the best grilled-cheese sandwiches in town, extra large, cut into thirds,

Dining 125

with a hefty side of french fries. A big basket of crackers and breadsticks comes with every meal. *Caesars Palace, 3570 Las Vegas Blvd. S, tel. 702/731-7110. AE, CB, D, DC, MC, V. Inexpensive–Moderate.*

Binion's Coffee Shop. Here's a place that serves "just good food," promises large portions and low prices, and always has a line of people waiting to get in. The specialties include Benny Binion's Natural (two eggs; ham, bacon, or sausage; home fries; toast; jelly; and coffee) and Binion's Delight (hamburger, cheese, lettuce, tomato, dressing, and fries). Chili, steaks, and soups fill out the menu. Western decor and keno boards cover the walls. *Binion's Horseshoe Hotel and Casino, 128 Fremont St., tel. 702/382-1600. AE, CB, D, DC, MC, V. Inexpensive.*

Food Fantasy. Food Fantasy lets you serve yourself, cafeteria style, while your eggs or hamburgers or roast-beef sandwiches are prepared to your specifications. This is one of the rare hotel restaurants that has a salad bar, and it is well stocked. Waffle fans take note: Extra-large, piping-hot waffles are made right before your eyes—a terrific evening treat when topped with vanilla ice cream. *The Flamingo Hilton and Tower, 3555 Las Vegas Blvd. S, tel. 702/733-3502. AE, CB, D, DC, MC, V. Open Mon.–Wed. 6 AM–9 PM, Thurs.–Sat. 24 hours. Inexpensive.*

Diners

Mary's Diner. Another venture of the Boyd Group, Mary's Diner at Sam's Town follows the same formula as Ralph's Diner at the Stardust. *Sam's Town Hotel and Casino, 5111 W. Boulder Hwy., tel. 702/456-7777. AE, CB, D, DC, MC, V. Inexpensive.*

Ralph's Diner. The folks who run the Boyd Group of hotels (California, Fremont, Sam's Town, and the Stardust) can spot a good American trend as well as anyone, and they responded quickly when the diner craze arrived. At Ralph's jukes are on the tables; the music is 1950s; and the food is chicken potpie, meat loaf, burgers, shakes, malts, floats, and Jello-O. The specialty to try is the Hangover: a grilled corn tortilla with three eggs any style, chili con carne and shredded cheddar cheese, home fries, and toast or biscuits. *Stardust Hotel and Casino, 3000 Las Vegas Blvd. S, tel. 702/456-7777. AE, CB, D, DC, MC, V. Inexpensive.*

French/Continental

Elaine's. On the second level of the Golden Nugget's elegant spa suite tower, far from the madding casino crowd, is a small dining room with curtained booths, well-spaced tables, and an expensive-looking decor—Venetian crystal chandeliers and paintings in the Impressionist style. Among the specialties are rack of lamb, quail stuffed with a mousse of veal, and chicken with wild mushrooms. *Golden Nugget Hotel and Casino, 129 E. Fremont St., 702/385-7111. Reservations advised. Jacket required. Dinner only. AE, CB, D, DC, MC, V. Expensive–Very Expensive.*

★ **Le Montrachet.** An elegant room with soft peach lighting, paintings of pastoral scenes, mohair booths, and fine linen, Le Montrachet gives you no indication that you're in Las Vegas. The menu changes with the season, approximately every three months. A recent bill of fare offered poached Dover sole stuffed with mousse of lobster, accompanied by lobster sauce on one side, a champagne caviar sauce on the other; broiled veal chops

Dining 126

with mussel puree; and rack of lamb. You won't find cigarette girls or gambling paraphernalia here, but you will find fresh flowers at every table. *Las Vegas Hilton, 3000 W. Paradise Rd., tel. 702/732–5111. Reservations advised. Jacket and tie advised. AE, CB, D, DC, MC, V. Dinner only. Expensive.*

★ **Palace Court.** This place is said to be the best "white glove" restaurant in town, which is another way of saying it's a fancy Caesars room with high prices. The Palace offers "fine" dining, with settings of crystal and silver, in a round room hung with portraits of the 12 Caesars, the work of the 17th-century painter Camillo Procaccini. A stained-glass skylight above the center of the restaurant glows brightly in the daytime. Recent menu selections have been veal Oscar (medallions with crab legs and white asparagus), breast of duck with a pink peppercorn sauce, fresh Maine lobster, and rack of lamb. The wine list is extensive. Dinner seatings at 6–6:30 PM and 9–9:30 PM. *Caesars Palace, 3570 Las Vegas Blvd. S, tel. 702/731–7547. Reservations required. Jacket required. AE, CB, D, DC, MC, V. No lunch Mon.–Wed. Expensive.*

Pamplemousse Restaurant. A small, quiet room that seats just 70, the Pamplemousse is popular with the convention trade—so popular that management suggests you make your reservations even before you start out for Las Vegas. The dominant color is red, orchestral music can be heard on the stereo system, and the food is classic French cuisine. Because the entrées change from day to day, there is no printed menu and the waiter recites the bill of fare. Recent offerings have included a Cajun-style salmon in lemon butter sauce with a mild curry; veal medallions in cream sauce with Dijon mustard; and roast duckling in red wine and banana rum sauce. All dinners include salad, basket of breads, steamed vegetables, and crudités. Dinner seatings at 6–6:30 PM and 9–9:30 PM. And *pamplemousse* is French for "grapefruit." *400 E. Sahara Ave., tel. 702/733–2066. Reservations required. AE, CB, D, DC, MC, V. Closed Mon. Expensive.*

German

★ **Alpine Village Inn.** A Vegas experience not to be missed, the Alpine Village is a full-service restaurant upstairs and a casual, collegiate rathskeller downstairs. The restaurant has been made to look like a Swiss chalet, with "snow" atop the "huts" that serve as booths. A giant replica of a gingerbread house stands in the middle of the room. The waiters wear lederhosen, the waitresses dirndls, and the patrons quaff their beer from quart glasses. The food is substantial German fare. All entrées are accompanied by relish bowl, hors d'oeuvres, soup, tossed green salad, red cabbage, Swiss potatoes, bread basket, cinnamon rolls, dessert (sherbet, ice cream, or strudel), and beverage. Prominent among the entrées are *Schweinebraten* (pork roast), *sauerbraten* (marinated beef), *Wienerschnitzel* (veal cutlet) and *Bratpfanne* (roast chicken). Dinner is served from 5 PM to midnight; at convention time or during a busy weekend, the wait can be one hour without a reservation, 15–30 minutes with one. Meanwhile, downstairs in the rathskeller, still more Alpine settings await. Here are red leather booths, red-and-white checked tablecloths, and an organist who sings while a miniature ski trolley travels back and forth before her. Three or four times a night she'll engage patrons in a sing-along version of "Las Vegas Schnitzelbank" (the lyrics are posted on the wall). The food is sim-

Dining 127

ilar to that served upstairs, but with smaller portions and lower prices. The gift shop upstairs has T-shirts, dolls, and clowns. Because the restaurant is right across the street from the Convention Center, it's a favorite of the convention crowd and is constantly busy. Be sure to call ahead, and be prepared for a wait. *3003 W. Paradise Rd., opposite the Las Vegas Hilton, tel. 702/ 734–6888. Reservations advised. AE, CB, D, DC, MC, V. Moderate.*

Italian

Andiamo. This is a bright restaurant, with white walls, gold columns, large plants, and salami and spices hanging from the walls of the kitchen, which is in the center of the room. You won't find a keno board or keno ticket here. The Northern Italian specialties include angel-hair pasta with tomatoes, spinach, mushrooms, and zuchini in a creamy sauce; and broiled breast of chicken seasoned with garlic, oregano, and lemon and topped with mozzarella. *Las Vegas Hilton, 3000 W. Paradise Rd., tel. 702/732–5111. Reservations advised. AE, CB, D, DC, MC, V. Expensive.*

★ **Primavera.** Homemade pasta and the Primavera hamburger are perfect for an afternoon in this pleasant, bright setting overlooking the enormous Garden of the Gods swimming pool at Caesars Palace. At dinnertime the mood is more restrained, the lights low, and, with seating for only 75, the tables hard to come by. The specialty of the house is fettuccine Primavera, tossed with sautéed vegetables, sweet butter, fresh cream, and Parmesan cheese. The notice that GENTLEMAN MUST WEAR PROPER ATTIRE merely means that shorts aren't allowed. A violinist and a guitarist provide an accompaniment in the evening, and the magician who works the room is Jimmy Grippo, the Caesars magician now in his nineties who specializes in close-up magic, performing coin tricks at your table. If he's not in the room when you're dining, be sure to ask for him, and he'll be there. *Caesars Palace, 3570 Las Vegas Blvd. S, tel. 702/731–7731. Reservations advised. AE, CB, D, DC, MC, V. Expensive.*

Battista's Hole in the Wall Italian Restaurant. A Vegas institution that was featured often on TV's "Vegas," Battista's is a *Hollywood* Vegas restaurant, one with celebrity photographs on the walls, alongside the wine bottles, garlic, and peppers. The fare is your basic Italian menu—ravioli, lasagna, and other pastas. All dinners include minestrone, garlic bread, salad, a pasta side dish, wine, and cappuccino. You'll hear opera on the stereo, and sometimes Battista Locatelli himself roams the restaurant, singing. His house rules prohibit tank tops, cigar smoking, and children under 4. *4041 Audrie St. at Flamingo Rd., tel. 702/732–1424. AE, CB, D, DC, MC, V. Dinner only. Moderate.*

Capozzoli's. The folks who run this rather new restaurant owned the Tower of Pizza restaurant opposite the Aladdin Hotel and Casino until a few years ago, when they closed it and retired. In 1989 they went back to work, opening this small yet comfortable Italian restaurant in a minimall a little more than a mile east of the Strip, at Maryland Parkway and Desert Inn Road. Capozzoli's, which stays open until 5 AM, is popular with local residents. The decor consists of red-and-white tablecloths, and wine bottles on the ceiling; the menu offers veal parmigiana, chicken, and tripe, with soups, salads, and breads made fresh daily. Sandwiches, subs, and pizzas are the lunchtime fare. The place

Dining 128

tends to be jammed on weekends and during conventions. *3333 S. Maryland Pkwy., tel. 702/731–5311. Reservations advised. AE, CB, DC, MC, V. Inexpensive–Moderate.*

Japanese

Oh No! Tokyo. This establishment regularly wins the award for best Japanese restaurant in the annual readers' poll of the *Las Vegas Review-Journal*. Four separate dining areas allow you the choice between Western seating (at tables) and traditional Japanese rooms, where you remove your shoes and sit on the floor on *tatami* (straw mats). The extensive Japanese bill of fare includes sushi, teriyaki, robata steaks, and cucumber salads. The restaurant is in the Tramp's Plaza shopping center at the corner of Flamingo Road and Arville Street, 1 mile west of the Strip. *4455 W. Flamingo Rd., tel. 702/876–4455. Reservations advised. AE, DC, MC, V. Moderate.*

Mexican

Santa Fe. A five-minute cab ride to the west of the Strip will bring you to a friendly Mexican restaurant with no slot machines or keno runners. The decor blends Mexican, Indian, and American West themes, and strolling mariachis complement the classic Mexican menu. In addition to the tacos, tostadas, and enchiladas are Santa Fe specialties such as chicken Daniel (seasoned chicken breast served on a flour tortilla with melted cheese), halibut and shrimp picado (served with onions, bell peppers, tomato, and mild chiles in a corn-tortilla basket), and drunken margarita duck (seasoned duck prepared in a tequila margarita sauce with pineapple, onion, bell pepper, and tomato, and served in a tortilla basket). *Renaissance Center, 4930 W. Flamingo Rd., tel. 702/871–7119. AE, CB, D, DC, MC, V. Moderate.*

Willy and Jose's Cantina. Two mean-looking Mexicans stand at the door of the cantina, guns in their holsters and arms ready to be tugged. Yes, the entrance to this restaurant at Sam's Town is guarded by two tall quarter slot machines that have jackpots of $5,000. Behind them is an old-fashioned Mexican-style fountain and a dining room with Spanish tile, baskets, and stuffed burros hanging from the ceiling. The fare is "early Californian" —large servings of chips, cheese, and salsa. *Sam's Town Hotel and Casino, 5111 W. Boulder Hwy., tel. 702/454–8044. Reservations advised. AE, CB, D, DC, MC, V. Dinner only. Moderate.*

★ **Margarita's Mexican Cantina.** This was a steak house until Margaret Elardi bought the Frontier and turned it into a grind joint. What do slot players like best? she asked. Not chops but tacos and margaritas. The new decor is classic Southwest, with turquoise and pink tiles, hardwood chairs, and pink and purple neon shading the ceiling. The look is an authentic one, except for the keno boards on the wall and the keno tickets and crayons at every table. The cuisine is classic upscale Mexican: tacos, enchiladas, chimichangas, burritos. At the "tortilleria" up front the chef prepares fresh tortilla chips that you can smell throughout the casino. For dessert there's Mexican deep-fried ice cream topped with strawberries, honey, and whipped cream. *Frontier Hotel, 3120 Las Vegas Blvd. S, tel. 702/734–0110. AE, CB, D, DC, MC, V. Inexpensive–Moderate.*

Dining 129

Only in Las Vegas

The Bacchanal. Caesars Palace's most elaborate restaurant turns food service into showbiz. To re-create a Roman feast in the atmosphere of a private villa, male guests are served wine by toga-clad "wine goddesses," who also deliver a massage before dessert. Two stone lions guard the room, and a lighted pool occupies the center. "I Caesar," the menu reads, "welcome you to the most resplendent arena of gustatory delights . . . the Bacchanal!" The seven courses of the fixed menu consist of appetizer, hors d'oeuvres, tureen of soup, a fish course, salad, the main course, vegetables, dessert, cheese, fruit, coffee, champagne, and all the wine you can drink. *Caesars Palace, 3570 Las Vegas Blvd. S, tel. 702/731-7110. Reservations advised. Dinner seatings at 6-6:30 PM and 9-9:30 PM. AE, CB, D, DC, MC, V. Very Expensive.*

The Sultan's Table. The former Dunes owner Major A. Riddle first heard The Magic Violins—six fiddlers who stop by your table and play ballads—in Mexico, decided they would be a hit in Vegas, and brought them here in 1958. In a hotel that has gone distinctly downscale since then, the expensive Sultan's Table still attracts a moneyed clientele. The motif is that of an Arabian pleasure palace, with blue-and-green stained-glass windows, a fountain at the center of the room, red booths, and orange lighting. The fare is eclectic: tournedos of prime beef Rossini in *sauce périgourdine; grenadins* of beef tenderloin sauté Bourguignon. *Dunes Hotel and Country Club, 3650 Las Vegas Blvd. S, tel. 737-4110. Reservations required. Jacket required. AE, CB, D, DC, MC, V. Dinner only. Very Expensive.*

Seafood

Dome of the Sea. The concept of serving fish in an undersea atmosphere is alive and well at the Dunes. Every night since this restaurant opened in 1958, a mermaid in a gondola plays the harp, while images of flying fish are projected on the wall as you dine. A fish tank and lagoon (where the harpist sits) are the first things you see on entering the round room, and the tables encircle them. Specialties include calamari steak with marinara sauce and angel-hair pasta; stuffed jumbo shrimp with tartar sauce and orange roughy sautéed with an orange ginger sauce. *Dunes Hotel and Country Club, 3650 Las Vegas Blvd. S, tel. 702/737-4110. Reservations advised. Jacket required. AE, CB, D, DC, MC, V. Dinner only. Very Expensive.*

★ **The Tillerman.** Its location on Flamingo Road, almost 3 miles east of the Strip, makes the Tillerman a quiet refuge from the casinos and a favorite with convention delegates. The garden setting, with a variety of oversize plants, places you under an open skylight on hot desert nights. Seafood and steak are the principal fare. *2245 E. Flamingo Rd., tel. 702/731-4036. No reservations. Dress: casual. AE, CB, D, DC, MC, V. Dinner only. Moderate.*

Steak Houses

★ **The Golden Steer.** One of the oldest restaurants in Las Vegas, the Steer caters to families with its San Francisco Barbary Coast motif, circa early 1900s, reflected in the red chairs and stained-glass windows. The grub is traditional steak-house

Dining　　　　　　　　　　　　　　　　　　　　　　*130*

fare: steaks, ribs, roast beef, and seafood, all served with baked potato and salad. The namesake's image appears on the sign out front. *308 W. Sahara Ave., tel. 702/384–4470. Reservations advised. AE, CB, D, DC, MC, V. Dinner only. Expensive.*

★ **The Steak House.** Believe it or not, the steak house set within the craziness of Circus Circus is one that many local residents contend is the best in town. The atmosphere here is totally unlike that of the rest of Circus Circus; the wood paneling and antique brass furnishings adorn a dark, quiet room reminiscent of 1890s San Francisco. The beef—aged 21 days—is displayed in a glassed-in area at the side; the cooking takes place over an open-hearth charcoal grill in the middle of the room. Steaks, chops, and roast beef make up the menu, and all entrées are accompanied by soup or salad, special or dark sweet breads, and baked potato. *Circus Circus, 2880 Las Vegas Blvd. S, tel. 702/734–0410. Reservations advised. AE, CB, D, DC, MC, V. Dinner only. Expensive.*

William B's Steakhouse. Aged beef is served in yet another room with turn-of-the-century decor, here with lower prices than you'll find at most hotel steak houses. Hearty portions of steak, ribs, chicken, and fish are served with salad and baked potato. No mementos of the Old West or the Barbary Coast here; it's just a dark, comfortable room with framed black-and-white Western drawings on the walls. William B. is Bill Boyd, president of the Boyd Group, which owns four Vegas hotels; Sam of Sam's Town is his dad. *Stardust Hotel and Casino, 3000 Las Vegas Blvd. S, tel. 702/732–6111. Reservations advised. AE, CB, D, DC, MC, V. Dinner only. Expensive.*

The Flame. A favorite of convention delegates, this is one of the few restaurants on the Strip that's not set in a hotel. Steak, chicken, seafood, and salads are served in a dark, quiet setting that will let you forget you're in Las Vegas. All entrées come with salad, french fries or baked potato, bread, and onion rings. Sandwiches are available at lunch, egg dishes in the wee hours, and the full dinner menu is served around the clock. *1 Desert Inn Rd., tel. 702/735–4431. No reservations. AE, CB, D, DC, MC, V. Moderate.*

8 Lodging

For many years the guiding principle in Las Vegas hotel construction was to make the rooms as loud and spectacular as possible, with no modern amenities such as a television set or a clock. The goal was to get the guest out of the room and into the casino. While some hotels still subscribe to that theory (Circus Circus is one that does), most Vegas hotels have entered the modern age and now provide TV, AM/FM radio, direct-dial telephones, and soft color schemes. (For the ultimate Vegas living experience, you'll have to go to Caesars Palace, where many of the rooms feature a round bed, a mirror on the ceiling, and a giant round bathtub.)

Throughout much of the 1980s, the four largest hotels in America were all in Las Vegas: the Las Vegas Hilton, Bally's, the Flamingo Hilton, and Circus Circus. Construction at the end of the decade and the start of the 1990s promises to create even larger hotels, with one or two reaching the 4,000-room mark. The great number and variety (in both price and style) of hotel and motel accommodations give the traveler a wide range of choice—at many times of the year.

Because most of its business came from nearby southern California on Friday and Saturday nights, the Vegas hospitality industry worked for decades to attract conventions that would fill the otherwise empty hotel rooms during the week. Convention facilities were built and conventions were booked in ever greater numbers. Today, in terms of available space and number of conventions, Las Vegas is the second-ranking convention city in the United States, after Chicago.

When a major convention has been scheduled, it can be difficult to find a room in Vegas. The worst weeks are the first week in January, the third week in April, and the first week in November. At other times you'll find plenty of rooms to choose from and rates that are lower than those in most other American resort and vacation cities. And in Vegas there are often rate discounts and package deals. When business is slow, many hotels offer reduced rates on rooms in their least desirable sections, sometimes with a buffet breakfast and a late-night show included. Most "sales" occur in December–February and July–August, the coldest and hottest times of the year. Circus Circus, for example, has had rooms for $18 for Monday–Thursday stays in January.

One useful guide to bargain rates is the Sunday "Calendar" section of the *Los Angeles Times*, where most of the Vegas hotels advertise. Another way to learn about specials is to call a hotel's toll-free number and ask what package deals it has for your vacation dates. When the hotel reservations clerks continually tell you they're sold out, try the **Las Vegas Tourist Bureau** (tel. 800/778–3427), the **Las Vegas Hotel Reservation Center** (tel. 702/736–1666 or 800/458–6161), or **The Travel Connection** (tel. 702/368–1488). For a fee, one of them may be able to place you in the hotel of your choice with a surcharge of only $5.

You can always get a room if you're willing to stay in one of the small motels that line the city. They tend to have adequate accommodations—tiny rooms with small beds and a working television set—for about $30 a night.

Highly recommended lodgings in each price category are indicated by a star ★.

Lodging 133

Category	Cost*
Very Expensive	over $100
Expensive	$70–$100
Moderate	$40–$70
Inexpensive	under $40

All prices are for a standard double room, excluding service charge and 7% tax.

The following credit card abbreviations are used: AE, American Express; CB, Carte Blanche; D, Discover Card; DC, Diners Club; MC, MasterCard; and V, Visa.

Hotels

Very Expensive
★ **Bally's Casino Resort.** When it opened in 1972, this was the big MGM Grand, patterned after the MGM movie *Grand Hotel* of 1932, with movie posters on every wall and Leo the Lion on every carpet. Since the Bally Corporation bought the hotel in 1985 some of the movie nostalgia has disappeared, but the film posters remain in every guest room and Leo the Lion's mug is on a plaque on every door. Bally's is still big: 2,900 rooms, two swimming pools, two showrooms each with seating for 1,000, and a 75,000-square-foot shopping arcade. The rooms may be the largest you'll see in Vegas, red and bawdy with flowered wallpaper, king-size beds, footrests, eating area, and expansive views of the Strip or the mountains. Some rooms have a bathtub on a pedestal in the center of the room; others have a raised bathroom with separate bathing and shower areas, two toilets, and a telephone. The nicest rooms, on the 26th floor, are reserved for star performers and big gamblers. (Sammy Davis, Jr., stays in the Ziegfeld Suite, where the living room is the size of a home.) Bally's is no place to stay for those who don't like to walk. It is enormous. Yet every floor has large couches, chairs, and tables for anyone who wants to rest. One of the showrooms offers a long-running variety production; the other features celebrity performers. The shopping arcade has an ice-cream parlor, T-shirt shop, video arcade, barbershop, old-time photo salon, and a shop with the loudest and most expensive men's clothing in Vegas (wait till you see Mort Yallin's $400 red, yellow, purple, and green sport coats). As the MGM Grand, this hotel was the site of a great fire in 1980, caused by faulty electrical wiring and made worse by the absence of a sprinkler system, which was not then required by law. Today sprinklers are the law in Las Vegas, and every hotel in town has an extensive sprinkler system. A remodeling in 1981 added 800 new rooms. *3645 Las Vegas Blvd. S, 89109, tel. 702/739–4111 or 800/ 634–3434; in CA, AZ, ID, OR, UT, 800/634–6363. Facilities: 7 restaurants, 10 tennis courts, 2 swimming pools, sauna, health club, lounge, comedy club, 2 showrooms. AE, CB, D, DC, MC, V.*

★ **Caesars Palace.** Welcome to the Las Vegas you saw in the movies *Rain Man* and *The Electric Horseman*. Round beds with mirrored ceilings and giant bathtubs grace your room, and a singing bellman croons Mario Lanza tunes as he delivers your luggage. If Las Vegas is a fantasy, Caesars does the best job of any resort of keeping the dream alive. The first thing you see at Caesars are the giant fountains out front; the hotel stands be-

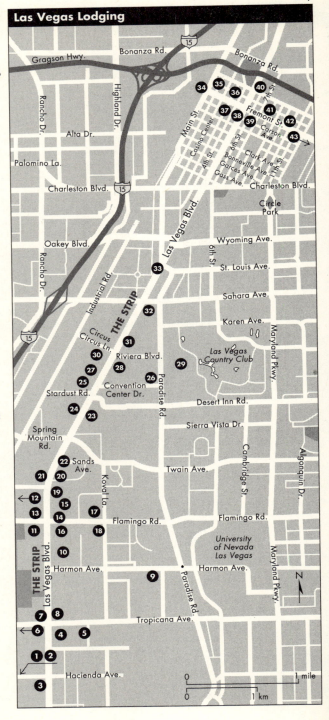

Las Vegas Lodging

Aladdin, **10**
Alexis Park, **9**
All-Star Inn, **6**
Bally's, **16**
Barbary Coast, **14**
Binion's Horseshoe, **36**
Caesars Palace, **13**
Circus Circus, **30**
Desert Inn, **23**
Dunes Hotel and Country Club, **11**
El Cortez, **42**
El Rancho Tower, **31**
Excalibur, **7**
Fitzgerald's, **39**
The Flamingo Hilton and Tower, **15**
Four Queens, **38**
Frontier, **24**
Gold Spike, **41**
Gold Strike, **2**
Golden Nugget, **37**
Hacienda, **3**
Holiday Inn, **20**
Imperial Palace, **19**
Lady Luck, **40**
Landmark, **26**
Las Vegas Club, **35**
Las Vegas Hilton, **29**
Marina, **8**
Maxim, **17**
The Mirage, **21**
Motel 6, **5**
Rio Suites, **12**
Riviera, **28**
Sahara Las Vegas, **32**
Sam's Town, **43**
Sands, **22**
Stardust, **25**
Town Hall/Vagabond Inn, **18**
Tropicana, **4**
Union Plaza, **34**
Vegas World, **33**
Westward Ho, **27**
Whiskey Pete's, **1**

Lodging 135

hind them, with blue-green lights showing at every window. Statues are everywhere, including an 18-foot white-marble replica of Michelangelo's *David* in the Appian Way shopping area. Caesars is meant to be an experience. Even the lowest-priced rooms have sink-in carpets, entire walls of mirrors, chaises, and, in some rooms, beds on raised platforms with steps and mirrored ceilings. The decor is Vegas garish—reds and purples, with the blue light from the window adding its glow to the room. The luxurious two-story Caesars suites, like the one shown in *Rain Man*, have a giant Jacuzzi on a pedestal before the picture window overlooking the Strip. In the film Dustin Hoffman and Tom Cruise arrived with $10,000 to play with at the blackjack tables and got the $750-a-night suite for free. In real life you'd have to be playing with at least $50,000 at Caesars to qualify for a freebie of that magnitude. But everyone can look forward to finding two big chocolate coins on his or her pillow at night. Caesars plans to open The Forum, an enclosed shopping complex of 150 stores, in August 1990; currently the Appian Way houses such upscale shops as Gucci, Ted Lapidus, and Caesars Only, which sells Caesars towels, robes, and teddy bears. Like Bally's, Caesars is so big that you must come prepared to do some walking. The Circus Maximus showroom features prominent entertainers. *3570 Las Vegas Blvd. S, 89109, tel. 702/731–7110 or 800/634–6661. 1,670 rooms. Facilities: 7 restaurants, 2 swimming pools, 4 tennis courts, health spa, lounge, movie theater, showroom. AE, CB, D, DC, MC, V.*

★ **Desert Inn Hotel and Casino.** One of the smaller hotels in town, the Desert Inn has 818 rooms, all of whose green smoked-glass windows overlook the golf course or the Frontier Hotel and the Strip. Howard Hughes lived here for four years (1966–70); those who would like to stay in his former digs on the ninth floor should ask for the $300-a-night Howard Hughes suite. While many establishments in Vegas call themselves resorts, the Desert Inn is one that truly qualifies. The hotel is up front, but many of the rooms and suites are spread out on the 200 acres of landscaped grounds, an arrangement similar to that of a Scottsdale or a Palm Springs resort. Some suites have a private swimming pool. The hotel rooms have a southwestern decor, with aqua pillows, dining areas, large beds with large dressing areas, and bathrooms with double sinks. Out on the greenery, the Wimbledon building is a glass and white-stucco pyramid with canvas awnings that houses six suites with private swimming pools ($250 a day). Looking out on the golf course, you can forget you're in Las Vegas, for there are no neon signs, tall buildings, or cigarette girls patrolling the grounds here. When you're ready for casino-games lessons, turn on the TV to channel 3. The Desert Inn opened in 1950 with 220 rooms, added 271 in 1960 and 329 more in 1978, and has no remodeling plans for the near future. The showroom features a variety of name entertainers. *3145 Las Vegas Blvd. S, 89109, tel. 702/733–4444 or 800/634–6906. 818 rooms. Facilities: 5 restaurants, 18-hole golf course, 10 tennis courts, lounge, health club, shuffleboard, showroom. AE, CB, D, DC, MC, V.*

Expensive **Alexis Park Resort Hotel.** Would businessmen and couples come to a luxury hotel in Las Vegas that had no neon, no gaming tables, and no slots? The Alexis Park opened in 1984 and discovered that the answer was yes. Located 2 miles from the convention center, this is a favorite spot for convention dele-

Lodging **136**

gates who want a "normal" living experience during their business day. The individual buildings of the all-suite desert hotel are two-story white-stucco blocks with red-tile roofs, all set in a water garden. Each room has a view of either a rock pool or a lawn. Every room has a wet bar; some have fireplaces. *375 E. Harmon Ave., 89109, tel. 702/796–3300 or 800/582–2228. 500 suites. Facilities: 3 restaurants, health spa, 2 tennis courts, 3 pools, 9-hole putting green, jogging track, lounge. AE, CB, D, DC, MC, V.*

★ **The Flamingo Hilton and Tower.** The Fabulous Flamingo that opened in 1946 with Jimmy Durante, Rose Marie, and Xavier Cugat as entertainers was a 98-room oasis with palm trees imported from California. The Flamingo has changed a lot since then, and today its three overbearing towers overlook the modest original motor hotel that was once so fashionable. The rooms in the back are the old Flamingo, made up of two-story motor hotels (now the Oregon, California, Arizona, Nevada, and New Mexico wings), all remodeled and updated. They offer the amenities of the tower without the hustle and bustle. If you want to feel powerful, ask for the $400 Presidential Suite; this was where Bugsy Siegel lived, on the fourth floor of the Oregon, the central building of the Flamingo in 1946. The suite, which overlooks the swimming pool, contains a pool table, a collection of Siegel's books, and the original olive-green wallpaper with palm-tree design. The more recent additions to the suite are a color TV, a wet bar, and elevator service. You'll do a lot of walking at the Flamingo, and you'll encounter lots of people, many of them taking advantage of the package rates for special tours that keep the hotel and casino busy. The Flamingo's color is pink—in the neon sign, in the flower vases, in the desk pens in the rooms, and in the lobby carpeting. The large rooms in the towers (decorated in rust, blue, green, beige/yellow, or peach) offer expansive views of the Strip. The swimming pool is one of the largest and prettiest in town, with a fountain in the center. Because the construction of the new Flamingo blocks the sun in the afternoon, a second pool has been added in an area where the sunlight comes through. For most of 1989 the front entrance of the Flamingo was closed for the expansion of the casino, and a new tower, with 28 floors, 770 rooms, and another 20,000 square feet of casino space, was scheduled to open in mid-1990. The Flamingo Hilton will then have 3,558 rooms. The registration area is on the side of the hotel near the elevators, so you won't have to carry your luggage through the casino. The showroom features a topless revue. *3555 Las Vegas Blvd. S, 89109, tel. 702/733–3111 or 800/732–2111. 3,558 rooms (as of mid-1990). Facilities: 6 restaurants, 2 swimming pools, health spa, 4 tennis courts, lounge, showroom. AE, CB, D, DC, MC, V.*

★ **Golden Nugget Hotel and Casino.** The Nugget was only a gambling hall with sawdust on the floors and no rooms when Steve Wynn took it over in the 1970s and decided to go after the high roller. Now red rugs flow over white marble, leading you to the lobby and a large public area with white marble columns, etched-glass windows, stained-glass panels, and fresh flowers in gold-plated vases. Almost everything here is gold—the telephones, the slots, the elevators. The large Victorian-style rooms have four-posters, period mirrors and furniture, a dining area, and uninspiring views of Fremont and 2nd streets. In addition to the standard double rooms, the Nugget has 27 du-

Lodging 137

plex suites and six two-bedroom apartments, each decorated in a different style. All suites are multilevel; some have a personal room-service waiter. The Nugget's one drawback is its out-of-the-way location. If you plan a lot of activities in Vegas, you'll have to endure the traffic when traveling between the Strip and downtown. This will be an irritation to those who are driving and a significant expense for those who use cabs. A small showroom features singers and comedians. The Nugget added 1,185 new rooms in 1987. *129 E. Fremont St., 89101, tel. 702/385–7111 or 800/634–3454. 1,918 rooms. Facilities: 4 restaurants, swimming pool, health club, lounge, showroom. AE, CB, D, DC, MC, V.*

Las Vegas Hilton. For years the Las Vegas Hilton has claimed to be the world's largest resort hotel. (The much bigger Rossiya in Moscow, with more than 5,000 rooms, is not a *resort* hotel.) New construction under way at four other Vegas hotels will soon make each of them larger than the Hilton. Yet even without the title, the Las Vegas Hilton is a sight to see—best of all by standing at its foot and staring up at the 375-foot tower, 29 floors, and three wings. The Hilton is so big that it's easily recognizable from anywhere in town. The rooms are of the basic Hilton hotel variety: large rooms with soft colors, large beds, and telephones in the lavatories. They can also be hard to find; the numbering system goes from hundreds to thousands and varies from wing to wing. Rooms on the higher floors have a great view of the city. This is another hotel where you can expect to do a lot of walking. For all its size, the hotel's services function remarkably well: Elevators run smoothly, operators answer the phone promptly (they could conceivably have hundreds of calls at one time), and plenty of parking is available. The Hilton's Youth Hotel, a dormitory for kids aged 3 to 18, supervised by counselors who serve meals and snacks, is the only facility of its kind in the area; kids can take part in fencing, tumbling, arts and crafts, table tennis, dance, basketball, tennis, volleyball, and magic shows. Rates are $4.50 per child per hour and $25 per child for overnight stays (midnight–8 AM). The Las Vegas Hilton added 391 rooms in 1982. The showroom features celebrity performers, who stay in the Elvis Suite on the 31st floor, where the King of Rock 'n' Roll resided when he played the Hilton (his white jumpsuit is on display in front of the showroom). The Hilton is adjacent to the Las Vegas Convention Center. *3000 Paradise Rd., 89109, tel. 702/732–5111 or 800/732–7117. 3,174 rooms. Facilities: 11 restaurants, 6 tennis courts, health spa, swimming pool, putting green, youth hotel and lounge. AE, CB, D, DC, MC, V.*

The Mirage. The newest hotel and casino on the Strip, the $630 million, 3,049-room Mirage opened in November 1989 and immediately became the most talked-about attraction in town. The lush, 31-story, South Seas–themed resort next door to Caesars Palace sits on 86 acres of grounds covered with 3,000 tropical plants, palm trees, banana trees, and lagoons. A rain forest occupies the atrium adjacent to the lobby. A 50-foot waterfall facing the Strip becomes an exploding volcano periodically during the evening hours, and a wide lawn allows lots of room for picture-taking. Six Himalayan white tigers owned by the showroom stars Siegfried and Roy roam a habitat enclosed in transparent plastic. In the spring six bottle-nosed dolphins were to inhabit a lagoon, with visitors able to watch their antics from a people-mover transport system above. Marble everywhere in the public areas indoors gives the Mirage a

Lodging 138

rich appearance. A day-care center and the audiovisual Jackson Attraction, a creation by Michael Jackson, are aimed at visiting families. The Mirage, not to be confused with La Mirage Hotel or the Mirage Motel, is the brainchild of Steve Wynn, the owner of the Golden Nugget, who was convinced there was room on the Strip for yet another luxury casino. *3400 Las Vegas Blvd. S, 89109, tel. 800/639–3403. 3,049 rooms. Facilities: 8 restaurants, swimming pool, 4 tennis courts, exercise facility, lounge. AE, CB, D, DC, MC, V.*

Rio Suites Hotel and Casino. Scheduled to open in January 1990, the Rio would be the first all-suite hotel in Vegas with a casino. (The all-suite Alexis Park has no casino.) Situated across the street from the Gold Coast Hotel on Flamingo Road, the Rio will be a 21-story structure with 430 suites and a Brazilian theme. *3700 W. Flamingo Rd., 89109, tel. 702/252–7777 or 800/874–6746. 430 suites. Facilities: swimming pool, 5 restaurants, lounge.*

Moderate **Aladdin Hotel and Casino.** New owners extensively renovated the 1,100 rooms of the Aladdin in 1986 and adopted a new motto: Your wish is our command. The rooms are standard hotel accommodations with low-key tan walls, dark pink carpeting and bedspreads, and a view of the Strip. Elevators opposite the registration area make long walks unnecessary. The principal attraction in the showroom is a magic show; next door, the 7,000-seat Aladdin Theatre for the Performing Arts features major performers who don't generally work Vegas showrooms—the likes of Fleetwood Mac, Tina Turner, and Anita Baker. *3667 Las Vegas Blvd. S, 89109, tel. 702/736–0111 or 800/634–3428. 1,100 rooms. Facilities: 6 restaurants, shopping arcade, pool, 2 tennis courts, lounge, showroom. AE, CB, D, DC, MC, V.*

★ **Barbary Coast Hotel and Casino.** The Barbary Coast has one of the most central locations in Vegas, across from Caesars, the Mirage, and the Dunes and next door to the Flamingo Hilton and Bally's. It's a fun place with a San Francisco Gold Rush theme—the Victorian-style rooms have brass four-posters with canopies, old-fashioned lamps, lacy curtains, eating areas, TV—and some of the best rates in town. The views are of the Strip or the Flamingo Hilton. Because there are only 200 rooms here, it's not always easy to get one. *3595 Las Vegas Blvd. S, 89109, tel. 702/737–7111 or 800/634–6755. 200 rooms. Facilities: 3 restaurants (including a McDonald's), lounge. AE, CB, D, DC, MC, V.*

Binion's Horseshoe Hotel and Casino. You'll look in vain for the brilliant red neon sign of the old Mint Hotel on Fremont Street; it was taken down in 1988 when the owners of Binion's Horseshoe bought the Mint, tore down the walls between the two casinos, and created a larger Horseshoe. The new neon signs are a turquoise Horseshoe legend and, up top, a revolving neon horseshoe. Inside, staff members speak of the old Mint building as the "east" Horseshoe, the original Horseshoe as the "west" side. Before the expansion, the Horseshoe had just 80 rooms upstairs—"nice, clean rooms," according to the owner, Benny Binion—and they were hard to get. "We don't take reservations," Binion told me once. "If I know you, you got a room. If I don't, you don't have a room." Today the 26-story hotel and casino has 300 rooms with some of the best views of downtown. While the rooms are available, they are often reserved for Binion's best gamblers. On the east side are modern, medium-

Lodging 139

size rooms decorated in light colors. The west side rooms, which you may never see, reflect the western style of the Horseshoe: They have a Victorian-style wallpaper and brass beds with quilted spreads. Binion's boasts that you won't find a cleaner room anywhere. *128 E. Fremont St., 89101, tel. 702/ 382–1600 or 800/237–6537. 380 rooms. Facilities: pool, 5 restaurants, lounge. AE, CB, DC, MC, V.*

Dunes Hotel and Country Club. Come to the Dunes for a sense of what Vegas was like in the 1950s, from the cocktail waitresses who patrol the floor in harem outfits and see-through pantaloons to the barker in the poker room who promotes five-card stud and Texas-hold-'em. The hotel opened in 1955 with 194 rooms and soon went into Chapter 11, but the opening of "Minsky's Burlesque," featuring seminude women, brought such crowds that the hotel quickly recovered. Today the Dunes is a 24-story high rise with 1,285 rooms, a swimming pool, and an 18-hole golf course. Like many Vegas establishments of its time, it began as a motor hotel with a casino; the tower was added in the 1960s. Tower rooms are of medium size, with yellow bedspreads, matching carpets, dark green upholstery, and a wide view of the Strip or the golf course. The smaller garden rooms present a green motif and views of the lawns and swimming pool or the golf course. *3650 Las Vegas Blvd. S, 89109, tel. 702/737–4110 or 800/777–7777. 1,197 rooms. Facilities: 4 restaurants, comedy club, 18-hole golf course, lounge, 4 tennis courts, 2 swimming pools. AE, CB, DC, MC, V.*

El Rancho Tower Hotel and Casino. A good place to call when everywhere else is full, El Rancho always seems to have rooms available. The casino has illustrations of cowboys, horses, and covered wagons on its walls and a buffet where the food is housed in covered wagons. The guest rooms upstairs are done in Vegas Pink: pink lamps, pink walls, and pink carpeting, with maroon bedspreads. Do the owners think of El Rancho as an unofficial annex of its neighbor, the very pink Circus Circus? El Rancho's location is great, provided you can stand a little pink in your life. *2755 Las Vegas Blvd. S, 89109, tel. 702/796–2222 or 800/634–3410. 1,000 rooms. Facilities: 4 restaurants, swimming pool, 52-lane bowling center, lounge. AE, CB, DC, MC, V.*

Excalibur. When it opens in mid-1990, opposite the Tropicana, the newest Vegas resort will have 4,000 rooms and the appearance of a medieval castle. The 100,000-square-foot casino on the first floor will be the largest in Las Vegas; the shopping arcade upstairs will replicate a medieval village, with minstrels and jugglers; downstairs, the "dungeon" fun zone will feature a minature-golf course, video arcade, movie theaters, jousting contests, games, and other events. *Address and telephone number to be announced. 4,000 rooms. Facilities: swimming pool, 6 restaurants.*

Fitzgerald's Hotel and Casino. The decor of the 34-story hotel, the tallest building in the state of Nevada, perpetuates the Irish theme of the casino. The marquee is green, the bellhops sport green pants and green ties, the cocktail waitresses wear green dresses, and you'll walk to your room on—you guessed it—green carpeting. But when you reach your room, you'll find that the door is orange and the bedspreads tan and the walls light brown—to complement the green curtains and carpets. The views are of Fremont Street or the neighboring Four Queens. *301 E. Fremont St., 89109, tel. 702/382–6111 or 800/*

Lodging · *140*

*274–5825. 650 rooms. Facilities: 3 restaurants, lounge. AE,
CB, D, DC, MC, V.*

Four Queens Hotel and Casino. This prominent downtown hotel
has one amenity you'll find nowhere else in Vegas: A security
guard stands at the elevator and asks to see your room key before you enter. The Queens rooms are furnished in Victorian
style with turn-of-the-century wallpaper, vintage lamps, four-
posters, and views of Fremont Street, Fitzgerald's, or the
Golden Nugget. Jazz is performed in the French Quarter
lounge on Monday evening. *202 E. Fremont St., tel. 702/385–
4011 or 800/634–6045. 720 rooms. Facilities: 2 restaurants,
lounge. AE, CB, DC, MC, V.*

Frontier Hotel. Without disturbing the basic Western character of the Frontier, a new owner in 1988 lowered the room rates,
reduced the gaming table minimums, and converted the showroom into a buffet with an all-you-can-eat policy. The Early
West motif prevails, as it did at the opening in 1942, but the
rooms have been updated and you won't find cactus or branding
irons on the walls. The medium-size rooms, decorated in earth
tones, have separate dining areas and views of the Strip or the
Frontier garden area. A 400-room tower was scheduled to open
in early 1990. *3120 Las Vegas Blvd. S, 89109, tel. 702/734–0110
or 800/421–7806. 1,400 rooms (with the opening of the new tower). Facilities: swimming pool, putting green, 4 restaurants, 2
tennis courts, lounge. AE, CB, D, DC, MC, V.*

Hacienda Hotel and Casino. The lonely hotel at the south end of
the Las Vegas Strip is the first hotel you'll see from the freeway
if you're driving here from southern California. A small establishment, the Hacienda is a refreshing alternative to some of its
bigger, more impersonal competitors farther up the Strip. For
one thing, it's the only hotel where you can park your car directly in front. Inside, the lobby decor is Spanish, and a loud
waterfall greets you upon entering. Rooms are small, with
white walls, twin beds, and eating areas; the views take in Las
Vegas Boulevard or the freeway. The showroom hosts a revue
production. *3950 Las Vegas Blvd. S, 89119, tel. 702/739–8911 or
800/634–6713. 840 rooms. Facilities: 3 restaurants, swimming
pool, 6 tennis courts, showroom, wedding chapel, lounge, RV
park. AE, CB, D, DC, MC, V.*

Holiday Inn Hotel and Casino. Believe it or not, this kitschy-
looking place with the Mississippi River gambling boat and a
Dixieland band out front is a Holiday Inn. The "ship on the
Strip" is the largest Holiday Inn in the world, and it will be
even bigger with the opening (scheduled for early 1990) of a
new 734-room tower with additional shopping and slots areas
and a health club. While the casino is as red and bawdy looking
as it can be, the rooms upstairs have an appearance as modest
as that of any other Holiday Inn: lavender doors, gray walls,
blue bedspreads and matching curtains, and dark wood furniture. The rooms look out on the Strip or onto Paradise Road. A
revue production plays in the showroom. *3475 Las Vegas Blvd.
S, 89109, tel. 702/369–5000 or 800/634–6765. 1,725 rooms. Facilities: swimming pool, 5 restaurants, exercise room, lounge,
showroom. AE, CB, D, DC, MC, V.*

Imperial Palace Hotel and Casino. The blue pagoda roof of this
curious-looking hotel announces the oriental motif, and the casino develops it with cocktail waitresses in short kimonos and
long-tongued dragon statues that seem to snarl at the slots
players. Stay here if you've tried every hotel and motel in town
and your only alternative would be to sleep in the car. The Im-

Lodging 141

perial Palace is noisy and messy, packed with tourists on package tours, a place that has never figured out how to route people efficiently. There's no direct walkway to the elevators; you'll have to carry your luggage through the casino, steering your way among the browsers, to reach the elevators to the rooms. The rooms themselves date from a period when garish decor was thought to be a spur in getting you out of the room and into the casino: The furniture is yellow and everything else is olive green. Ice cubes from the machine in the hall will cost you 50¢. The hotel has been adding towers for several years; the 547 rooms in the tower that was scheduled to open in late 1989 bring the room count to 2,637. The showroom offers a revue in which performers impersonate deceased celebrities. *3535 Las Vegas Blvd. S, 89109, tel. 702/731–3311 or 800/634–6441. 2,637 rooms. Facilities: swimming pool, 4 restaurants, lounge, antique-car museum, showroom. AE, CB, DC, MC, V.*

Lady Luck Casino and Hotel. The addition of a 25-story 400-room tower in 1989 made this the third-largest hotel property downtown. The new tower is across the street from the 17-story tower addition that opened in 1986, and visitors travel from the old Lady to the new Lady via a glass-enclosed pedestrian bridge on the third-floor level. Lady Luck has small, bright rooms with white walls and half-windows that look out on Ogden Street. A free shrimp cocktail awaits your arrival. *206 N. 3rd St., 89109, tel. 702/477–3000 or 800/634–6580. 800 rooms. Facilities: swimming pool, exercise facility, 5 restaurants. AE, CB, D, DC, MC, V.*

Landmark Hotel and Casino. This hotel was intended to be monumental, a sort of Space Needle of Las Vegas. It's a 31-story round building with what looks like a spaceship on top, and when the hotel opened in 1969, the spaceship was the casino and it revolved like some rooftop restaurants do. That took so much getting used to that the turning was halted and the casino was made stationary. Today only *you* will be going around, looking for your room when you get off the elevator. Those coming to Las Vegas for a convention will find the Landmark an excellent place to stay—across the street from the Las Vegas Convention Center and two blocks from the Strip. The Landmark often has rooms during convention periods when other hotels are booked, and the rooms have some of the best views in town. The medium-size rooms—with cream-colored walls, green carpeting, and curved picture windows—look out over the Strip or Paradise Road. A magic show with singing and dancing is the showroom attraction. *364 Convention Center Dr., 89109, tel. 702/733–1110 or 800/634–6777; in CA, 800/458–2946. 500 rooms. Facilities: 3 restaurants, swimming pool, lounge, showroom. AE, CB, D, DC, MC, V.*

Las Vegas Club Hotel and Casino. A sports theme prevails everywhere but in the guest rooms. The coffee shop is the Dugout, the lobby walls bear a sports hall of fame display with baseball and basketball photos and memorabilia, and a gift shop offers a wide selection of baseball shirts. The small rooms—no baseballs here—have a light brown finish, the beds have small awnings, and the tiny half-windows overlook Fremont Street. *18 E. Fremont St., 89109, tel. 702/385–1664 or 800/634–6532. 224 rooms. Facilities: lounge, 2 restaurants. AE, CB, DC, MC, V.*

Marina Hotel and Casino. The advantages of this medium-size hotel are its proximity to the Tropicana next door and the ab-

Lodging   **142**

sence of crowds on the golf course and in the casino. The rooms are some of the smallest in town, with half-windows overlooking the small pool or the parking area. The telephones have rotary dials. Special rates and packages are the Marina's way of attracting guests, and you could find a bargain here when you want to travel. A revue plays the showroom. A renovation has been announced for 1991. *3805 Las Vegas Blvd. S, 89109, tel. 702/739–1500 or 800/634–6169. 705 rooms. Facilities: lounge, 3 restaurants, swimming pool, showroom. AE, CB, DC, MC, V.*

Maxim Hotel and Casino. Situated just two blocks off the Strip, this is a good place to try when other establishments have no room. The Maxim's medium-size rooms are decorated in earth tones. Because the swimming pool—blue, with a big M on the bottom—is right on Flamingo Road, one of the busiest streets in town, you'll notice the exhaust fumes while you're in the water. The showroom offers a sexy rock revue. *160 E. Flamingo Rd., 89109, tel. 702/731–4300 or 800/634–6987. 795 rooms. Facilities: 2 restaurants, swimming pool, lounge, showroom. AE, CB, D, DC, MC, V.*

Riviera Hotel. Once upon a time there was a nice little casino hotel on the Strip that styled itself after the Miami resorts of the 1950s yet tried to capture the feeling of the French Riviera. It appealed to the upper crust of society. Then, one day, a new owner added a Burger King to the hotel. The critics denounced the move, complaining that fast food didn't belong in a casino, but it was successful nevertheless. The Riviera made more money than ever, and the owner decided to expand by adding towers to the nine-story hotel. He put a tower in the back, he put a tower in the front, and he's still at it. One could argue that he would have done better to tear it all down and start over, for today the Riviera looks like a house to which too many rooms have been added. The layout is confusing; you'll walk and walk and walk through the Riviera with no idea where you're going. The lobby is in the middle of the hotel, with acres of slots on both sides, and you must navigate the casino to reach the elevators. Yet the rooms are large, modern affairs with maroon bedspreads and carpeting, teak furniture, dining areas, and views of the Strip or El Rancho next door (be sure to ask for a room overlooking the Strip). The owner plans to make the Riviera the largest hotel in Vegas; a new 43-story tower will add 1,600 rooms when it opens in 1992. Five showrooms, each with seating for 100 to 500, showcase name entertainers, variety shows, and topless revues. *2901 Las Vegas Blvd. S, 89109, tel. 702/734–5110 or 800/634–6753. 2,200 rooms. Facilities: swimming pool, health club, 2 tennis courts, 3 restaurants, five showrooms. AE, CB, DC, MC, V.*

Sahara Las Vegas Hotel. Like many of its neighbors, the Sahara began as a small motor hotel and built itself up by adding towers (571 rooms were new in 1988). Unlike many of its neighbors, however, the Sahara has retained a small, gardenlike ambience. A walk through the lobby will take you past the pool, with its sunbathers and huts where you can sit and have a drink. The original rooms are small, in the motor-hotel style, with a dining area, a medium-size window, and utilitarian furniture; all the old garden rooms overlook the pool, greenery, and artificial grass. The tower rooms are bigger, with king-size beds and mauve colors; they overlook the Strip or Paradise Road. In the shopping area you can have your own oil portrait painted in an hour for $75. Female impersonators appear in the showroom.

Lodging 143

2535 Las Vegas Blvd. S, 89101, tel. 702/737–2111 or 800/634–6666. 1,505 rooms. Facilities: 5 restaurants, 2 swimming pools, health club, lounge, showroom. AE, CB, D, DC, MC, V.
Sands Hotel and Casino. Frank Sinatra, Dean Martin, Sammy Davis Jr., Peter Lawford, and Joey Bishop hung out here in 1960 during the filming of the quintessential Vegas movie, *Ocean's 11.* The Sands is another 1950s landmark, the first circular building in town, with 730 rooms on nine floors. Originally it consisted of 11 low-rise buildings clustered around the pool, all named after racetracks. The old buildings still stand, with their medium-size rooms overlooking the garden and the pool. Shaped like a V (for Vegas), with a platform in the middle for sunbathers, the pool was the setting for the classic 1950s Vegas publicity photograph that showed a group of fun-loving men and women shooting craps in it—truly a "floating" crap game. The Sands pool today has strict rules for its use: Women must wear caps, no glass or chewing gum in the pool, no eating near the pool, no running on deck, and no pins or clips in the pool. (The rules notice adds, "Only fools don't obey rules." Ready for camp, anyone?) The 700-room tower atop the casino is an experience. Because the hotel's structure is round, everything you do takes you in a circle. Looking for the elevator? Walk in a circle until you find it. On leaving the elevator, you walk in a circle to reach your room. Tower rooms are twice the size of garden rooms, with red bedspreads, walls, and curtains, Early American–style furniture, and views of the Strip and the Desert Inn. The presidents John Kennedy, Richard Nixon, and Ronald Reagan were guests in the Sands Presidential Suite. *3355 Las Vegas Blvd. S, 89109, tel. 702/733–5000 or 800/634–6901. 750 rooms. Facilities: 2 pools, 4 restaurants, putting green, 6 tennis courts, health club, lounge, showroom. AE, CB, D, DC, MC, V.*
Stardust Hotel and Casino. Just a block from the Convention Center, this hotel is conveniently located for convention delegates. The original Stardust was a series of small motor hotels whose rooms have economy-class furnishings: twin beds, table, mirror, TV. The rooms of the newer nine-story tower are of medium size with a blue color scheme, a couch, a small dining area, and views of the Strip or the hotel garden. A 32-story, 1,465-room tower scheduled to open in 1990 will more than double the present size of the Stardust. A long-running revue is booked in the showroom. *3000 Las Vegas Blvd. S, 89109, tel. 702/732–6111 or 800/634–6757. 1,326 rooms. Facilities: pool, 4 restaurants, lounge, RV park, showroom. AE, CB, D, DC, MC, V.*
Tropicana Resort and Casino. "The Tiffany of the Strip" when it opened in 1957, the old Tropicana motor hotel still stands, with rooms that are typically small motel units. But successive owners have added 22-story towers that have raised the room count to more than 1,900, doubled the size of the casino, and introduced a plush European-style decor. Today the Tropicana's legend is "the Island of Las Vegas"; its principal attraction is the Island water park, where you'll find the best swimming pool in the city. The large pool has two sections, each with rock constructions in the center upon which swimmers can climb and sunbathe, Jacuzzis built among the rocks, and a waterfall. A bridge across the pool divides the areas. Five ponds and lagoons are stocked with fish and other aquatic life. Furnishings in the tower rooms reflect a tropical theme in the bamboo trim, bedspreads, and the pastel hues of the carpeting. Tower rooms overlook the Island or the lower Strip. A topless revue occupies

Lodging 144

the showroom. *3801 Las Vegas Blvd. S, 89109, tel. 702/739–2222 or 800/634–4000. 1,908 rooms. Facilities: 6 restaurants, 2 swimming pools, 4 tennis courts, 18-hole golf course, putting green, health club, lounge, showroom. AE, CB, D, DC, MC, V.*

Union Plaza Hotel. One of the newer downtown hotels, opened in 1971, the Union Plaza anchors Fremont Street and can be seen in nearly every photo of it. Its roof is the base of activities for broadcasts of the Vegas New Year's celebrations. Rooms on the sixth floor have a superb view of the backs of Vegas Vic and Sassy Sally, the neon symbols of downtown Las Vegas. And you'll have to be assertive here and demand a room overlooking Fremont Street; otherwise you'll have a view of the train tracks. This is one hotel where it's relatively easy to get a room at the time of a big convention. A green decor and mirrors above the bed characterize the medium-size rooms. Those taking the train to Vegas will find themselves in the hotel when they step off the train. The showroom has booked an ice follies revue. *1 Main St., 89109, tel. 702/386–2110; 800/634–6575; in California, 800/634–6821. 1,037 rooms. Facilities: 3 restaurants, swimming pool, 4 tennis courts, wedding chapel, jogging track, lounge, Amtrak depot, showroom. AE, CB, D, DC, MC, V.*

Vegas World Hotel and Casino. The Vegas World theme, announced in the painting on the face of the building, is the space age. The registration desk is in a darkened area, where plastic columns of red and blue neon send up water bubbles, creating a *Star Wars* look. The decor of the medium-size guest rooms is spacesuit silver, with matching bedspreads, curtains, and furniture; many of the rooms overlook the residences that border Las Vegas Boulevard. And the elevators speak: "Going up. Next floor . . . four." Celebrity impersonators perform in the showroom. *2000 Las Vegas Blvd. S, 89109, tel. 702/382–2000 or 800/634–6277. 1,270 rooms. Facilities: swimming pool, lounge, 2 restaurants, showroom. AE, CB, D, DC, MC, V.*

Inexpensive   **Circus Circus.** You can *always* find a room at Circus Circus; if they don't have one for you, they'll locate one. But beware, this place is truly a madhouse. Circus Circus opened in 1968 as a casino with a circus, and subsequent owners added to it; now it can be hard to figure out where you're going, and you'll run into crowds of people trying to do the same. While the registration area is out in front, under the pink porte cochere, the room elevators are all the way to the back, allowing you a long, busy stroll through the casino. Upstairs you'll find painted circus tents in the hallway and some of the most garishly appointed guest rooms in Vegas: king-size beds, bright red carpets, matching red chairs, pink walls, and, on one wall, red-, pink-, and blue-striped wallpaper. The casino attracts so many visitors that drivers will find it a major achievement just getting into the Circus Circus parking lot. On a Saturday night, the nearby stretch of Las Vegas Boulevard leading up to the Circus is usually gridlocked. Those who despair of finding a parking space may turn to the parking valet up front; even when the FULL sign is out, you may be able to get help—for a toke. Circus Circus is a favorite of families: Parents can drop the kids off at the midway on the second floor to play games or watch the circus acts while the adults go off to play slots. You can take advantage of this service without being a guest of the hotel. Performances are scheduled from 11 AM to midnight, with five-minute shows followed by 20-minute intermissions. *2880 Las Vegas Blvd. S,*

Lodging 145

89109, tel. 702/734–0410 or 800/634–3450. 2,793 rooms. Facilities: wedding chapel, carnival midway with live circus acts, RV park, 3 swimming pools, 4 restaurants. AE, CB, D, DC, MC, V.

El Cortez Hotel. Here is one of the great Las Vegas deals: a room for two in the heart of the downtown area for $23 a night—available on a walk-in basis only, and not on Saturday. The two floors of tiny rooms have twin beds, a small TV, and a narrow window with a view of Fremont Street. 600 E. Fremont St., 89109, tel. 702/385–5200 or 800/634–6703. 315 rooms. Facilities: 2 restaurants. AE, CB, D, DC, MC, V.

Gold Spike Hotel and Casino. Jackie Gaughan owns both El Cortez and the Gold Spike, and the latter is much the nicer place to stay. The hotel is billed as "Las Vegas as It Used to Be," with penny slots, nickel keno, and $1 blackjack tables. The Spike charges only $20 a night, every night, for a small, plain double room with twin beds, a nightstand, TV, and a view of East Ogden Avenue. A suite for $30 a night adds a four-poster, couch, and balcony. All rates include breakfast for each guest and two-for-one dinners in the Gold Spike Diner. 400 E. Ogden Ave., 89109, tel. 702/384–8444 or 800/634–6703. 110 rooms. Facilities: coffee shop. AE, CB, D, DC, MC, V.

Sam's Town Hotel and Casino. Sam's is far from the center of activity, and that's what makes the trip here so interesting. The hotel's attempt to present Vegas as it once was, with an Old West theme, seems more authentic here, where you're closer to the desert. Sam's Town is named for a gambler, an old-timer who has been in town since the 1950s, running and operating hotels such as the Sahara and Union Plaza. His Boyd Group now owns Sam's, the Fremont, the California, and the Stardust. Sam's excels at producing the Western theme. Everyone wears garters and string ties, the food is inexpensive, the rooms comfortable. It's one of the few Vegas hotels where you'll wake in the morning to look out at the desert mountains in the distance. And Boulder Highway offers a wonderful backroad route to Boulder Dam and Lake Mead. 5111 W. Boulder Hwy., 89109, tel. 702/456–7777 or 800/634–6371. 204 rooms. Facilities: swimming pool, bowling alley, 4 restaurants, lounge, RV park. AE, CB, D, DC, MC, V.

Out of Town Two casino hotels on Interstate 15 serve those traveling the Los Angeles–Las Vegas route who want a break from driving.

Gold Strike Hotel and Gambling Hall. Only 30 minutes from Vegas, the Gold Strike has rooms for $29 a night and a weird white-and-orange facade that has to be seen in full daylight to be appreciated. The casino has a strong Old West ambience. 1 Main St., Jean 89019, tel. 702/477–5000. 300 rooms. Facilities: pool, restaurant, lounge. AE, CB, D, DC, MC, V.

Whiskey Pete's Casino and Hotel. That you can see the neon image of Pete at night while you're still 15 minutes away is an indication of how dark the desert and how bright the neon sign. Inside you'll find a noisy, surprisingly busy state-line casino with lounge bands, cheap food, and rooms for only $19. The rooms are large, with king-size beds, cable TV, direct-dial phone, and small bathrooms. When you're headed for Vegas, the stop at Pete's will leave you 45 minutes of driving time in the morning. Box 93718, Las Vegas 89193, tel. 702/382–4388 or 800/528–1234. 262 rooms. Facilities: swimming pool, lounge, 2 restaurants. AE, CB, D, DC, MC, V.

Lodging 146

Motels

Motels offer you the opportunity to save some money and the chance to park just outside your room. Those who dread having to search for a parking space and then trek long distances through halls and casinos to reach their hotel room may prefer the compactness of the motel. Don't be concerned that staying in a motel will take you away from the action; all the motels listed here are near casinos, so when you have the gambling urge, you can cross the street and start dropping quarters.

All-Star Inn. Similar in character to a Motel 6, All-Star has the advantage that fewer people know about it, and thus it's easy to find a room here, even when there's a big convention in town. Another plus for drivers is that All-Star is just off the Tropicana exit from I-15. When you're tired after a long drive, you won't have to begin your Vegas visit by battling the Tropicana Avenue traffic looking for a motel; get off the freeway, turn left, and you're there. The rooms are identical to those of Motel 6—tiny, with a TV set on a platform near the ceiling. *5085 S. Industrial Rd. (just south of Tropicana Ave.), 89118, tel. 702/739-6747. MC, V.*

Motel 6. Welcome to the largest Motel 6 in the United States, with 877 rooms, a pool, and a neon sign. If you're comfortable staying at the low-price national lodging chain, you'll love this Vegas edition, which has rooms that look like those of any other Motel 6—small and spare, with the TV mounted on a platform near the ceiling. When travelers think in terms of cheap rooms, they think Motel 6, so the rooms here tend to go pretty fast. *195 E. Tropicana Ave., 89109, tel. 702/798-0728. AE, D, DC, MC, V.*

Town Hall/Vagabound Inn (formerly Mini-Price Motor Inn). This is a great location for convention delegates. Town Hall is directly behind Bally's, within walking distance of the Four Corners (Flamingo Road and Las Vegas Boulevard), and a short cab ride to the Las Vegas Convention Center. The three-story building has 360 basic motel rooms and a casino. *4155 Koval La., 89109, tel. 702/731-2111 or 800/634-6541. Facilities: coffee shop, swimming pool. AE, DC, MC, V.*

Westward Ho Motel and Casino. The largest motel in the world, with seven swimming pools and a casino, the Ho is strategically located between the Stardust and Circus Circus for your entertainment pleasure. Parking spaces are in front of the rooms. The one drawback here is the location: On Saturday night this part of town is gridlocked, and returning to your room by car will take considerable time. *2900 Las Vegas Blvd. S, 89109, tel. 702/731-2900 or 800/634-6803. 1,000 rooms. MC, V.*

9 Nightlife

The very name "Vegas" has come to be synonymous with a certain kind of showbiz ever since Jimmy Durante was the first headliner at Bugsy Siegel's Fabulous Flamingo Hotel in 1946. Over the years the list of Vegas stars has included Frank Sinatra, Noel Coward, Louis Prima and Keely Smith, Sammy Davis Jr., Dean Martin, Lola Falana, Shecky Greene, Siegfried and Roy, Don Rickles, Randy Travis, Nat King Cole, Billy Eckstine, Diana Ross, David Copperfield, Paul Anka, Jerry Lewis, Harry Belafonte, Joan Rivers, Julio Iglesias, Joe E. Lewis, Milton Berle, George Burns, and of course Mr. Las Vegas himself, Wayne Newton, the Midnight Idol.

In the not-so-old days the major Las Vegas hotels offered a dinner show early in the evening and a late-night cocktail show at 11 or 11:30 PM. The only hotels that still offer a dinner show today are the Flamingo Hilton and the Tropicana on the Strip and the Union Plaza downtown. There's little reason to mourn the passing of this tradition; the mass-produced meal that was served was expensive, generally cold, and nearly tasteless. At the cocktail shows you'll get two drinks with your admission, and you can always buy peanuts and chips from the cigarette girls who patrol the showrooms.

Back when Las Vegas began to promote itself as the Entertainment Capital of the World, the shows were loss leaders, much as the buffets and hotel rooms are today: They were intended to draw patrons who would eventually wind up in the casino. Admission prices to shows were dirt cheap, and the programs were fairly short (which drove guests back into the casino that much sooner). Nowadays it may cost you $45 to see Wayne Newton, and tickets to a big production such as "Donn Arden's Jubilee" are often $30. Yet many of the smaller shows have much lower admission prices; at press time, tickets to "Melinda's Follies Revue" are $14.95, "Playboy's Girls of Rock and Roll" costs $12.95, and you can get into "Boy-lesque" for $9.95. Las Vegas publicists are fond of pointing out that tickets even to the top draws are cheaper than those for Broadway productions—and two drinks are included in the admission price!

There are several kinds of shows in Las Vegas. The major stars who appear in the "big rooms" are the headliners who command the $35–$40 ticket prices and attract audiences of 1,000 to 1,500. The big-production spectaculars—90 minutes of singing, dancing, topless show girls, specialty acts, special effects, and vintage show tunes—are revues that are extremely popular with the increasing numbers of international tourists who have descended on the city over the last decade. Foreign visitors also seem to love magic shows; two of the most popular performers in town are Siegfried and Roy, magicians who make things disappear while saying hardly a word—so you don't have to understand English to enjoy them. The same is true for the revues, of course, which rely less on script than on musical numbers and the ubiquitous topless show girl, whose blatant charms can be appreciated in any language.

You don't need to buy a ticket to get into the showrooms, but you will need to make a reservation and then stand in line for at least 30 minutes. Once you've been seated at a table, before the show begins, you'll be asked to pay your bill, which covers two drinks. (Don't forget to include a tip for your waiter.) On weekends it can be tough getting in to see such top acts as Siegfried and Roy, Sammy Davis, and Wayne Newton. Half of the room is usually re-

Nightlife 149

served for big-spending gamblers, who get in for free. Your chances of getting a seat are usually better when you're staying—and gambling—at the hotel. Here's where you can use whatever "juice" you've pulled together on your trip: If you're spending a good deal of time in the casino, ask the pit boss (the man with folded arms who stands between the tables watching the action) for a free ticket to the show. If that works, or even if it doesn't, ask him for a line pass. It will allow you to go straight to the VIP line outside the showroom, which means you won't have to spend the half-hour waiting in line. The worst the pit boss can do in this situation is to say no.

Once in the showroom door, you should tip the maître d' or captain $5 to $20 to get a booth or a good seat. The choice seats are always the booths, which are many times more comfortable than the tables. The majority of the places are at long tables that seat 10 to 15 people facing each other. When the show begins, you have to shift your body toward the stage and into a position that's likely to give you a neckache by the end of the night. However, if the showroom isn't very crowded, the captain may seat you wherever you like.

If you're looking to spend a little more money, the tuxedo-clad women who patrol the showrooms with large cameras will take portrait photographs of couples for $25 or so. The photos will be ready when the show is over.

Las Vegas–Style Revues

Abracadabra (Aladdin Hotel and Casino, 3667 Las Vegas Blvd. S, tel. 702/736–0111). When Siegfried and Roy announced in 1988 that they were leaving Las Vegas to tour for a year and a half, the management of Aladdin figured there would still be a hunger for magic in town, so they built a show around it. The spectacle begins when a large magic lamp appears on stage, with the illusion of a giant genie emerging from the lamp. He grants his own wish, and a dance number follows. Singers sing, dancers dance, and magicians make things levitate and disappear. The star of the show is Kirby Van Burch, who calls himself the Prince of Magic (Siegfried and Roy call themselves the Kings of Magic; Melinda, of "Melinda and Her Follies Revue," calls herself the First Lady of Magic). On stage Van Burch levitates a woman, locks himself in a cage with a motorcycle, and makes both woman and motorcycle disappear. He also takes a stab at Harry Houdini's classic water-torture stunt, in which a huge tank is filled with water and the magician's hands and feet are shackled and lowered into the water. He is given two minutes to get out, and of course he does.
Boy-lesque (Sahara Las Vegas Hotel, 2535 Las Vegas Blvd. S, tel. 702/737–2111). Kenny Kerr stars in this long-running revue, impersonating Barbra Streisand, Diana Ross, Ann-Margret, Carol Channing, and other famous ladies. The show played for years at the Silver Slipper until, in 1988, the casino was torn down and Kerr moved across the street.
City Lites (The Flamingo Hilton and Tower, 3555 Las Vegas Blvd. S, tel. 702/733–3111). The "City Lites" format follows the basic revue formula: topless show girls, specialty act, singer, show girls, specialty act, show girls, finale. If you like Broadway musicals, "City Lites" is the show for you. You'll hear songs like "42nd Street," "Dames," "New York, New York," "Cabaret," and "Lullaby of Broadway" in this very nostalgic

Nightlife   150

tribute to the Great White Way. (The name of the show comes from the song "City Lites," a tune featured in the Liza Minnelli vehicle *The Act.*) Besides old show tunes, "Lites" also features a sight that has to be seen to be believed: bare-breasted ice skaters wearing pink headdresses. Later they switch to topless green kimonos for an Oriental ice-skating session, and at the end they don clothes and top hats to sing "City Lites" together, at which point they kick up their heels in a Radio City Music Hall Rockettes–style line. In between the gals is comedy, magic by Joseph Gabriel (a "Tonight Show" regular who works with doves), and the Garza Brothers, whose act consists of putting silver paint on their bodies and transforming themselves into human sculptures. Accompanied by low lights and dramatic music, they stand atop each other, extending their bodies into replications of famous statues.

Crazy Girls (Riviera Hotel, 2901 Las Vegas Blvd. S, tel. 702/734–5110). This is the dirtiest show in town, and it was created to be that way. Unlike other shows, which feature a mixture of topless and clothed show girls, "Crazy" has a cast of women who wear practically nothing at all times. The basic formula is a chorus line of nine topless women who lip-sync songs, gyrate to the music, and roll on the floor. The only break from this activity comes when one of the girls sings and another tells jokes. The show is designed to remind one of the Crazy Horse Saloon in Paris, which Crazy Girls' producers claim is dirtier than any Las Vegas show, including their own.

Donn Arden's Jubilee (Bally's Casino Resort, 3645 Las Vegas Blvd. S, tel. 702/739–4111). Arden, who has been producing shows in Vegas since 1952, put together this spectacular stage tribute to Hollywood for the MGM Grand Hotel in 1981; it was all set to go when the devastating fire occurred. The show finally opened six months later and has been running ever since, while the MGM Grand has become Bally's Casino Resort. "Jubilee" is the largest show in town, with a cast of more than 100 performing in a showroom with 1,100 seats. It offers great special effects: The sinking of the *Titanic* is re-created; Samson destroys the temple and the wreckage goes up in flames. Show girls parade about in the largest collection of feathers and bare breasts you've ever seen. The $5,000 headdresses weigh an average of 40 pounds each, and the costumes were designed by Hollywood veteran Bob Mackie, who is perhaps best known for the outrageous dresses he has invented for Cher. As is standard for a Donn Arden show, a tribute to the good old days includes songs made famous by Eddie Cantor, Al Jolson, Bing Crosby, and Judy Garland; a short classical ballet uses the music of Johann Strauss. Between the numbers, jugglers, magicians, and specialty performers do their thing in front of the curtain while the stagehands change the set. "Jubilee" is one Las Vegas spectacle that may also be a victim of its own bigness: The show is so large that it loses some of the live, up-close excitement you get with a show such as "Lido."

Folies Bergere (Tropicana Resort and Casino, 3801 Las Vegas Blvd. S, tel. 702/739–2222). A French topless revue like the "Lido," this is presented in a slightly larger showroom, with music that's a tad more modern—there is a tribute to the sounds of the 1950s—but on the whole it's your standard T & A show, with singers, dancers, comedians, jugglers, and a can-can finale. "Folies" also stars an excellent magician, Lance Burton, who pulls doves from his sleeves and turns them into

Nightlife 151

handkerchiefs. (He also appears on the "Tonight Show" once or twice a year.)

Legends in Concert (Imperial Palace Hotel and Casino, 3535 Las Vegas Blvd. S, tel. 702/731–3311). For those who like the old-timers and aren't content merely to watch them on video-cassette, "Legends" features impersonators of Elvis Presley, Marilyn Monroe, Buddy Holly, Judy Garland, Louis Armstrong, Hank Williams, and, more recently, Liberace and Roy Orbison. (The rule is that only dead "legends" can be depicted in the show. The Liberace impersonator was added a few days after Mr. Showmanship died, and Roy Orbison was cloned in April 1989, four months after his death.) The show is basically wall-to-wall music; the finale features Elvis, as played by Tony Roi, in his white jumpsuit, singing "Viva Las Vegas."

Lido de Paris (Stardust Hotel and Casino, 3000 Las Vegas Blvd. S, tel. 702/732–6111). Imported from Paris in 1958 by the Las Vegas producer Donn Arden, the "Lido" was the first show in town to feature topless show girls. (The year before, "Minsky's Burlesque" at the Dunes had shown breasts decorated only with tassels.) The concept of nudes on stage caught on quickly, and the "Lido" was followed by "Nudes on Ice," "Xstasy on Ice," "Razzle Dazzle," and other topless shows. More than naked breasts and oversize feather headdresses, the "Lido" is the prototypical Vegas revue, presenting dancing, singing, special effects, and specialty acts in a small, intimate showroom. Although it's often lumped together with "Folies Bergere" and "City Lites" as "the French T & A shows," the "Lido" offers the best entertainment of the three. The reason is simple: Audience members feel they're a part of the show. A runway from the stage stretches into the audience, allowing the show girls to strut their stuff right before you. The only negative is Bobby Berosini's orangutan act, which is sophomoric and not very funny. Some say the "Lido" has gone downhill over the years; it's true, yet the show is still a classic of its kind.

Melinda and Her Follies Revue (Landmark Hotel and Casino, 364 Convention Center Dr., tel. 702/733–1110). Twenty-four-year-old Melinda Saxe used to go to sleep at night and dream about being a magician. Now she's the star of her own revue, produced by Bonnie Saxe, her mom. Melinda's story began a few years back when she quit her job dancing in Siegfried and Roy's show and convinced the owners of the small Bourbon Street Casino to let her try out her act in their 100-seat showroom. She pulled in the audiences, and now her name—and bare buttocks—shine from the marquee of the Landmark Hotel, where she has been performing since 1988. Melinda, the first female magician to attain star billing in Vegas, levitates her sister, makes doves appear out of thin air, and creates the illusion of making a yellow VW Bug vanish. Anthony Gatto, a young juggler who used to appear in the "Jubilee" show at Bally's, is also in her revue, along with the impressionist Gordie Brown.

Playboy's Girls of Rock and Roll (Maxim Hotel and Casino, 160 E. Flamingo Rd., tel. 702/731–4300). One of the best deals in town, this show is no naughtier than the "Lido" or "Jubilee." Its topless show girls, semidressed in glittery rock-and-roll outfits, sing current musical material; a comedian and a magician also perform. For price and value, "Girls" is a Vegas bargain.

Splash (Riviera Hotel, 2901 Las Vegas Blvd. S, tel. 702/734–5110). This isn't a traditional Vegas T & A show in any sense, for

Nightlife   152

the large numbers of female dancers are clothed. Instead of wearing the usual showgirl costume of headdress, fishnet stockings, and feather boas, the "Splashgirls" dress as serpents, clams, mermaids, and other amphibious creatures. In time to the music, they jump into a 65,000-gallon water tank, climb out, dry off, and dance in front of fountains that spout from various parts of the stage. Not only do the dancers get wet, so do showgoers in the front seats. The music in "Splash" is more contemporary than that of any other Vegas revue production; the producer Jeff Kutash deliberately presents a Top 40 sound, hoping to appeal to younger audiences and to create a new wave of Strip entertainment. "Splash" also features magicians, country fiddlers-singers-dancers, motorcycle daredevils who whirl around inside a giant steel "Globe of Death," and the "acro-balancing" act of Murillo and Ulises, who balance atop each other's heads while telling jokes. In 1989 Kutash revamped his show: The original finale—a tribute to America and the Statue of Liberty—came out, and in its place he put a 23-minute salute to Broadway and Hollywood, with medleys from *Cats*, *Little Shop of Horrors*, *A Chorus Line*, *Phantom of the Opera*, and *Dirty Dancing*.

Showroom Stars

Whenever you ask Las Vegas entertainment directors why their showrooms don't book more contemporary stars, they tell you that the Whitney Houstons, Billy Joels, and Elton Johns won't play Vegas. Or they insist that the kind of audiences who come to Las Vegas wouldn't pay money to see Tone-Lōc, the Fine Young Cannibals, or Debbie Gibson. Las Vegas showrooms have become a tad more modern over the past few years: Eddie Murphy has played the Las Vegas Hilton, and other recent acts have included Randy Travis, Jeffrey Osborne, Gladys Knight, Natalie Cole, Barbara Mandrell, and Willie Nelson. In general, Las Vegas stars are a curious mix of performers who haven't had a hit record in years (Engelbert Humperdinck, Paul Anka, the Four Seasons) and well-established personalities who could sell tickets anywhere (Sammy Davis Jr., Frank Sinatra, Wayne Newton).

The "big rooms" of Vegas, where the headliners appear, are five in number: Bally's, Caesars Palace, the Desert Inn, the Golden Nugget, and the Las Vegas Hilton. Performance schedules vary with the star and the season, but most performers appear at least Thursday through Sunday nights. The giveaway tourist magazines in hotels and gift shops will tell you what stars are in town and where and when they're performing during the week.

The headliners who command the most attention in Vegas these days are:

Ann-Margret. In 1960 she was discovered in Las Vegas by George Burns, who hired her to open his show at the Sahara Hotel. Hollywood talent scouts saw her act there and signed her for starring parts in the films *Bye-Bye Birdie* and *Viva Las Vegas*, in which she co-starred with Elvis Presley. Over the years she has developed a must-see Vegas act that features many male dancers and irresistible energy. She took a sabbatical from the Vegas stage in 1982, to return in 1988 with a brand-new show.

Nightlife 153

Sammy Davis Jr. The Candyman is also a Vegas must-see. Celebrating his 60th anniversary in show business in 1989, Davis was singing better than ever—and dancing again. He's at his best when, as the stage lights shine on his tiny body, he whips off his tuxedo jacket, loosens his bow tie, and belts out "Birth of the Blues." You'd think that after all these years he'd be tired of it, but Davis seems to come alive on stage, talking to the audience about his life, loves, and wishes, thanking them for their support over the years, telling them what's been on his mind lately, and crooning the vintage hits "Mr. Bojangles" and "The Candyman." Lately Davis has been performing with Jerry Lewis, who does an hour of comedy to Davis's hour of singing, and then the two do comedy together and sing a duet of "Rockabye Your Baby with a Dixie Melody."

Engelbert Humperdinck. When you go to see "The Hump" at the Las Vegas Hilton, where he performs frequently, you'll notice a large group of women up front. This is his fan club, a pack of women who travel all over the West to see him, no matter where. When he plays Las Vegas, they come for the weekend, they're first in line, and they see three or four shows, sitting together in the front row. Such is the devoted following for a man whose last hit, "After the Lovin'," was way back in 1977. On stage he delivers a friendly show, pleasing his audiences with such past hits as "Release Me," "There Goes My Everything," "The Last Waltz," and "Am I Easy to Forget?" Over the years Humperdinck has seasoned into a fine performer, and recently he added a tap-dance segment, donning a top hat to sing Fred Astaire tunes.

Tom Jones. Another Vegas veteran who is getting better with age, Jones may still split his pants to please the blue-haired ladies, but he refuses to sing only his hits. Sure, he'll throw in "Green, Green Grass of Home" and "It's Not Unusual," but he also performs such current tunes as his own remake of Prince's "Kiss," Robert Cray's "Ain't Nothing But a Woman," and Paul Simon's "You Can Call Me Al."

Wayne Newton. Mr. Las Vegas, the Midnight Idol, the King of the Strip, Wayne Newton plays the Las Vegas Hilton 12 weeks a year and is in many ways the epitome of the Las Vegas headliner. A homegrown phenomenon, he has been performing here since his teens, when he did an act with his brother Jerry at the Fremont's Carnival Lounge. On stage, Newton gives it the Al Jolson treatment, working and sweating his way through two hours of show—singing, telling jokes, playing the guitar, violin, and trumpet. Whatever one thinks of the kind of music Newton is known for, no one would dispute the fact that, after all these years, he knows how to entertain his audience. Seeing a Wayne Newton show is as much a part of the experience of visiting Vegas as gambling and visiting Hoover Dam. You have to know that you've been part of a "very special" audience, and only the Wayne Man can tell you that.

Siegfried and Roy. A trip to Las Vegas is truly complete only when you've seen the master illusionists Siegfried and Roy strut their stuff—provided you can get in. As the stars of "Beyond Belief" at the Frontier from 1981 to 1988, they sold out every show over a seven-year run, and the seats were always hard to get. They left to tour for a year and a half, but Steve Wynn has signed them to a $55.5 million contract to star at his new Mirage Hotel, where they were scheduled to debut with an entirely new show in December 1989. In their shows, Siegfried and Roy have made elephants and motorcycles disappear and

Nightlife 154

have levitated each other as well as the lions and tigers who are their roommates in Las Vegas.

Lounges

The lounges of the Las Vegas casino hotels were once places where such headliners as Frank, Sammy, Dean, and the gang would go after their shows, taking a seat in the audience to laugh at the comedy antics of Shecky Greene or Don Rickles or to enjoy the music of Louis Prima and Keely Smith. Now the lounges have been reduced to small bars within the casino, where bands play Top 40 hits and dancing is encouraged. Virtually every casino has such a spot; all you need to do is buy a drink or two and you can listen to the music all night long. One good choice is **Top of the Place** at the Landmark Hotel (364 Convention Center Dr., tel. 702/733–1110), which offers panoramic views of the Strip.

Comedy Clubs

Since the demise of the days when comedians reigned in the casino lounges, comedy has suffered. It's thriving again, however, in the 1990s version of the Vegas lounge: the comedy club. There are three in town, and all are doing big business.

Catch a Rising Star (Bally's Casino Resort, 3645 Las Vegas Blvd. S, tel. 702/739–4397). Generally, three comedians play week-long engagements here, in what was a movie theater when Bally's was the MGM Grand.
The Comedy Store (The Dunes Casino Theater, 3650 Las Vegas Blvd. S, tel. 702/737–4741). Each week a different lineup of five comedians takes the stage.
An Evening at the Improv (Riviera Hotel, 2901 Las Vegas Blvd. S, tel. 702/794–9300). Three shows a night, each with a different comic, fill the stage at the Riviera's small club in the Mardi Gras Center.

Dancing

Chaz features live bands, a $500,000 sound system, and a spaceship at the center of the dance floor on Friday and Saturday. A DJ spins records the rest of the week. *1650 E. Tropicana Ave., tel. 702/736–2020. Open Tues.–Thurs. 9 PM–4 AM, Fri.–Sat. 9 PM–6 AM.*
Cleopatra's Barge offers dancing on a big boat in the Caesars Palace casino. Live bands perform hits every night except Monday. *Caesars Palace, 3570 Las Vegas Blvd. S, tel. 702/731–7110. Live band 9 PM–3 AM.*
Shark Club is a trendy, young, dark club on three levels, each with a dance floor and live music. *75 E. Harmon Ave., tel. 702/795–7525. Open Sun.–Thurs. 7 PM–6 AM, Fri.–Sat. 7 PM–8 AM.*
Tramps, voted the No. 1 dance club in Las Vegas by readers of the *Las Vegas Review-Journal*, is where university students and the young local folk come to watch music videos and dance to music played by DJs. *4405 W. Flamingo Rd., tel. 702/871–1424. Dancing nightly 11 PM–4 AM.*

Nightlife 155

Music

Country and Western **Dance Hall and Saloon** offers live country-and-western music every night except Tuesday, when big-band tapes play. Country-and-western dance lessons are given free on Sunday, Monday, Wednesday, and Thursday at 6:30 PM. *Gold Coast Hotel, 4000 W. Flamingo Rd., tel. 702/357–7111. Open 7–11:30 PM.* **Western Dance Hall** is another spot for country-and-western dancing to live bands. You can expect to hear renditions of recent country hits by George Strait, Randy Travis, and Buck Owens. *Sam's Town Hotel and Casino, 5111 Boulder Hwy., tel. 702/458–0096. Open nightly 7 PM–4 AM.*

Irish Music The Irish Showband plays Wednesday through Sunday in the lounge of the **Barbary Coast Hotel** (3595 Las Vegas Blvd. S, tel. 702/737–7111).

Jazz The French Quarter room in the **Four Queens Casino** (202 E. Fremont St., tel. 702/385–4011) has live jazz Monday and many other evenings as well. New Orleans jazz plays nightly in the lounge of the **Bourbon Street Casino** (120 E. Flamingo Rd., tel. 702/737–7200).

Movies

A lot of movies play Las Vegas—there are 12 theaters and 67 screens in town—but you won't see film marquees on the Strip. The easiest cinemas to find will be the **Gold Coast Twin** (4000 W. Flamingo Rd., tel. 702/367–7111), which is at the Gold Coast Hotel and Casino, a couple of blocks west of the Strip; and the **Parkway 3** (3768 S. Maryland Pkwy., tel. 702/734–8151), near the Boulevard Shopping Mall, a short trek from the Strip.

In the heart of downtown, in "Glitter Gulch," are:
UA Cinemas 1-2-3 (410 E. Fremont St., tel. 702/382–2626).
Century 21 (2606 S. Lamb Blvd., tel. 702/641–2500).
Cinedome 6 (3200 S. Decatur Blvd., tel. 702/362–2133).
Cinema 8 (3025 E. Desert Inn Rd., tel. 702/734–2124).
Huntridge Theaters (1250 E. Charleston Blvd., tel. 702/382–3314).
Mountain View 3 (3400 S. Jones Blvd., tel. 702/362–4848).
Paradise 6 (3330 E. Tropicana Ave., tel. 702/451–7373).
Caesars Palace (3570 Las Vegas Blvd. S, tel. 702/731–7110) shows movies every day in a big, shiny dome outside its casino; the immense Omnimax screen shows 70mm movies. Films available in this format usually have such subjects as trips to Hawaii, travel on a space shuttle, and exploring the Grand Canyon. If you've never seen a film this way, you owe it to yourself to have a look, for the larger-than-life images are breathtaking.

Strip Club

The **Palomino Club** is the home of "Girls, Girls, Girls," where performers dance topless and strip for male and female guests. *Playboy* magazine has called this the best strip club in Vegas. *1848 Las Vegas Blvd. N., tel. 702/642–2984. Open 24 hours.*

Nightlife   *156*

The Graveyard Shift

An entirely different aspect of Vegas nightlife is the routine of casino operations during the graveyard shift, the hours from 2 AM to 10 AM. The crowds are much diminished from the evening hours, yet the games and the entertainment continue through the night, and a stroll around a casino can lead to new and revealing perspectives.

These are the hours when the slots are emptied, when the money is counted, when hotel public relations officials must be wakened at home and told to come to the casino because a slot player has just hit a jackpot. The winner must stand by the slot until the p.r. person arrives, a photo can be taken, and the player interviewed for a press release that will demonstrate that folks do actually win jackpots in Las Vegas.

The busiest man in the casino during the graveyard shift is the shift manager. He essentially runs the casino in the absence of the casino manager, who at this hour is home in bed but within hearing of a beeper or a phone that may waken him several times in the course of a night. The shift manager's main function is to be skeptical; he's there to thwart those persons who would try to rip off the casino. He also evaluates gamblers' requests for credit, and he sees that everything runs smoothly.

Dice and cards are examined closely by the shift manager, who looks for nicks or cuts on the dice and for bent or shaved cards and other signs of tampering. On the casino floor, he watches the betting patterns of the gamblers, looking for unusual behavior; when a player suddenly graduates from $5 to $100 bets, it can be a signal that some monkey business is in the works. He watches out for teams of players working the dice tables and trying to pull fast ones on the dealers.

One part of the shift manager's domain is the "eye in the sky" area, the upstairs room from which the entire casino is monitored by closed-circuit cameras. The "eye" misses nothing; cameras survey every twenty-one, roulette, craps, keno, bingo, slot, and baccarat area, videotaping everything on giant banks of VCRs and retaining all records for three days.

In "the sky," as elsewhere in the house, personnel maintain a constant search for cheats. "That's what a lot of people come here for," one supervisor explained. "They like to bend the cards of certain hands so that they can recognize them when they are shuffled in the deck. They will put foreign substances on cards, and they will try to work with other players—or dealers—by making signals behind their backs. If a dealer signals the players, we'll see it from here, and we'll go down and pull him off and prosecute him.

"But most dealers want to keep their jobs. This is their livelihood. They're not going to jeopardize it for a couple of bucks. Integrity is very important in the gambling business."

Most of the shift manager's time is spent on the casino floor. "On a typical night," a former Frontier shift manager told me, "I'd come in, see who our players were, monitor the pit for a while, see that everything was going all right, and then go back to the cage and do evaluations on our customers." No, he wasn't evaluating all the customers, just those who were being "comped." To qualify for free rooms, meals, and shows, players have to agree to play a cer-

Nightlife 157

tain amount of money for a certain amount of time. It's the shift manager's job to tally the player's action and to determine what freebies the player has earned.

Folks who have families to support generally don't like working the graveyard shift. Many other Vegans prefer it for the mellower atmosphere, with the reduced levels of noise and smoke.

10 Reno and Lake Tahoe

Reno

Smaller, less crowded, friendlier, and prettier than Las Vegas, Reno is one of the nicest places to visit in Nevada. The casinos here have more amicable dealers, lower table minimums, and large numbers of vintage slot machines from the 1950s, which can be a lot of fun to play (the Nevada Club and Harold's Club have the best selection). Some considerate Reno casinos also provide entire nonsmoking gaming areas. Reno hotels have striking views of the snowcapped Sierra Nevada; beautiful Lake Tahoe is 45 minutes away; and Reno is a convenient starting point for excursions to the former mining towns of Virginia City and Carson City nearby.

The first permanent settlement in the area was Mormon Station, east of Lake Tahoe, in what is Genoa today. Yet Nevada was known for little more than its hot deserts until June 1859, when gold was found in Virginia City. The Comstock Lode, one of the richest bodies of gold and silver ore ever discovered, drew so many people to the area that Nevada became a territory in 1861 and a state in 1864. Virginia City is said to have had 25 saloons before it had 4,000 residents. In 1863 a young reporter on Virginia City's *Territorial Enterprise*, Samuel Clemens, signed his name "Mark Twain" for the first time in writing about the legislature in Carson City.

Reno's beginnings were in 1859, when Charles Fuller built a toll bridge across the Truckee River. Two years later Myron Lake bought the bridge, rebuilt the trading station, and added an inn and tavern. About four blocks up the street from where Lake's businesses once were is today's bustling Virginia Street and the Reno arch. After the railroad came through town in 1868—to connect with the Virginia and Truckee railroads that carried the silver from the Comstock in Virginia City—the first building lot was sold and the city named in honor of General Jesse Reno, a northern Civil War hero. The present-day Reno arch, with its legend, THE BIGGEST LITTLE CITY IN THE WORLD, is the fourth since 1926, when the first arch commemorated the highway's passage through town.

Gambling came to northern Nevada in 1868 when the railroad reached Reno. By 1910 gaming had been outlawed throughout the state, but by 1930 lawmakers were being urged to legalize it again as a source of income for the state treasury. In 1931 the gambling bill was signed into law; in 1935 the first major casinos, Harold's Club and Bill Harrah's Tango Club (later called Harrah's), opened their doors on Virginia Street in Reno. The casino owners, Raymond "Pappy" Smith (with his son Harold) and Bill Harrah, strived to make their large new properties more accessible to the common man than the backroom gambling houses of yore had been. Their casinos were brightly lighted and the activity open to view from the sidewalk, giving the impression that there was nothing to hide and no unsavory atmosphere within.

Because the first major casinos were opened in Reno, by the early 1950s it had come to be known as the gambling capital of the state. The area was also known as a divorce haven. Nevada law permits divorces to residents of the state, and residency can be attained by living in the state for six consecutive weeks. For many years, before divorce laws elsewhere were liberalized, married women came to northern Nevada dude ranches, vacationed under the sun

Reno and Lake Tahoe   *160*

for six weeks, and left for home as single women. In a ritual known as Renovation, a newly free woman would toss her old wedding ring from the Virginia Street Bridge into the Truckee River. It was also customary to plant lipstick kisses on the pillars of the Washoe County Courthouse in celebration of Divorce Day.

All gambling in Nevada comes under the jurisdiction of the Nevada Gaming Control Board in Carson City, the state capital. The board rules on new kinds of games, decides whether an individual is fit to have a gaming license, and collects the state's share of the table and slot winnings. The GCB also regulates Megabucks, the arrangement whereby progressive slots at participating casinos are joined together as one super slot machine that offers enormous jackpots.

Important Addresses and Numbers

Tourist Information
Reno-Sparks Convention and Visitors Authority (4590 S. Virginia St., Reno, NV 89504, tel. 702/827–7366 or 800/367–7366). **Reno Tahoe Visitors Center** (135 N. Sierra St., tel. 702/348–7788) is open weekdays 9–5.

Emergencies
Police, fire, ambulance (tel. 911).

Hospital Emergency Rooms
Veteran's Hospital (1000 Locust St., tel. 702/786–7200) and **Washoe Medical Center** (77 Pringle Way, tel. 702/328–4100) have 24-hour medical service.

Late-Night Pharmacy
Shopko (6139 S. Virginia St., tel. 702/852–0730) is open 24 hours.

Getting Around

Reno, accessible by air, rail, and road, is a small town you can walk about comfortably. Most major hotels are on or near Virginia Street, and the majority of the gambling action is within a four-block radius of downtown. A car will come in handy for those who want to see the mountains, Virginia City, or Lake Tahoe. A number of bus companies serve the area, making it easy to arrange an excursion to a nearby city. If gambling action is all you seek, you'll find downtown Reno a five-minute drive from the airport.

By Plane
Reno-Cannon International Airport (tel. 702/322–0927 or 800/356–7220), on the east side of the city, serves the area.

America West Airlines (tel. 702/348–2777 or 800/247–5692), **American Airlines** (tel. 702/329–9217 or 800/433–7300), **Continental Airlines** (tel. 702/323–1661 or 800/525–0280), **Delta Air Lines** (tel. 702/323–1661 or 800/221–1212), **Northwest Airlines** (tel. 800/225–2525), **United Airlines** (tel. 702/329–1020 or 800/241–6522), and **USAir** (tel. 800/428–4322) are the principal airlines that fly into Reno.

Airport Transportation
LTR Stage Lines (tel. 702/323–3088) provides service from the airport to Lake Tahoe, and **Airport Minibus** (tel. 702/786–3700) has service to Reno and surrounding areas.

By Car
To reach downtown Reno from the airport, take Route 395N to Interstate 80 and head west on I–80 to the N. Virginia exit for downtown Reno.

By Taxi
Reno-Sparks Cab Co. (tel. 702/333–3333), **Whittlesea Checker Taxi** (tel. 702/323–3111), and **Yellow Deluxe Cab Co.** (tel. 702/

Reno
161

331–7171) serve the Reno area. The base charge is $1.40 plus $1.20 per mile.

By Train **Amtrak** (tel. 702/329–8638 or 800/872–7245) provides twice-daily service on the *California Zephyr,* westbound to San Francisco in the morning and eastbound toward Chicago in the evening. Passengers arrive downtown at 135 E. Commercial Row, across from Harrah's Casino.

By Bus **Greyhound Lines** (155 Stevenson St., tel. 702/322–2970) offers nationwide service, with frequent runs to the San Francisco Bay Area and other points in California.

Reno Citifare (333 Center St., tel. 702/348–7433) operates local buses in Reno 24 hours a day. The local fare is 60¢.

Escorted Tours **Sierra Nevada Stage Lines/Gray Line Tours** (2570 Tacchino St., tel. 702/329–2877 or 800/822–6009) has daily tours in Reno and from Reno to Virginia City and Lake Tahoe. Passengers are picked up at, and returned to, their hotels.

The **Sierra Tahoe Connection** (141 N. Virginia St., tel. 702/323–1820), another large tour operator, takes visitors to Virginia City, Carson City, and Lake Tahoe.

Exploring Reno

Numbers in the margin correspond with the numbered points of interest on the Reno map.

Reno's climate, much milder than that of Las Vegas, lures visitors the year around. In the winter people come to the area to ski and gamble. In the summer they come to enjoy the scenery and gamble. No matter what the season, laying a bet is the Number One activity in downtown Reno, and a tour of the city is principally a tour of the casinos, which are located on and near Virginia Street.

❶ **Club Cal-Neva** (38 E. 2nd St., at Virginia St., tel. 702/323–1046). This casino is home to the record-breaking $6.8 million slot jackpot, and Cal-Neva won't let you forget it. Reminders are posted everywhere in the casino and on the marquee out front. In spite of all the promotion, Cal-Neva is a rather nice, low-key gambling hall with an emphasis on slots that are housed in large railroad cars. The gaming tables tend to have lower minimums than those at Harrah's across the street.

❷ **Harrah's** (219 N. Center St., tel. 702/786–3232). Opened by Bill Harrah in 1935 as The Tango Club and now owned by the Holiday Inn Corporation, Harrah's is the second oldest casino in the state. This is the ritziest, snazziest joint in town, the house where the biggest entertainers play and the wealthy come for upscale treatment. To Harrah's credit, you can still find the occasional $1 blackjack table, nickel slot, friendly people, and friendly service here. Large and sprawling, Harrah's extends over several floors. The front Harrah's casino has an entrance on Virginia Street. To the back, out the door and across the alley, another Harrah's building has a hotel atop it and another casino, a showroom, a steak house, and the elevators that lead to the rooms.

❸ **Nevada Club** (224 N. Virginia St., tel. 702/329–1721). Here is my favorite place to gamble in Reno, if not in the entire state. If you want to step into a time machine that can show you what life

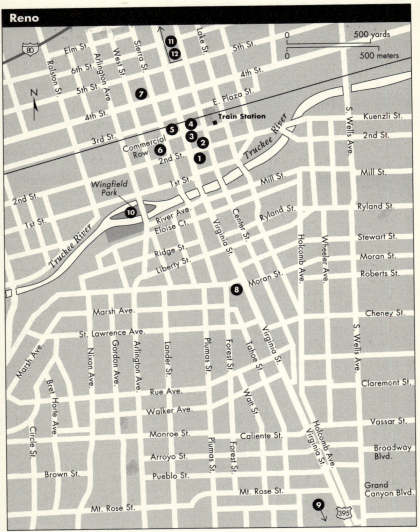

Circus Circus, **7**
Club Cal-Neva, **1**
Fitzgerald's, **5**
Flamingo Hilton, **6**
Fleischmann
Planetarium, **11**
Harold's, **4**
Harrah's, **2**
Nevada Club, **3**
Nevada Historical
Society, **12**
Peppermill, **9**
Ponderosa, **8**
Wingfield Park, **10**

was like in the 1950s, you'll love the Nevada Club. Virtually every slot here is a 1950s three-reel classic—a silver-plated contraption in which you deposit a dime and watch it fall into a large collection of dimes behind plate glass. Pull the handle and line up three cherries or three bells, and you might win a jackpot of $250 or $500. The Nevada Club's minimums at the table games are consistently the lowest in town, and fans of burgers, flapjacks, and shakes should enjoy the 1950s-style diner on the second floor.

4 Harold's (250 N. Virginia St., tel. 702/329–0881). This was the first major casino in Nevada, begun by Raymond "Pappy" Smith and his son Harold in 1935. It was the establishment that advertised HAROLD'S CLUB OR BUST on billboards across California. Today Harold's is still prominent at Virginia Street and Casino Center, in front of the Reno arch. Harold's has no hotel rooms, just casino space and restaurants with nonsmoking sections. Like the Nevada Club, Harold's has many three-reel slots from the 1950s, along with a collection of more than 500 historic guns, the oldest dating to the 1500s. Out front you'll see one of the prettiest murals in town, a portrayal of pioneers camped out in the mountains, with flowing blue water separating them from the Indians on the opposite bank. Harold's, the legend says, is dedicated in all humility to those who blazed the trail.

5 Fitzgerald's (255 N. Virginia St., tel. 702/786–3663). The concept of the Fitz, now extended to Vegas, had its start in Reno, where the original stands proudly on Virginia Street opposite Harold's. The large green casino is the home of good luck, Irish themes, and leprechauns. On the second floor, in the Blarney Castle, patrons can walk wishing steps, rub the belly of Ho-Tei (the god of good fortune), and touch a lucky horseshoe. But don't be conned—more people lose here than win every day, or the Fitz would have closed long ago.

6 Flamingo Hilton (255 N. Sierra St., tel. 702/322–1111). What was originally Del Webb's Sahara in the 1970s, and the Reno Hilton for much of the 1980s, was transformed into the Flamingo Hilton in 1989. A multimillion-dollar remodeling brought a carbon copy of the Vegas Flamingo to the Biggest Little City in the World. The large pink-feather neon signs that hang outside cast a bright pink neon glow in the casino, and the tables are newly plushed with green felt. While there are a few $2 tables, most minimums are $3 or more.

7 Circus Circus (500 N. Sierra St., tel. 702/329–0711). At the northern end of Virginia Street stands the familiar large neon clown waving hello and sucking a lollipop. This version of the Circus Circus sign—and the casino—is a lot smaller than the one in Las Vegas, but it's just as unfriendly to the motorist. There is no car entrance up front, and it's difficult to find the parking facilities, especially if you aren't a registered guest of the hotel. Yet for visitors with children, Circus Circus is easily the best Virginia Street stop. Complete with clowns, games, funhouse mirrors, and circus acts, the midway (overlooking the casino floor) is open from 9 AM to 2 AM. While this Circus Circus is a lot less crowded than the one in Las Vegas, it's still packed, and the floor layout is confusing.

8 Ponderosa (515 S. Virginia St., tel. 702/786–6820). The owners of this new casino came up with a great idea for Nevada gaming:

Reno and Lake Tahoe 164

a 100% smoke-free hotel. Cigarettes, pipes, and cigars are not allowed on the premises, and the effect is breathtaking. A small casino on the southern end of Virginia Street, the Ponderosa has shopping mall–style parking out front and plenty of $2 twenty-one tables and nickel slots inside.

⑨ Peppermill (2707 S. Virginia St., tel. 702/826–2121). Those who prefer the gaudy, glitzy craziness of Las Vegas to the more sedate Reno scene will love the Peppermill. In terms of both noise and decor, this is the loudest casino in town. Neon signs sit atop each section of the room, and the dealers wear shiny vests that sparkle in the neon light. Unlike most other Reno casinos, the Peppermill captures the Vegas touch in the cigarette girls who patrol the room with "Cigarettes, cigars, tiparillos?"

For a breath of fresh air and relief from the casinos and crowds, walk about four blocks west along the Truckee River until you **⑩** reach **Wingfield Park.** From here you can catch a beautiful glimpse of the river and its environs.

To explore Reno further, head north on Virginia Street until you reach the University of Nevada's Reno campus. The university, founded in Elko, Nevada, in 1874, moved to Reno in 1885 and now enrolls more than 10,000 students. Best known for its business and mining schools, the Reno campus sprawls over more than 200 acres.

⑪ Further north is the **Fleischmann Planetarium,** with a 6-foot-diameter model of the earth and moon, computer-based exhibits, a telescope, and science quiz games. In the meteorite collection is one meteor that you can handle. The planetarium programs special shows that change periodically. *1600 Virginia St., tel. 702/784–4812. Admission: $4 adults, $2.50 children under 13 and senior citizens. Children under 6 not admitted to evening shows. Open weekdays from 8 AM, weekends from 10:30 AM.*

⑫ At the northern end of the university grounds, the **Nevada Historical Society** has much to satisfy the visitor interested in Nevada's past. A permanent exhibit surveys mining activities, gambling, the Victorian era, and Native Americans. Additional special exhibits change regularly. Native American artifacts, beadwork, and basketry are also on display, and a research library that specializes in Nevada and the Great Basin is open to the public. *1650 N. Virginia St., tel. 702/789–0190. Contribution: $1. Open Tues.–Sat. 10–5, Sun. noon–5. Research library closed weekends.*

Exploring Virginia City

Numbers in the margin correspond with the numbered points of interest on the Virginia City map.

Head south from Reno on U.S. 395 and take the Highway 341 turnoff to Virginia City.

The Comstock Lode, one of the largest gold and silver ore discoveries of the 19th century, created a boomtown in Virginia City as the prospect of wealth lured new residents by the thousands and led to the construction of mansions and saloons alike. Today Virginia City looks just like the 1870s Gold Rush community it used to be. The streets are made of wood, and the city adheres firmly to the Old West theme.

Bucket of Blood Saloon, **4**
Chamber of Commerce, **1**
Chollar Mansion, **9**
Delta Saloon, **5**
Mackay Mansion, **8**
Mark Twain Museum of Memories, **3**
Mark Twain Museum, **2**
Virginia and Truckee Railroad, **7**
The Way It Was Museum, **6**

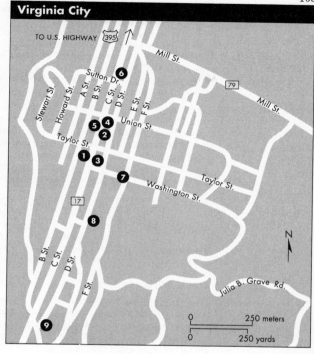

Because the town is so small—there's only one commercial street, and business establishments don't always have numbered addresses—parking spaces are hard to find. When you arrive, it's best to park where you can and spend your time walking about town. Most visitors will stroll for a couple of hours on C Street, take a 30-minute railroad ride, look for souvenirs, and grab a bite to eat before going on to Carson City.

❶ To orient yourself, you might well begin at the Virginia City **Chamber of Commerce** (N. C St., tel. 702/847-0311), which will probably direct you down C Street to the Mark Twain Museum.

Samuel Clemens, then in his twenties, lived in the area for a couple of years and reported on the legislature and other subjects for the *Territorial Enterprise* and other local newspapers. It was here that he first used the name "Mark Twain," and later he wrote of those early days in *Roughing It*. His memory lives
❷ on in the **Mark Twain Museum,** where you'll find his copy desk, typewriter, an original printing press, and other artifacts. *S. C St., tel. 702/847-0525. Admission: $1 adults, 50¢ children, free under 12. Open daily 10-5.*

One block south, at the corner of C and Taylor streets, a second
❸ museum, the **Mark Twain Museum of Memories,** commemorates Twain's career in Virginia City through many period items and exhibits on Virginia City history. *C and Taylor Sts., tel. 702/847-0454. Open March-Sept., daily 10-5.*

Reno and Lake Tahoe 166

For a thirst quencher and a taste of Old West "hospitality," consider the **Bucket of Blood Saloon** (N. C St., tel. 702/847–0322), the host to many a Friday night brawl back in 1876 (and that's how it got its name). Today it offers drinks and gaming, a wonderful view of the mountains, and a piano-banjo duo that plays the old tunes. The original 30-foot wood bar still stands, along with old pictures, guns, bottles, and swords. The Bucket of Blood T-shirt is a classic.

Another Old West establishment, the **Delta Saloon** (N. C St., tel. 702/847–0789), is home to the famous "suicide table." Actually a faro table that was later converted into a blackjack table, it was here that three owners committed suicide. Folks line up to see this free attraction even though it isn't much to look at. Following the viewing, you might have a drink in the saloon or play the slots. There are video games to occupy the kids.

For further insight into local history, walk north to the intersection of D and Sutton streets, where you'll find **The Way It Was Museum.** A 16-minute color video describes the history of the Comstock Lode, and the museum holds an extensive collection of mining artifacts, among them a working model of an early water-powered stamp mill, costumed mannequins, mining equipment, and a blacksmith shop. *D and Sutton Sts., tel. 702/847–0766. Admission: $1.50. Open daily 9–5:30.*

Turn now and walk southeast toward F and Washington streets and the celebrated old **Virginia and Truckee Railroad.** In its heyday it had as many as 45 trains arriving and departing Virginia City daily. Completed in 1869, the line hauled millions of dollars in gold and silver ore from the Comstock mines. Today the steam-powered train makes 30-minute rail trips 10 times a day through the old mining area. Passengers have the choice of riding in the open car or in the partially covered car. *Washington and F Sts., tel. 702/847–0380. Admission: $3.25 adults, $1.50 children, free under 5. Open Memorial Day–Sept., daily; first ride at 10:30, last ride at 5:45.*

Head over to D Street to visit the history-rich **Mackay Mansion.** Tours of this Victorian-style home are offered. *D and Flowery Sts., tel. 702/847–0173. Admission: $3. Open Memorial Day–Sept., daily 10–6; Oct.–May, daily 11–5.*

Continue along to the junction of D and C streets for a look at the **Chollar Mansion** (565 S. D St., tel. 702/847–9777). Built in 1861, the former office of a mine superintendent is now a bed-and-breakfast. The old Comstock offices have been converted into bedrooms decorated in a Victorian style that lends to the charm of the building. Three rooms are available for boarding.

Exploring Carson City

For the trip to Carson City, head south on Highway 341, turn west on U.S. 50, and continue for about 3 miles until you come to U.S. 395.

While there's little to do in Carson City, you'll always be able to boast that you visited the smallest state capital in America, where Nevada gambling was legalized in 1931. Today the city is almost a ghost town, with only a few places open for business among the boarded-up stores and casinos. Ormsby House is the major hotel and casino; other attractions include the Carson

Reno 167

Nugget Casino, the Carson Station Casino, the State Capitol Building, a state history museum, a number of handsome 19th-century mansions, and the governor's residence. For shopping and other activities, local residents leave town for the strips of shopping malls, K Marts, and fast-food chains that line the roads to and from the city.

A visit to the **Nevada State Museum**—the former Carson Mint, across from the Carson Nugget Casino—will brief you on local history. During the Civil War era, in an attempt to raise money for the Union, Congress authorized the hasty construction of this mint, where some $50 million in silver and gold was coined in the mid-1800s. Today the museum hosts exhibits on early mining days, antique gaming devices, and a gift shop well stocked with Nevada souvenirs. *600 N. Carson St., tel. 702/885–4810. Admission: $1.50 adults. Open daily 8:30–4:30.*

While you're in the town center, you might take a self-guided tour of the **State Capitol Building.** With its impressive dome, large green lawn, Alaskan marble halls, and interesting murals, this is easily one of the prettiest capitols in the country. The murals depict Nevada history and contain drawings of gold, silver, sulfur, nickel, iron, and other ores significant to Nevada's past. While the governor still maintains an office here, most governmental activity takes place across the street, in the newer legislative building. *101 N. Carson St., tel. 702/885–5030. Admission free. Open daily 8–5 for self-guided tours.*

About 2 miles south of the capital complex, off U.S. 395, the **Nevada State Railroad Museum,** a branch of the Nevada State Museum, features four antique locomotives that ride the tracks alongside the highway. *2180 S. Carson St., tel. 702/885–5168. Contribution. Open Wed.–Sun. 8:30–4:30.*

What to See and Do with Children

Circus Circus. This is one of Reno's big kiddie attractions. Styled like the Las Vegas casino, the second floor boasts free circus acts, funhouse mirrors, and a large midway with carnival games. Parents can dump the kids upstairs if they choose and head downstairs to hit the slots and games. *500 N. Sierra St., tel. 702/329–0711. Midway open daily 9 AM–2 AM.*

Wild Waters. Opened in 1989, this is the first water park in the Reno-Sparks area. Its 11 acres feature slides and body flumes, and there's a kiddie wading-area. *250 Boxington Ave., Sparks, tel. 702/359–2927. Admission: $12.95 adults, $9.95 children 4–11. Open Memorial Day–Labor Day, daily 11–7.*

John Ascuaga's Nugget. This isn't much, but kids who like to see elephants can catch a free glimpse of Bertha. *1100 Nugget Ave., Sparks, tel. 702/356–3300. Open daily 10–2.*

The Great Basin Adventure. A covered children's history park, the Great Basin has seven exhibits that include a mining area, a dinosaur pit, and a children's petting zoo. *1502 Washington St., Reno, tel. 702/785–4844. Admission: $2 adults, $1 children. Open May–Sept., Tues.–Sun. 10–5.*

Harrah's Auto Museum. Only a shell of what it once was when William Harrah was alive, the collection still features more than 220 antique and classic automobiles. Harrah began buying

Reno and Lake Tahoe
168

vintage autos in 1948 with the purchase of a 1911 Maxwell and a 1911 Ford. When Holiday Inn bought the company in 1986, many of the jewels of the collection were sold. Among those that remain are Elvis Presley's 1973 Cadillac Eldorado, John Wayne's 1953 Corvette, and Al Jolson's Cadillac. Harrah's moved to a new address late in 1989. *10 Lake St. S, Reno, tel. 702/333-9300. Admission: $6.50 adults, $5.50 senior citizens, $2.50 children 6–15. Open daily 9:30–5:30; closed Christmas.*

Wedding Chapels

Like Las Vegas, the Reno area is flush with wedding chapels that take advantage of Nevada's liberal marriage laws. A marriage license can be obtained in the state of Nevada without blood test or waiting period, and it's valid anywhere in the state. A license may be obtained for $27 (cash only) at the Marriage Bureau in the Washoe County Courthouse for anyone 18 years of age or older. Legal ID with proof of age is required. Couples age 16–18 can obtain marriage licenses with their parents' or a legal guardian's consent, given in person or in writing (and notarized) to the county clerk.

Civil marriages in Reno and Sparks are performed by the **commissioner of civil marriages** (195 S. Sierra St., Reno 89510, tel. 702/328-3275).

Many wedding chapels in Reno offer quick à la carte weddings that begin at around $50 for the service (photos, music, and food are extra) plus a $25 tip for the minister. Three wedding chapels on Virginia Street are: **Cupid's Chapel of Love** (629 N. Virginia St., tel. 702/323-2930), **Reno Wedding Chapel** (655 N. Virginia St., tel. 702/323-5818), and **Wedding Bells Chapel** (17 S. Virginia St., tel. 702/329-0909).

Shopping

Park Lane Mall (310 Plumb La. at Virginia St., tel. 702/825-7878). Anchored by Sears and Weinstock's and located between downtown Reno and the airport, the Park Lane is the largest mall in town. In addition to the department stores, there are toys, jewelry, men's and women's apparel, book shops, and fast food.

Old Town Mall (4001 S. Virginia St., tel. 702/826-2141). The mall closest to downtown Reno, Old Town is just two blocks from the Reno-Sparks Convention Center. Among the 25 shops are Birkenstocks of Reno, Brenners, and a Cinema III theater.

Harold's Club Antique Slots (250 N. Virginia St., tel. 702/329-0881). Want to take home a classic slot machine? That can be arranged at Harold's, where prices begin at around $1,000.

Parker's Western Wear (151 N. Sierra St., tel. 702/323-4481). The oldest and certainly the largest Western shop in town extends from one end of Sierra Street to the other. Established in 1919, Parker's is an old-fashioned shop with hardwood floors, autographed celebrity photos on the wall, and large stocks of jeans, boots, shirts, jackets, and other cowboy and cowgirl duds.

Reno

Sports and Fitness

Biking This being the land of big hills and mountains, mountain biking seems to be the preferred mode of cycling, yet one can take leisurely rides through Reno along the paths that follow the Truckee River. Bicycle rentals are available at **Bikes Etc.** (901 W. Moana La., tel. 702/827–2128) and **Reno Bicycle Center** (418 W. 5th St., tel. 702/323–1221).

Boating National parks and resorts in close proximity to Reno offer boat, water-ski, and jet-ski rentals. Two boating facilities in the Reno and Lake Tahoe area are **Anchorage Marina** (Hwy. 89, 2½ mi north of the "Y," South Lake Tahoe, tel. 916/541–1777) and **North Tahoe Marina** (7360 N. Lake Blvd., Tahoe Vista, tel. 916/546–8248).

Golf When it comes to teeing off, Reno cannot match the year-round sunny desert terrain of Las Vegas, yet several 18-hole courses are in the area. These courses operate seasonally, most of them closing in the winter, so it would be wise to phone ahead before planning a visit to **Lakeridge Golf Course** (1200 Razor Back Rd., Reno, tel. 702/825–2200), **Wildcreek Golf Course** (3500 Sullivan La., Sparks, tel. 702/673–3100), or **Incline Village Golf Course** (955 Fairway Blvd., Incline Village, tel. 702/832–1144).

Hiking Many hiking trails have been established in the Sierra Nevada. Detailed information about hiking in the Reno–Carson City area is available from the **Carson Ranger District, U.S. Forest Service** (tel. 702/882–2766). For information about hikes in Lake Tahoe, contact the **Lake Tahoe Basin Management Unit, U.S. Forest Service** (tel. 916/573–2600).

Trails **Mt. Rose.** One of the highest peaks hereabouts, Mt. Rose offers panoramas of Lake Tahoe, the Sierra Nevada, and Reno. The 5-mile trail's trailhead is located at the Mt. Rose summit on the right side of Highway 431, en route to Lake Tahoe from Reno, where you'll find a dirt road next to the maintenance building.

Ophir Creek. Here the trail leads to two lakes, Rock and Price, and views of Carson City and Washoe Valley. The start is at Davis Creek Park, 17 miles south of Reno on U.S. 395, and for 5 miles the walk is uphill.

Mariette Lake. A 5-mile hike by the lake shows off the west side of Lake Tahoe. The trail begins at Spooner Lake Park on Highway 28, north of the junction with Highway 50.

Rafting Gliding down the Truckee River on a raft from Tahoe City can be a pleasant way to cool off in the summer heat. Raft tours and/or rentals are available at **Fanny Bridge Raft Rentals** (185 River Rd., Tahoe City, CA, tel. 916/583–3021) and **Truckee River Rafting Center** (205 River Rd., Tahoe City, CA, tel. 916/583–5606).

Skiing Cross-country skiing is a great way to escape the crowds and *Cross-Country* still experience the winter wonderlands. **Spooner Lake Cross-Country Ski Area** (tel. 702/749–5349), 12 miles south of Incline Village, offers 30 miles of varied terrain and guided tours as well.

Downhill The Reno and Lake Tahoe area, with a larger concentration of ski resorts than anyplace else in the country, has been rated Number One for skiing in the United States by Rand McNally. The 16 alpine resorts here offer many varieties of terrain, and

Reno and Lake Tahoe 170

most of the resorts are within 45 minutes of Reno. With a season's average snowfall of 350 inches, skiing is usually available six months of the year.

Alpine Meadows Ski Area (Box 5279, Tahoe City, CA 95730, tel. 916/583-4232 or 800/824-6348). This resort 45 miles from Reno has the longest season in the area. It has a height of 8,637 feet, a vertical drop of 1,800 feet, 13 lifts, and 100 trails.

Heavenly Valley Ski Resort (Ski Run Blvd., Box AT, South Lake Tahoe, CA 95705, tel. 916/541-1330). With nine mountain peaks and 20 square miles of ski terrain, this resort offers the highest peak in Tahoe: 10,100 feet, with a vertical drop of 3,600 feet.

Squaw Valley USA (Box 2007, Olympic Valley, CA 93730, tel. 916/583-6985). The site of the 1960 Winter Olympics, Squaw Valley has 8,300 acres of skiable terrain; its highest peak reaches 8,900 feet, with a vertical drop of 1,502 feet.

Ski rentals are available at **Alpine Sports** (971 W. Moana La., Reno, tel. 702/827-3205), **Hyatt Lake Tahoe Ski Shop** (111 Country Club Dr., Incline Village, tel. 702/831-1111), and **Outdoorsman of Lake Tahoe** (910 Tahoe Blvd., Incline Village, tel. 702/831-0446).

Snowmobiling **Mt. Lake Adventures** (288 Village Blvd., Incline Village, tel. 702/831-4202 or 800/433-5253) offers 100 miles of snowmobile tours through the wilderness.

Tennis **Lakeridge Tennis Club** (6000 Plumas St., Reno, tel. 702/827-4500) has 12 outdoor courts and four indoor courts. **Bally's Reno** (2500 E. 2nd St., Reno, tel. 702/789-2000) has five outdoor courts and three indoor courts. **Tahoe Marina** (N. Lake Blvd., Tahoe City, CA, tel. 916/583-2365) has six outdoor courts.

Windsurfing One of the thrills of coming to the Reno and Lake Tahoe area is partaking in the sport of windsurfing. The most popular spots for this activity are on Lake Tahoe, Washoe Lake, and the lake at Paradise Park in Reno. Lessons and rental equipment are available at **Alpine Sports** (971 W. Moana La., Reno, tel. 702/825-8803) and **Bobo Sheehan's Ski Co.** (1200 S. Wells Ave., Reno, tel. 702/786-5111).

Dining

The number of restaurants in the Reno area may be smaller than that in Vegas, but the kinds of dining opportunities are similar, from the hotel restaurants, buffets, and coffee shops to the steak houses and ethnic eateries. Restaurants are listed in order of their price category.

Category	Cost*
Very Expensive	over $18
Expensive	$15–$18
Moderate	$7–$15
Inexpensive	under $7

average cost of a three-course dinner, per person, excluding drinks, service, and 7% sales tax

Reno   171

The following credit card abbreviations are used: AE, American Express; CB, Carte Blanche; D, Discover Card; DC, Diners Club; MC, MasterCard; and V, Visa.

Harrah's Steak House. Located within the usually busy Harrah's casino, this dark, romantic eatery has no view of slot machines to disrupt the warm ambience of the plush red booths and candlelight. Burgers, BLTs, and chicken sandwiches are available for lunch; the steaks, chops, chicken, and fish at dinner come with soup or salad and vegetables. *219 N. Center St. at Virginia St., tel. 702/786–3232. Reservations advised. Dress: casual, but no shorts. AE, CB, D, DC, MC, V. Very Expensive.*

Rapscallion Seafood House & Bar. Up to 30 varieties of fresh seafood are on the menu daily at this traditional French restaurant. Rapscallion prepares steaks and pastas, too, but the specialty is definitely fish. Calamari Rapscallion is deep-fried squid served with scallions and mushrooms; the Rapscallion Stew is made with clams, mussels, crab, shrimp, scallops, fish fillets, leeks, tomatoes, garlic, white wine, and fish bouillon. All entrées are served with soup or salad and vegetables. Salads, burgers, fish, and steak sandwiches are available at lunch. *1555 S. Wells Ave., tel. 702/323–1211. Reservations advised for dinner. Dress: casual. AE, MC, V. Expensive.*

Cantina Los Tres Hombres. In a small shopping plaza south of downtown you'll find this Mexican restaurant with bamboo and wood beams, round tables, a large bar with giant-screen TV, and free nachos during the bar's happy hour. Tacos, enchiladas, and tostadas are the main fare, and there's a make-your-own-burrito bar. Patio dining is available outdoors under the umbrellas. *7111 S. Virginia St. at Green Acres Plaza, tel. 702/852–0202. Reservations required for 8 or more. Dress: casual. AE, MC, V. Moderate.*

Christmas Tree Inn. This restaurant, about 30 miles from Reno en route to Lake Tahoe, stands 7,100 feet up in the mountains. It's a quiet lodge with a large stone fireplace and picture windows, a place where every day is Christmas. A well-decorated Christmas tree stands in the middle of the room, and ornaments hang all over the restaurant. The kitchen specializes in mahogany-broiled steaks and in chicken, chops, and fish; all entrées come with salad, bread, and baked potato. Hot toddies are also served. *20007 Mt. Rose Hwy., tel. 702/849–0127. Reservations advised. Dress: casual (but no shorts). Dinner only; cocktails from 3 PM. AE, MC, V. Moderate.*

John Ascuaga's Nugget. Although the buffets here are relatively expensive at $12–$14 per person, they are the best. The food is fresh, and carvers are ready to serve you. *1100 Nugget Ave., Sparks, tel. 702/356–3300 or 800/648–1177. Reservations advised 1 hour before buffet begins; parties of 10 or more must call ahead. Dress: casual. AE, MC, V. Moderate.*

19th Hole Restaurant. Located right on the Lakeridge golf course, the 19th Hole is where local residents send those who appreciate great views. At night, seated in the plush red chairs of the restaurant atop a hill, you can see the sights of Reno through picture windows. At lunchtime you can watch golfers at work, the mountains in the background. The lunch menu consists of sandwiches and burgers; seafood, steaks, and chicken are served at dinner. All entrées come with soup du jour or salad and vegetable. *1200 Razor Back Rd., tel. 702/825–1250. Reservations advised. Dress: casual. AE, MC, V. Moderate.*

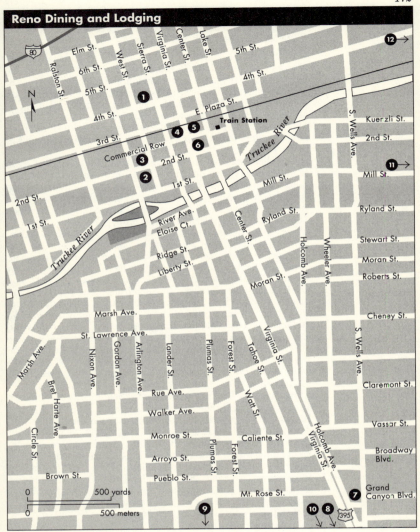

Bally's Reno, **11**
Cantina Los Tres Hombres, **10**
Circus Circus, **1**
Comstock Hotel, **2**
Fitzgerald's Hotel, **4**
Flamingo Hilton, **3**
General Store (Nugget), **12**
Harrah's, **6**
Harrah's Steak House, **6**
John Ascuaga's Nugget, **12**
19th Hole Restaurant, **9**
Peppermill Hotel, **8**
Presidential Car, **5**
Rapscallion Seafood House & Bar, **7**

Reno

Presidential Car. The Presidential Car, on the seventh floor of Harold's Club, is another dining room with picture windows that reveal the city of Reno. The decor has a dark, 1900s-era look, with lots of wood. The fare is steaks, veal, fish, and chicken, all served with soup or salad, baked potato or rice. *Harold's Club, S. Virginia St., tel. 702/329–0881. Reservations advised. Dress: casual. AE, MC, V. Moderate.*

Circus Circus. As in Las Vegas, every major hotel and casino here has low-priced buffets that offer lots of food for very little money. Circus Circus has the most famous of them, with breakfast for $2.50 and dinner (40 items) for $3.50. *500 N. Sierra St., tel. 702/329–0711. No reservations. Dress: casual. No credit cards. Inexpensive.*

General Store. One of the better coffee shops in town is the General Store at the Nugget, a large, Barbary Coast–style setting. Open 24 hours, it offers an extensive children's menu along with your basic coffee-shop fare: burgers, chicken-fried steak, Jell-O, salads. *1100 Nugget Ave., Sparks, tel. 702/356–3300. No reservations. Dress: casual. AE, CB, DC, MC, V. Inexpensive.*

Lodging

Hotel rooms in Reno are as plentiful as they are in Las Vegas, but they can be more difficult to obtain during the peak season, from July 4 to Labor Day. Still, the principle remains one of getting you in the door and into the casino, and special deals on rooms are common. When planning your trip, your first move should be to call the hotel's toll-free 800 reservation number and ask what package rates are available.

Category	Cost*
Very Expensive	over $80
Expensive	$60–$80
Moderate	$50–$60
Inexpensive	under $50

All prices are for a standard double room, excluding service charge and 7% tax.

The following credit card abbreviations are used: AE, American Express; CB, Carte Blanche; D, Discover Card; DC, Diners Club; MC, MasterCard; and V, Visa.

Flamingo Hilton. The former Reno Hilton was spruced up in 1989 and given a new casino, new neon signs out front, new restaurants, and remodeled accommodations. The Flamingo's medium-size guest rooms have white walls and green curtains, and from either side of the hotel the rooms overlook the Reno mountains. The Flamingo is one block west of Virginia Street. *255 N. Sierra St., 89501, tel. 702/322–1111 or 800/732–2111. 604 units. Facilities: 4 restaurants, lounge. AE, D, DC, MC, V. Expensive.*

Bally's Reno. The tallest (26 floors) hotel in Reno is quite literally in the middle of nowhere. While most Reno hotels are in downtown Reno (the Nugget is in downtown Sparks), Bally's is out near the airport, tucked away in its own corner of the city, surrounded by a huge parking lot and little else of interest. The

Reno and Lake Tahoe 174

former MGM Grand Hotel still has Leo the Lion on its doors, and carpets and large portraits of movie stars in the hallways. The rooms are gaudy in the Vegas manner yet quite large, with green or orange color schemes and king-size beds. The picture windows offer spectacular views of the mountains. Bally's has the largest casino in Reno, 100,000 square feet of tables and slots, and a large shopping area downstairs where T-shirts, jewelry, clothing, and leather goods are to be found. In 1989 the showroom embarked on a star-performer policy, and the likes of Wayne Newton and Frank Sinatra now play the Bally. *2500 E. 2nd St., 89595, tel. 702/789-2000. 2001 units. Facilities: tennis courts, pool, 24-hour bowling alley, 7 restaurants, lounge, shopping arcade, health club, showroom. AE, CB, DC, MC, V. Moderate.*

Fitzgerald's Hotel. Across the street from Harrah's and the Reno arch stands a large green hotel of Irish luck. Unlike the Las Vegas version, which offers green rooms, the Reno Fitz accommodations have a maroon color scheme—with green in the curtains. The owners of the Fitz also own Harold's Club and the Nevada Club casinos on the other side of Virginia Street. *255 N. Virginia St., 89513, tel. 702/786-3663 or 800/648-5022. 345 units. Facilities: 2 restaurants. AE, DC, MC, V. Moderate.*

Harrah's. The largest hotel in downtown Reno is the most luxurious. Harrah's large rooms are decorated in a conservative white and brown, with king-size beds and plush bedspreads. Both sides of the hotel offer picture windows with views of the mountains. Because the lobby is on the second floor, you'll have to lug your bags through the casino. Stars such as Bill Cosby, Sammy Davis Jr., and Jay Leno perform in Harrah's showroom. *219 N. Center St. at Virginia St., tel. 702/329-4422 or 800/648-3773. 565 units. Facilities: showroom, pool, tennis courts, health club, 4 restaurants. AE, MC, V. Moderate.*

John Ascuaga's Nugget. Don't let the out-of-the-way location in downtown Sparks put you off; the Nugget has a lot going for it. As if to compensate for the distance from Reno, the management and staff appear to try harder. Moreover, the Nugget has some of the largest and most luxurious rooms in town—and at lower rates than Harrah's. The Nugget began in 1958 as a small casino and coffee shop and grew to be one of the larger properties in town. A convention center area was added in 1989. One nice touch has the elevators adjacent to the check-in section, thereby eliminating long, baggage-laden treks through the casino. The Nugget has free shuttle bus service to downtown Reno, and kids will enjoy seeing Bertha, the elephant who lives at the Nugget. *1100 Nugget Ave., Sparks 89520, tel. 702/356-3300 or 800/648-1177. 610 units. Facilities: pool, 6 restaurants, showroom, lounge. AE, DC, MC, V. Moderate.*

Peppermill Hotel. The home of Reno's most garish casino has plush, sedate rooms upstairs with dark blue curtains, lampshades, bedspreads, and furniture. While the Peppermill is 3 miles from downtown, it's near the shopping centers, and local residents love it. The singles bar and the slots regularly win top honors in the *Reno Gazette*'s "best of Reno" awards. *2707 S. Virginia St., tel. 702/826-2121 or 800/648-6992. 542 rooms. Facilities: pool, 3 restaurants, lounge. AE, DC, MC, V. Moderate.*

Circus Circus. Although this is a smaller version of the giant Las Vegas property, it still has two sprawling towers. The mar-

Reno 175

quee promises: ROOMS AVAILABLE. IF NOT, WE'LL PLACE YOU. (On a recent visit I found another notice at the registration desk: PLACEMENT SERVICE CLOSED.) If you do get a room here—and these are easily the most inexpensive rooms in a major downtown Reno hotel—you'll find the decor a bit more conservative than that of the Vegas Circus Circus; the small rooms have orange wallpaper, twin beds, and views of the mountains. *500 N. Sierra St. at Virginia St., 89513, tel. 702/329–0711 or 800/648–5010. 1,625 units. Facilities: 2 restaurants, lounge, wedding chapel, free circus acts, carnival midway for children. AE, CB, DC, MC, V. Inexpensive.*

Comstock Hotel. Two blocks west of Virginia Street is another in a series of Nevada casinos that aims to re-create the Old West. Here the subject is the mining activity of the 1860s and 1870s in nearby Virginia City and Ely. The glass-walled elevators give the impression that you are riding in mine shafts. The rooms, small and conservative, have blue bedspreads and views of the mountains. *200 W. 2nd St., 89501, tel. 702/329–1880 or 800/648–4866. 309 units. Facilities: 3 restaurants, pool, lounge. MC, V. Inexpensive.*

Lake Tahoe

The largest alpine lake in North America, Lake Tahoe offers the visitor a terrain strikingly different from the desert landscapes that characterize much of Nevada. At an elevation of 7,000–9,000 feet in the Sierra Nevada range, lush green trees abound and the mountains remain snowcapped most of the year. While Lake Tahoe is shared by California and Nevada, and most of the lodging opportunities are on the California side, this guide explores the Nevada side of the lake.

Exploring Lake Tahoe

Numbers in the margin correspond with the numbered points of interest on the Lake Tahoe map.

To reach Lake Tahoe from Reno, travel south on U.S. 395 to the Mt. Rose Highway turnoff (431).

● A drive of about an hour will take you into **Incline Village,** one of the most pleasant (and most expensive) places to visit in the North Tahoe area. Since it's up in the mountains, it's not as hot as Reno, and being a "planned" community, it has only one casino, the Hyatt Lake Tahoe. Incline is a small town with a shopping center and restaurants nearby, a classic wood-lodge community, very low key, a nice place to take in the sights. The Incline Village **Chamber of Commerce** (702/831–4440 or 800/468–2463) or the Douglas **Chamber of Commerce** (702/588–4591) can provide further information about the area.

● Two miles southwest of Incline, on Highway 28, the attractive community of **Crystal Bay** has two casinos where the atmosphere is more relaxed than that of the gaming houses in Reno.

The **Cal-Neva Lodge** (2 Stateline Rd., Crystal Bay, tel. 702/832–4000) is the hotel and casino that Frank Sinatra co-owned for a short time in the 1950s, until he was seen in the company of a prominent gangster. The Nevada Gaming Control Board forced Sinatra to sell his share in the property, on the grounds that it was illegal for gaming licensees to hobnob with known mobsters. Of all the North Tahoe hotel and casinos, the Cal-Neva best suggests Yosemite—a classic wood lodge in the mountains with stuffed deer and elk mounted on the wall above the stone fireplace. A welcome touch are the picture windows that look out on the lake, interspersed with rows of slots and table games.

● Fans of the longtime television series "Bonanza" will want to travel east from Incline on Highway 28 to visit the **Ponderosa Ranch.** Here are the Cartwrights' ranch house, a Western town, and a saloon. Horseback riding and hayrides are available. *Hwy. 28, tel. 702/831–0691. Admission: $6.50 adults, $4.50 children 5–11. Open daily 9:30–5.*

● Traveling south along the east side of the lake, you'll come across **Sand Harbor Beach,** a popular recreation area that often reaches capacity by 11 AM on weekends (be here early). In July the beach is host to a pop music festival; in August it's the site of a **Shakespeare festival** (tel. 916/583–9048) whose performances take place on the beach under the stars.

177

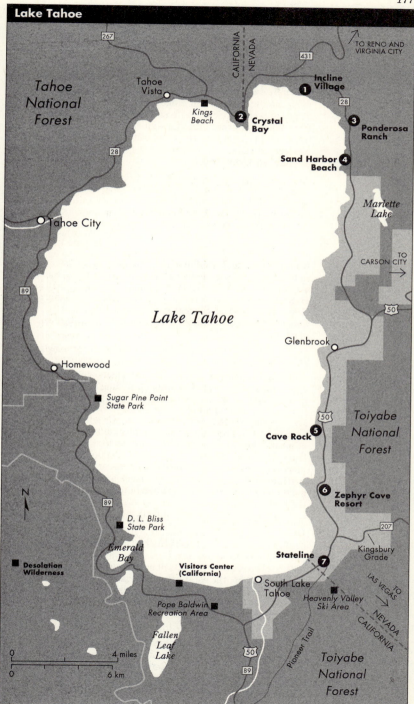

Reno and Lake Tahoe

Next you'll meet U.S. 50 again and encounter scenic vistas. The
⑤ road passes through **Cave Rock,** 25 yards of solid stone. Four
⑥ miles beyond Cave Rock you'll come to **Zephyr Cove Resort** (tel.
702/588–6644), whose beach and marina are home to tour boats.
Just ahead you can see the towers of the casinos at Stateline.

When folks think of Nevada's Lake Tahoe, they tend to have the
⑦ South Tahoe town of **Stateline** in mind. Stateline is a city to
drive into, park the car in a hotel parking lot, and stroll around.
There are only five casinos here, and visitors tend to gravitate
from one to the other. Yet Stateline has more games, entertainment, and restaurants than any other lakeside community in
western Nevada, so it is often crowded; in the summertime it
can be a zoo of activity.

Although gaming brought fame to the area, the town of
Stateline drew widest attention in 1960, when the Winter
Olympic Games were held at nearby Squaw Valley. In spite of
the prestige involved, the community remains small enough
that nearly all businesses give Stateline and Highway 50 as
their address (even though many use post office box numbers
for out-of-state mailings).

Gaming came to Stateline in the mid-1940s when the entrepre-
neur Harvey Gross opened Harvey's Wagonwheel Saloon and
Gambling Hall. Bill Harrah joined the fray in 1955 with
Harrah's Tahoe across the street. Then came the Sahara Tahoe
(1965; now the High Sierra) and Caesars Tahoe (1980). As in so
many Nevada communities, an exploration of Stateline is a tour
of casinos.

If you come into town from the right direction, **Harvey's Resort
Hotel and Casino** (Hwy. 50 and Stateline, tel. 702/588–2401), on
the Stateline border, will be the first casino you meet. Tahoe's
oldest casino is a huge, bustling, sprawling affair that occupies
several floors. A plan downstairs tells you where everything is,
but finding it amid all the hubbub may not be easy. Harvey's
accommodates visitors with a video guide and staff positioned
near the front door (a welcome addition). Table minimums, as
at most Tahoe casinos, tend to be on the high side, but because
Harvey's is the easiest to figure out, you may find playing here
more comfortable than elsewhere. With Caesars and Harrah's
getting most of the tour bus traffic, Harvey's might also be a
good place to visit first, particularly when you hope to get into
the restaurants.

The biggest casino in Stateline, **Harrah's Lake Tahoe Casino
Hotel** (Hwy. 50 and Stateline, tel. 702/588–6606), has the most
confusing layout. Yet this is the house where the biggest stars
perform—Bill Cosby, Jay Leno, Sammy Davis Jr.—and the
hotel has an excellent reputation and draws the largest crowds.
Opened in 1955, the establishment has expanded over the years
and now seems to go on for miles. Like most Nevada casinos,
Harrah's Lake Tahoe has signs telling you where to go that are
of little help.

Business was so good at Harrah's that its owners, the Holiday
Inn Corporation, built another casino next door. **Bill's** (Hwy.
50 and Stateline, tel. 702/588–2455) is named for Bill Harrah,
the late owner of Harrah's, who died in 1978. There are no hotel
rooms here, just 10¢ popcorn, a McDonald's, and slots and table
games galore. The crowds are usually smaller than those at the
other, more famous Tahoe casinos.

Lake Tahoe 179

Of the four big Stateline casinos, **Del Webb's High Sierra Casino Hotel** (Hwy. 50 and Stateline, tel. 702/588–6211) is the one with the Old West theme that is so prevalent at Nevada gaming properties. The casino, however, is very much in the Vegas style, dark but glitzy with neon. Low minimums at the tables are rare here, for the South Tahoe area is usually busy, especially in the summertime.

Caesars Tahoe (Hwy. 50 and Stateline, tel. 702/588–3515) offers an experience quite different from that of the Vegas Caesars. Yes, the theme is Roman and the casino is packed, but few oval images are to be seen, the dealers wear bow ties instead of the green Roman shirts of Vegas, the cocktail waitresses don't wear their hair in buns, and no singing bellman is to be found. The house does have plenty of gaming tables and slot machines.

Dining

The price categories for restaurants in the Tahoe area are the same as those for the Reno area.

North Tahoe Area **Hugos.** A Hyatt restaurant, Hugos is the one place on the North Shore to come for dining with a view. Under the pressure of local fears of overcommercialization, this establishment has maintained its environment. Hugos is on the lake, and consequently it specializes in fish and duck dishes, along with steaks and salads. The large windows allow diners to enjoy the view, from a dark, woodsy, romantic setting. *111 Country Club Dr., Incline Village, tel. 702/831–1111. Reservations advised. Dress: casual. AE, CB, D, DC, MC, V. Dinner only. Very Expensive.*

Hacienda de la Sierra. A neighborhood taco bar with wood booths and floral wallpaper, Hacienda offers traditional Mexican eats (tostadas, burritos, fajitas, tacos) in a slightly upscale fashion. *933 Tahoe Blvd., Incline Village, tel. 702/831–8300. Reservations unnecessary. Dress: casual. AE, MC, V. Moderate.*

Alpine Jack's. Located downstairs in the Hyatt, this comfortable coffee shop offers breakfast, lunch, and dinner with little view other than that of the grounds. As there are no fast-food restaurants in Incline, Jack's is the only place you'll find a kids' menu (spaghetti, peanut butter and jelly, grilled cheese, burgers) at reasonable prices in an establishment where adults will feel comfortable. For the adults there are burgers, sandwiches, salads, and full-course dinners; meals are prepared with salt-free margarine and low-calorie salad dressing on request. *111 Country Club Dr., Incline Village, tel. 702/831–1111. No reservations. Dress: casual. AE, CB, D, DC, MC, V. Inexpensive.*

Cal-Neva Coffee Shop. Eggs, burgers, salads, and steaks are served from 7 AM until midnight before a wide lakeside view. *2 Stateline Rd., Crystal Bay, tel. 702/832–4000. Reservations unnecessary. Dress: casual. AE, CB, DC, MC, V. Inexpensive.*

South Tahoe Area **Summit/Forest.** Occupying rooms on the 18th floor of Harrah's, the Summit offers the best view in town and the option to dine buffet-style at the Forest for a more moderate price. The interior simulates a forest, with mock trees at each booth and picture windows overlooking the area. The dining-room menu

Reno and Lake Tahoe 180

includes steak, chicken, fish, and veal. *Harrah's, Hwy. 50 and Stateline, South Lake Tahoe, tel. 702/588–6611. Reservations required; expect a long wait for the buffet in the summer. Jacket advised. AE, CB, D, DC, MC, V. Very Expensive.*

Top of the Wheel. Yet another restaurant with a fantastic view, Top of the Wheel, on the 26th floor of Harvey's, faces the lake and the mountains. Among the Top's specialties are chicken breast teriyaki with pineapple and sesame seeds (and soup or salad, rice, potato or vegetable) and prime rib in a creamed horseradish sauce. *Harvey's, Hwy. 50 and Stateline, South Lake Tahoe, tel. 702/588–2411. Reservations advised. Dress: casual (but no shorts). AE, CB, D, DC, MC, V. Very Expensive.*

El Vaquero. Harvey's Mexican restaurant is downstairs, in the hotel shopping arcade, far from the slots and games tables. Decorated with wrought iron, a fountain, tiles, and an Old Mexico feel, El Vaquero serves traditional Mexican fare—enchiladas, etc.—and allows you the opportunity to put together your own taco. *Harvey's, Hwy. 50 and Stateline, South Lake Tahoe, tel. 702/588–2411. Reservations accepted. Dress: casual. AE, CB, D, DC, MC, V. Moderate.*

Primavera. This Caesars' Italian restaurant isn't as fancy as the one in Las Vegas, but its location in a corner of the hotel, beside the indoor swimming pool and health club, permits diners to watch the activity in the pool. The fare is classic Italian: chicken parmigiana, veal parmigiana, pizzas, salads, soups. *Caesars Tahoe, Hwy. 50 and Stateline, tel. 702/586–2025. Reservations required. Dress: casual (but no shorts). AE, CB, D, DC, MC, V. Moderate.*

Sierra. The Harrah's coffee shop features burgers, sandwiches, breakfasts, and full dinners. Its decor is Old West, with dark wood and plush blue booths. Specialties include grilled chicken marinated in lemon and garlic sauce, served with spinach, mushrooms, and tomatoes, and topped with smoked melted cheese; and the Arizona mixed grill—lamb chops, quail, and beef tournedos with béarnaise sauce. Both come with soup or salad, vegetables, and potato. Expect a wait in summertime. *Harrah's, Hwy. 50 and Stateline, South Lake Tahoe, tel. 702/588–6611. No reservations. Dress: casual. AE, CB, D, DC, MC, V. Inexpensive.*

Lodging

The price categories for accommodations in the Tahoe area are the same as those for the Reno area.

North Tahoe Area **Hyatt Lake Tahoe.** The one lakeside resort in the community has been undergoing reconstruction, a $10 million renovation intended to upgrade the guest rooms, all of which have a view of the lake. What were once basic hotel rooms have taken on a classic lodge feel, with dark wood, wood four-posters, and furniture to match. The hotel is a block from the beach, the only Nevada hotel and casino with beach access. The beach is available to guests, along with snack bar, motor sports rentals, and a lakeside restaurant—the only such establishment in North Tahoe. Day care for kids 3–12 is available free at nighttime and for $25 during the day. Of course, all these features will cost you; the Hyatt is the most expensive place to stay in North Lake Tahoe, with rates averaging $190 a night in the summer and $150 a night during other seasons. *111 Country Club Dr.,*

Lake Tahoe 181

Incline Village 89450, tel. 702/831-1111 or 800/233-1234. 460 units. Facilities: health club, tennis courts, lake, pool, 2 restaurants. AE, CB, D, DC, MC, V. Very Expensive.

Cal-Neva Lodge. At the Cal-Neva the rooms are decorated in Victorian fashion and have views of the lake. There is no official access to the lake, but hotel officials point out that Tahoe is only a five-minute walk away. *2 Stateline Rd., Crystal Bay 89402, tel. 702/832-4000 or 800/225-6382. 220 rooms. Facilities: pool, tennis courts, 3 restaurants. AE, CB, DC, MC, V. Expensive.*

Tahoe Biltmore. The former Nevada Club sits across the street from the Cal-Neva Lodge, and it's clearly a bargain for those seeking an alternative to the hustle and bustle of South Lake Tahoe and the expense of the Hyatt. Room rates average $50 a night and can be as low as $25, and the lake isn't far off. Built in 1946, the hotel is a 1950s-style resort, with dark wood and a rustic lodge feel, yet it isn't nearly as nice or as well kept as its more expensive neighbor across the street. The large, smoky casino has low table minimums and lots of slots. *5 Hwy. 28, Crystal Bay 89402, tel. 702/831-0660 or 800/245-8667. 95 rooms. Facilities: pool, 2 restaurants. AE, MC, V. Inexpensive.*

South Tahoe Area **Caesars Tahoe.** Finding your way to the registration desk at the back of the hotel is just half the battle; then you must walk several flights of stairs and pass many sections of the hotel before reaching the elevator. Once upstairs, you'll find plush, garish rooms whose dominant color is dark blue. Few rooms have round beds or mirrored ceilings, unlike the Vegas Caesars. The pool is indoors, and that can be delightful in December and February, when the mountains are covered with snow and the air is brisk. *Box 5800, Stateline 89449, tel. 702/588-3515. 446 units. Facilities: showroom, lounge, indoor pool, tennis courts, health club, 6 restaurants. AE, CB, DC, MC, V. Very Expensive.*

Del Webb's High Sierra Casino Hotel. The exterior of the High Sierra maintains the Old West theme, while indoors the Victorian-style rooms contribute further to the romantic alpine setting. *Box C, Stateline 89449, tel. 702/588-6211 or 800/648-3322. 537 units. Facilities: tennis courts, handball, racquetball, outdoor pool, health club, 3 restaurants. AE, MC, V. Very Expensive.*

Harrah's Lake Tahoe Casino Hotel. Although Harrah's has an inconvenient floor plan, with the registration desk at the back of the hotel and the elevators in the middle, the luxurious surroundings upstairs make up for the aggravation. Oriental art hangs on the walls, plush carpets greet you at the elevator, and the accommodations are rose colored, with curved picture windows that look onto the mountains and the lake. Some rooms have TV in the bathroom, and there's a sitting area beside every elevator. *Box 8, Stateline 89449, tel. 702/588-6606 or 800/648-3773. 540 units. Facilities: pool, tennis courts, 6 restaurants, showroom, lounge. AE, MC, V. Very Expensive.*

Harvey's Resort Hotel and Casino. Harvey's rooms are decorated with Colonial-style furniture, and they have round eating areas in front of the curved picture windows that overlook the mountains and the lake. *Box 128, Stateline 89449, tel. 702/588-2411 or 800/648-3361. 575 rooms. Facilities: pool, tennis courts, 5 restaurants, lounge. AE, MC, V. Very Expensive.*

Reno and Lake Tahoe

Nightlife

Most major casinos have showrooms where big-name entertainers perform nightly. Check Harrah's, Bally's Reno, John Ascuaga's Nugget, and Caesars Tahoe for performance times.

Rock-and-Roll Clubs
Del Mar Station (701 S. Virginia St., Reno, tel. 702/322–7200) has live music nightly.
Paul Revere's Kicks (tel. 702/786–7500) presents dance music and special theme nights throughout the week.
Turtles Night Club (Round Hill Mall, Hwy. 50, tel. 702/588–6766) offers live music, three bars, and several dance floors for a very "in" crowd.

Bars
Scruples Bar and Grill (9 W. Plum La., Reno, tel. 702/322–7171), a sports bar, is open 24 hours and attracts 49ers' fans.
The Fresh Ketch (Tahoe Keys Marina, South Lake Tahoe, tel. 916/541–5683) is popular spot with both local residents and visitors.

Cocktails
Top of the Wheel (Harvey's Resort Hotel and Casino, Lake Tahoe, tel. 702/588–2411) offers a pleasing view of the lake, soft dinner and dance music, and a big band night.

Index

Abracadabra (show), *149*

Ace Loan Company, *112*

Adams Western Store, *113*

Airports
Las Vegas, *13*
Reno, *160*

Airport to hotel transportation
Las Vegas, *14–15*
Reno, *160*

Aladdin Hotel and Casino
casino facilities, *69*
hotel facilities, *138*
nightlife, *149*

Alan Bible Visitor Center, *102*

Alexis Park Resort Hotel, *135–136*

All-Star Inn, *146*

Alpine Jack's (restaurant), *179*

Alpine Meadows Ski Area, *170*

Alpine Village Inn, *126–127*

Anchorage Marina, *169*

Andiamo (restaurant), *127*

Ann-Margaret, *152*

Arden, Donn, *150*

Art galleries and museums, *97*

Automatic Teller Machines (ATMs), *6–7*

Auto racing, *5, 117*

Baby-sitting services, *8–9*

Baccarat, *48–51*

Bacchanal (restaurant), *129*

Bally's Casino Resort
casino facilities, *70*
hotel facilities, *133*
nightlife, *150, 154*
sports facilities, *117*

Bally's Reno (casino hotel), *173–174*

Barbary Coast Hotel and Casino
casino facilities, *71*
hotel facilities, *138*
nightlife, *155*

Baseball, *117*

Basketball, *117*

Battista's Hole in the Wall Italian Restaurant, *127*

B. Dalton (shop), *111*

Beaches, *176*

Best Western Driftwood Lodge, *106*

Big Six (Wheel of Fortune), *56–57*

Biking
Las Vegas, *116*
Reno, *169*

Bill's (casino), *178*

Bingo, *54–56*

Binion, Benny, *80*

Binion's Horseshoe Hotel and Casino
casino facilities, *80*
hotel facilities, *138–139*
restaurants, *121, 125*

Blackjack (Twenty-one), *20, 21*
bet limits, *21*
betting procedure, *23*
burning a card, *24, 40*
busting percentages, *27–28*
card counting, *35*
card counting (10-values), *35–38*
card counting (aces), *38–40*
cheating, *23*
chips, purchase of, *21–23*
cutting the cards, *24*
dealer options, *25–26, 42*
decks in play, *23*
double-exposure blackjack, *42*
doubling down, *29–30, 32, 42*
etiquette for, *65*

fluctuation in bets, *37–38*
hard holding strategy, *26–29*
hit, *25*
insurance, *34*
luck and, *29*
money management, *40–41*
natural blackjack, *24–25*
position at the table, selection of, *21, 39–40*
rules, basic, *24–35*
rule variations, *41–42*
sharing information with other players, *40*
soft holdings, *30–32*
splitting, *32–34, 42*
stand, *25*
surrender, *35, 42*
table, layout of, *22*
table changing, *41*

BLM Visitor Center, *105*

Boating
Las Vegas, *116*
Reno, *169*

Bonanza "World's Largest Gift Shop," *90, 109, 111*

Bonnie Springs Motel, *105*

Bonnie Springs Ranch, *105, 116*

Books on Las Vegas, *13*

Bookstores, *111, 112*

Boulder City, Nevada, *102*

Boulevard Mall, *111*

Bourbon Street Hotel and Casino
casino facilities, *70*
nightlife, *155*

Bowling
facilities for, *116*
professional, *118*

Boxing, *118*

Boy-lesque (show), *149*

British travelers, tips for, *3–4*

Index

184

Bryce Canyon National Park, *106–107*
Bucket of Blood Saloon, *166*
Business hours, *16*
Bus travel
disabled travelers, *10*
to Las Vegas, *10, 12, 15*
local buses, *17*
older travelers, *12*
to Reno, *161*
tours, *17*

Caesars Palace (casino hotel)
casino facilities, *70–71*
hotel facilities, *133, 135*
movies, *155*
restaurants, *123–125, 126, 127, 129*
sightseeing in, *88*
sports facilities, *117*
Caesars Tahoe (casino hotel)
casino facilities, *179*
hotel facilities, *181*
Cafe Michelle, *121, 123*
Cafe Roma, *124–125*
California Hotel and Casino, *80*
Cal-Neva Coffee Shop, *179*
Cal-Neva Lodge (casino hotel)
casino facilities, *176*
hotel facilities, *181*
Candlelight Wedding Chapel, *90, 96*
C&R Clothiers, *111*
Cantina Los Tres Hombres (restaurant), *171*
Capozzoli's (restaurant), *127–128*
Car rentals, *15*
Carson City, Nevada, *166–167*
Car travel
to Las Vegas, *15*
in Las Vegas, *16–17, 85*
to Reno, *160*
Cash machines, *6–7*
Cashman Field, *93, 117*

Casino Clothiers of Nevada, *111*
Casinos, *64*
beyond the Strip, *78–79*
disabled people, accommodations for, *10–11*
downtown, *79–83*
etiquette for, *64–66*
gambling lessons, *64*
gift shops in, *109*
graveyard shift in, *156–157*
Lake Tahoe area, *176, 178–179*
in Laughlin, *105*
maps of, *68, 81*
photography in, *65, 99, 101*
in Reno, *161, 163–164*
smoking in, *66*
the Strip, *67–78*
Catch a Rising Star (comedy club), *154*
Cave Rock, *178*
Center Stage (restaurant), *121*
Chamber of Commerce (Las Vegas), *2, 16*
Chaz (club), *154*
Chemin de fer. *See* Baccarat
Children, attractions for
Las Vegas, *94, 98*
Reno, *167–168*
Children, traveling with, *7–9*
hotel accomodations, *8, 94, 137*
Chin's (restaurant), *124*
Chocolate shops, *111*
Chollar Mansion, *166*
Christmas Tree Inn, *171*
Churches, *89, 95*
Circus Circus (casino hotel, Las Vegas)
casino facilities, *77*
hotel facilities, *144–145*
restaurants, *123, 130*
sightseeing in, *90*
Circus Circus (casino hotel, Reno)
casino facilities, *163*

children, attractions for, *167*
hotel facilities, *174–175*
restaurants, *173*
City Lites (show), *149–150*
Clark County Fair, *5*
Clark County Library, *93*
Clark County Marriage License Bureau, *96*
Clark County Southern Heritage Museum, *97*
Cleopatra's Barge (club), *154*
Cleveland Boys, *73–74*
Climate, *4–5*
Clothestime (shop), *111–112*
Clothing for the trip, *6*
Clothing shops
Las Vegas, *111–112*
Reno, *168*
Club Cal-Neva (casino), *161*
Colorado Belle (casino), *105*
Comedy clubs, *154*
Comedy Store (comedy club), *154*
Come-ons, *91*
Comps, *66*
Comstock Hotel, *175*
Contempo Casuals (shop), *112*
Cornero, Tony, *75*
Craps, *45–48*
Crazy Girls (show), *150*
Crystal Bay, *176*
Cupid's Chapel of Love, *168*
Customs and duties, *3*

Dance Hall and Saloon, *155*
Dancing, *154, 155*
Davis, Sammy, Jr., *153*
Dealers
school for, *90–91*
talking with, *65*
Dealers Room Casino Clothiers, *111*

Index

Del Mar Station (club), *182*
Delta Saloon, *166*
Del Webb's High Sierra Casino Hotel
casino facilities, *179*
hotel facilities, *181*
Dentists, *16*
Desert Inn Hotel and Casino
casino facilities, *73–74*
hotel facilities, *135*
sports facilities, *124*
Dining. *See* Restaurants
Disabled travelers, hints for, *9–11*
Discount stores, *112*
Discovery: The Children's Museum, *94*
Divorce and marriage laws, *96*
Doctors
Las Vegas, *16*
Reno, *160*
Dome of the Sea (restaurant), *129*
Donn Arden's Jubilee (show), *150*
Downtown
casinos, *79–83*
sightseeing, *91–93*
Dunes Hotel and Country Club
casino facilities, *70*
hotel facilities, *139*
nightlife, *154*
restaurants, *129*
sports facilities, *116*

Edgewater (casino), *105*
Elaine's (restaurant), *125*
El Cortez Hotel
casino facilities, *83*
hotel facilities, *145*
Electricity, *4*
El Rancho Tower Hotel and Casino
casino facilities, *78*
hotel facilities, *139*
sports facilities, *116*
El Vaquero (restaurant), *180*
Emergencies
Las Vegas, *16*
Reno, *160*

Empress Court (restaurant), *123–124*
Escorted tours, *161*
Ethel M Chocolates, *111*
Etiquette for Las Vegas, *64–66*
Evening at the Improv (comedy club), *154*
Excalibur (casino hotel)
casino facilities, *67, 69*
hotel facilities, *139*
Excursions from Las Vegas, *102–107*

Fairs, *5*
Fashion Show Mall, *88–89, 109*
Festivals and seasonal events, *5–6*
First Baptist Church, *95*
First Southern Baptist Church, *95*
Fitzgerald's Hotel (Reno)
casino facilities, *163*
hotel facilities, *174*
Fitzgerald's Hotel and Casino (Las Vegas)
casino facilities, *82*
hotel facilities, *139–140*
The Flame (restaurant), *130*
Flamingo Hilton (casino hotel, Reno)
casino facilities, *163*
hotel facilities, *173*
Flamingo Hilton and Tower (casino hotel, Las Vegas)
casino facilities, *71–72*
hotel facilities, *136*
nightlife, *149–150*
restaurants, *121, 125*
Flamingo Room (restaurant), *121*
Fleischmann Planetarium, *164*
Folies Bergere (show), *150–151*
Food Fantasy (restaurant), *125*
Food shops, *112*

Football betting, *59*
handicapping, *59–60*
money management, *60*
point spread, *61–62*
types of bets, *60–61*
Foot Locker (shop), *113*
Forts, *95*
Four Queens Hotel and Casino
casino facilities, *81–82*
hotel facilities, *140*
nightlife, *155*
FREE ASPIRIN AND TENDER SYMPATHY sign, *87*
Free attractions, *93*
Fremont Hotel and Casino, *82*
Fresh Ketch (bar), *182*
Frontier Hotel and Gambling Hall
casino facilities, *74*
hotel facilities, *140*
restaurants, *128*
Fun books, *66*
Furs by Le Nobel of Athens, *112*
Fur shops, *112*

Gambler's Book Store, *112*
Gamblers General Store, *112*
Gambling lessons, *64*
Gambling memorabilia, *112*
Games of chance. *See also* Blackjack
baccarat, *48–51*
Big Six (Wheel of Fortune), *56–57*
bingo, *54–56*
craps, *45–48*
dealers, talking with, *65*
football betting, *59–62*
keno, *51–54*
money management, *40–41, 60, 66*
roulette, *43–45*
slot machines, *57–59*
General-interest tours, *2*
General Store (restaurant), *173*
Gift shops, *109*

Index

Gold Coast Hotel and Casino
casino facilities, *79*
nightlife, *155*
sports facilities, *116*

Golden Nugget (casino, Laughlin), *105*

Golden Nugget Hotel and Casino (Las Vegas)
casino facilities, *81*
hotel facilities, *136–137*
restaurants, *123*, *124*, *125*

Golden Steer (restaurant), *129–130*

Gold Spike Hotel and Casino
casino facilities, *83*
hotel facilities, *145*

Gold Strike Hotel and Gambling Hall, *145*

Golf
Las Vegas, *116*
professional, *5*, *118*
Reno, *169*

Great Basin Adventure (history park), *167*

Guardian Angel Cathedral, *89*, *95*

Guided tours, *17*

Guinness World of Records Museum, *97*

Hacienda de la Sierra (restaurant), *179*

Hacienda Hotel and Casino
casino facilities, *67*
hotel facilities, *140*

Harold's (casino)
casino facilities, *163*
restaurants, *173*

Harold's Club Antique Slots (shop), *168*

Harrah's (casino hotel)
casino facilities, *161*
hotel facilities, *174*

Harrah's Auto Museum, *167–168*

Harrah's Lake Tahoe Casino Hotel
casino facilities, *178*

hotel facilities, *181*
restaurants, *179–180*

Harrah's Steak House, *171*

Harris and Frank Clothing, *111*

Harvey's Resort Hotel and Casino
casino facilities, *178*
hotel facilities, *181*
nightlife, *182*
restaurants, *180*

Health clubs, *116*

Heavenly Valley Ski Resort, *170*

Helicopter tours, *17*

Helldorado Days and Rodeo, *5*

Hiking
Las Vegas, *116*
Reno, *169*

Hock Shop Ltd., *113*

Holiday Inn Hotel and Casino
casino facilities, *72–73*
hotel facilities, *140*
restaurants, *123*

Hoover Dam, *102*
guided tours, *17*

Horseback riding, *116–117*

Horsehoe Hotel. *See* Binion's Horseshoe Hotel and Casino

Hospitals
Las Vegas, *16*
Reno, *160*

Hotels
children, accommodations for, *8*, *94*, *137*
disabled people, accommodations for, *10–11*
on Interstate 15, *145*
Lake Tahoe area, *180–181*
in Las Vegas, *132–146*
in Reno, *173–175*

House of Antiques and Slots (shop), *112*

Ho Wan (restaurant), *124*

Hughes, Howard, *74*, *75*, *135*

Hugos (restaurant), *179*

Humperdinck, Engelbert, *153*

Hyatt Lake Tahoe (hotel), *180–181*

Imperial Palace Automobile Museum, *88*

Imperial Palace Hotel and Casino
casino facilities, *72*
hotel facilities, *140–141*
nightlife, *151*

Incline Village, *176*

Incline Village Golf Course, *169*

Insurance
for British travelers, *3*
for luggage, *14*

James R. Dickinson Library, *93*

Jaycee Park, *97*

Jerry Lewis Muscular Dystrophy Telethon, *5*

Joan of Arc (church), *95*

Joe's Bayou (restaurant), *123*

Jogging, *117*

John Ascuaga's Nugget (casino hotel)
children, attractions for, *167*
hotel facilities, *174*
restaurants, *171*

Jones, Tom, *153*

Keno, *51–54*

Kinney (shop), *113*

K Mart, *112*

Kyle Canyon, *105–106*

Lady Luck Casino and Hotel
casino facilities, *82–83*
hotel facilities, *141*

Lake Mead, *102–104*, *116*

Lakeridge Golf Course, *169*

Lake Tahoe, *176*
boating, *169*
hotels, *180–181*
map of, *177*
nightlife, *182*
restaurants, *179–180*
sightseeing, *176–179*

Landmark Hotel and Casino
casino facilities, *75–76*

Index

187

hotel facilities, *141*
nightlife, *151*
Las Vegas Air Charter Terminal, *87*
Las Vegas Art Museum, *97*
Las Vegas Athletic Club, *116, 117*
Las Vegas Club Hotel and Casino
casino facilities, *80*
hotel facilities, *141*
Las Vegas Convention and Visitors Authority, *2, 15–16*
Las Vegas Convention Center, *89*
Las Vegas High School, *93*
Las Vegas Hilton (casino hotel)
casino facilities, *76*
children's accommodations, *94, 137*
hotel facilities, *137*
nightlife, *153*
restaurants, *125–126, 127*
Las Vegas Invitational golf tournament, *5, 118*
Las Vegas Municipal Golf Course, *116*
Las Vegas Museum of Natural History (Las Vegas Blvd.), *87*
Las Vegas Museum of Natural History (Maryland Pkwy.), *93*
Las Vegas Nevada Temple of the Church of Jesus Christ of the Latter-day Saints, *95–96*
Laughlin, Nevada, *104–105*
Lee Canyon, *106, 117*
Legends in Concert (show), *151*
Le Montrachet (restaurant), *125–126*

Liberace Museum, *97*
Libraries, *93*
Lido de Paris (show), *151*
Lillie Langtry's (restaurant), *124*
The Limited (shop), *111*
Limousines, *15*
Little Caesar's Gambling Casino, *69*
Little Church of the West, *96*
Little White Chapel, *96*
Lodging. *See* Hotels *and* Motels
Lorenzi Park, *97–98*
Lost City Museum, *104*
Lucky (shop), *112*
Luggage
airline regulations, *6*
insurance for, *14*

McCarran International Airport, *13, 87*
Mackay Mansion, *166*
Major Video (shop), *113*
Mansions, *166*
Maps
casinos (downtown), *81*
casinos (Strip), *68*
hotels, *134*
Lake Mead, *103*
Lake Tahoe, *177*
Reno, *162, 172*
restaurants, *122*
shopping, *110*
sightseeing (downtown), *92*
sightseeing (Strip), *86*
Virginia City, *165*
Margarita's Mexican Cantina, *128*
Mariette Lake, *169*
Marina Hotel and Casino
casino facilities, *69*
hotel facilities, *141–142*
Marinas
Lake Mead, *104, 116*
Lake Tahoe, *169*
Mark Twain Museum, *165*

Mark Twain Museum of Memories, *165*
Marriage licenses, *96*
Marshall-Rousso (shop), *111*
Mary's Diner, *125*
Maxim Hotel and Casino
casino facilities, *69–70*
hotel facilities, *142*
nightlife, *151*
The Meadows (mall), *111*
Melinda and Her Follies Revue, *151*
Miller Stockman (shop), *113*
The Mirage (casino hotel)
casino facilities, *73*
hotel facilities, *137–138*
nightlife, *153*
Money management, *66*
blackjack, *40–41*
football betting, *60*
Mormon temples, *95–96*
Motels, *146*
Motel 6, *146*
Mt. Charleston, *105–106*
Mt. Charleston Inn, *106*
Mt. Charleston Restaurant and Lounge, *106*
Mt. Charleston Stables, *116–117*
Mt. Rose, *169*
Movies, *94, 155*
Munari, Geno, *91*
Museums
art, *97*
automobile, *88, 167–168*
Believe It or Not, *92*
in Carson City, *167*
for children, *94*
history, *97, 164, 166, 167*
Indians, *104*
in Las Vegas, *87, 88, 92, 93, 94, 97*
Liberace, *97*
natural history, *87, 93*
railroad, *167*
in Reno, *164, 167–168*
Twain, Mark, *165*

Index

Museums *(continued)*
in Virginia City, *165,
166*
world records, *97*
Music, *155*

**National Finals of
Rodeo,** *5, 118*
Neon shows, *75*
Neon sign makers, *94*
Nevada Club (casino),
161, 163
**Nevada Commission
on Tourism,** *2*
**Nevada Historical
Society,** *164*
**Nevada State
Museum,** *167*
**Nevada State
Museum and
Historical Society,**
97
**Nevada State
Railroad Museum,**
167
Newton, Jerry, *82*
Newton, Wayne, *82,
153*
New Year's Eve, *5–6*
Nightlife
comedy clubs, *154*
dancing, *154, 155*
graveyard shift,
156–157
Lake Tahoe area, *182*
in Las Vegas, *148–157*
lounges, *154*
movies, *94, 155*
music, *155*
revues, *149–152*
showroom stars,
152–154
strip clubs, *155*
**19th Hole
Restaurant,** *171*
Nissan Mint 400
(road race), *5, 117*
North Tahoe Marina,
169

Oh No! Tokyo
(restaurant), *128*
Older travelers, hints
for, *11–12*
Old Mormon Fort, *95*
Old Nevada Ranch,
105
Old Town Mall, *168*
Omnimax Theater, *94*
Ophir Creek, *169*

O'Sheas Casino, *72*
**Package deals for
independent
travelers,** *3*
Palace Court
(restaurant), *126*
**Palace Station Hotel
and Casino**
casino facilities, *79*
restaurants, *123*
Palomino Club, *155*
**Pamplemousse
Restaurant,** *126*
**Paradise Valley
County Park,** *98*
**Parker's Western
Wear** (shop), *168*
Park Lane Mall, *168*
Parks, city
Las Vegas, *97–98*
Reno, *164*
Parks, national,
106–107
**Parks, state and
county,** *98, 104*
Passports, *3*
Paul Revere's Kicks
(club), *182*
**Paul-Son Dice and
Card** (shop), *112*
**Paul-Son School of
Gaming,** *90–92*
Pawn shops, *112–113*
Peppermill Casino
(Las Vegas), *74–75*
Peppermill Hotel
(Reno)
casino facilities, *164*
hotel facilities, *174*
**Peppermill Shopping
Center,** *89*
Pharmacies
Las Vegas, *16*
Reno, *160*
Photography
cameras and film,
99–100
in casinos, *65, 99, 101*
subjects for, *100–101*
traveling with film, *7*
Photography shops,
112
Pioneer Hotel, *105*
Planetariums, *164*
Plane travel
airlines, *13*
airports, *13*
airport to hotel
transportation, *14–15*
from Britain, *3–4*

with children, *8*
luggage insurance, *14*
luggage regulations, *6*
to Reno, *160*
smoking, *13–14*
**Playboy's Girls of
Rock and Roll**
(show), *151*
Ponderosa (casino),
163–164
Ponderosa Ranch,
176
Presidential Car
(restaurant), *173*
Presley, Elvis, *76*
Primavera
(restaurant, Lake
Tahoe), *180*
Primavera
(restaurant, Las
Vegas), *127*
Princess Furs (shop),
112

Racquetball, *117*
Rafting, *169*
Railroads, *166, 167*
Ralph's Diner, *125*
Ramada Express
(casino), *105*
Ranches, *105, 176*
**Rapscallion Seafood
House & Bar,** *171*
Record shops, *113*
Record Surplus
(shop), *113*
Red Rock Canyon,
105
Regency Casino, *105*
Reno, *152*
emergencies, *160*
excursions, *164–167*
history of, *159–160*
hospitals, *160*
hotels, *173–175*
maps of, *162, 172*
pharmacies, *160*
restaurants, *170–173*
shopping, *168*
sightseeing, *161–164,
167–168*
sports and fitness,
169–170
tourist information,
160
transportation,
160–161
wedding chapels, *168*
**Reno Wedding
Chapel,** *168*

Index

189

Restaurants
American, *121, 123, 171, 173*
buffets, *123*
Cajun, *123*
Chinese, *123–124*
coffee shops, *124–125, 179, 180*
diners, *125*
French/continental, *125–126*
German, *126–127*
Italian, *127–128, 180*
Japanese, *128*
Lake Tahoe area, *179–180*
in Las Vegas, *120–130*
Mexican, *128, 171, 179, 180*
in Reno, *170–173*
seafood, *129, 171*
steak houses, *129–130, 171*
Rio Suites Hotel and Casino, *138*
Ripley's Believe It or Not Museum, *92*
Riverside Resort, *105*
Riviera Hotel
casino facilities, *76–77*
hotel facilities, *142*
nightlife, *150, 151–152, 154*
Rock formations, *106*
Rodeos, *5, 118*
Roulette, *43–45*
Ruby's Inn, *107*

Sahara Las Vegas Hotel
casino facilities, *78*
hotel facilities, *142–143*
nightlife, *149*
St. George, Utah, *106*
Saloons, *166*
Sam's Town Gold River (casino), *105*
Sam's Town Hotel and Casino
casino facilities, *83*
hotel facilities, *145*
nightlife, *155*
restaurants, *123, 125, 128*
sports facilities, *116*
Sam's Town Western Emporium (shop), *113*

Sand Harbor Beach, *176*
Sands Hotel and Casino
casino facilities, *73*
hotel facilities, *143*
Santa Fe (restaurant), *128*
Sarno, Jay, *71, 77*
Sassy Sally (neon cowgirl), *91*
Scandia Family Fun Center, *94*
Scruples Bar and Grill, *182*
Senior Classic golf tournament, *5*
Shakespeare festival, *176*
Shark Club, *154*
Shoe shops, *113*
Shopping
Las Vegas, *109–113*
Reno, *168*
Showboat Invitational Bowling Tournament, *118*
Shows. *See* Nightlife
Siegel, Bugsy, *71, 136*
Siegfried and Roy, *153–154*
Sierra (coffee shop), *180*
Sightseeing, *85*
checklists for, *95–98*
children, attractions for, *94, 98, 167–168*
downtown, *91–93*
excursions from Las Vegas, *102–107*
excursions from Reno, *164–167*
free attractions, *93*
Lake Tahoe area, *176–179*
off the beaten track, *94*
in Reno, *161–164, 167–168*
the Strip, *85–91*
Silver City (casino), *76*
Silver Dragon (restaurant), *124*
Sinatra, Frank, *176*
Skiing
Las Vegas area, *117*
Reno area, *169–170*

Skye Room (restaurant), *121*
Slot machines, *57–58*
progressive slots, *58–59*
Slots-A-Fun (casino), *77–78*
Snowmobiling, *170*
Southern Nevada Zoological Park, *98*
Special-interest tours, *2–3*
Splash (show), *151–152*
Spooner Lake Cross-Country Ski Area, *169*
Sports and fitness
Las Vegas, *116–118*
Reno, *169–170*
Sports Club–Las Vegas, *116, 117*
Squaw Valley USA (ski resort), *170*
Stardust Hotel and Casino
casino facilities, *75*
hotel facilities, *143*
nightlife, *151*
restaurants, *125, 130*
State Capitol Building, *167*
Stateline, Nevada, *178–179*
The Steak House, *130*
Stoney's Loan and Jewelry (shop), *112–113*
the Strip
casinos, *67–78*
maps of, *68, 86*
shopping, *109, 111*
sightseeing, *85–91*
Strip clubs, *155*
Stupak, Bob, *69, 78–79*
Sultan's Table (restaurant), *129*
Summit/Forest (restaurant), *179–180*
Sunset Park, *98*
Swimming, *117*
Synagogues, *96*

Tahoe. *See* Lake Tahoe
Tahoe Biltmore (casino hotel), *181*
Target (shop), *112*

Index

Taxis
Las Vegas, *14, 17*
Reno, *160–161*
Temple Beth Sholom,
96
Tennis
Las Vegas, *117*
Reno, *170*
Tiffany Furs (shop),
112
The Tillerman
(restaurant), *129*
Timing the visit, *4–5*
Tipping, *66*
Top of the Place
(lounge), *154*
Top of the Wheel
(restaurant), *180,
182*
Tour groups, *2–3*
Tourist information
Las Vegas, *2, 15–16*
Reno, *160*
Tower Records
(shop), *113*
**Town Hall/
Vagabound Inn,**
146
Toy shops, *113*
Toys 'R Us (shop),
113
**Trader Ann's Trading
Post,** *90*
Train travel
disabled travelers,
9–10
to Las Vegas, *15*
older travelers, *12*
to Reno, *161*
Tramps (club), *154*
**Tropicana Resort
and Casino**
casino facilities, *67*
hotel facilities,
143–144
nightlife, *150–151*
restaurants, *123*

sports facilities, *116,
117*
Turtles Night Club,
182
Twain, Mark, *165*
Twenty-one. *See*
Blackjack

Union Plaza Hotel
casino facilities, *80*
hotel facilities, *144*
restaurants, *121*
Union Premiums
(shop), *112*
**University of
Nevada–Las Vegas,**
117

**Valley of Fire State
Park,** *104*
Vans of California
(shop), *113*
Vegas Vic (neon
cowboy), *91*
**Vegas World Hotel
and Casino**
casino facilities, *78–79*
hotel facilities, *144*
Video arcades, *94*
Video Park (shop),
113
Video shops, *113*
**Virginia and Truckee
Railroad,** *166*
**Virginia City,
Nevada,** *164–166*
Visas, *3*
Visitors Center, *87*

**Waldenbooks and
More** (shop), *111*
Walking, *85*
Water parks
Las Vegas, *90*
Reno, *167*
**The Way It Was
Museum,** *166*

Weather information,
5
**Wedding Bells
Chapel,** *168*
Wedding chapels
Las Vegas, *90, 96*
Reno, *168*
WELCOME TO LAS VEGAS
sign, *85, 87*
Western Dance Hall,
155
Western goods, *113*
**Westward Ho Motel
and Casino**
casino facilities, *75*
motel facilities, *146*
**Wet 'N Wild water
park,** *90*
**Whiskey Pete's
Casino and Hotel,**
145
**Wildcreek Golf
Course,** *169*
Wild Waters (water
park), *167*
**William B's
Steakhouse,** *130*
**Willy and Jose's
Cantina,** *128*
Windsurfing, *170*
Wingfield Park, *164*
**World Series of
Poker,** *5, 92*
Wynn, Steve, *81*

**Young Electric Sign
Company,** *94*
Youth Hotel, *94*

Zephyr Cove Resort,
178
**Ziedler and Ziedler
Ltd.,** *111*
Zion National Park,
106
Zoos, *98*

Personal Itinerary

Departure *Date*

Time

Transportation

Arrival *Date*   *Time*

Departure *Date*   *Time*

Transportation

Accommodations

Arrival *Date*   *Time*

Departure *Date*   *Time*

Transportation

Accommodations

Arrival *Date*   *Time*

Departure *Date*   *Time*

Transportation

Accommodations

Personal Itinerary

Arrival *Date*   *Time*

Departure *Date*   *Time*

Transportation

Accommodations

Arrival *Date*   *Time*

Departure *Date*   *Time*

Transportation

Accommodations

Arrival *Date*   *Time*

Departure *Date*   *Time*

Transportation

Accommodations

Arrival *Date*   *Time*

Departure *Date*   *Time*

Transportation

Accommodations

Personal Itinerary

Arrival *Date* *Time*

Departure *Date* *Time*

Transportation

Accommodations

Arrival *Date* *Time*

Departure *Date* *Time*

Transportation

Accommodations

Arrival *Date* *Time*

Departure *Date* *Time*

Transportation

Accommodations

Arrival *Date* *Time*

Departure *Date* *Time*

Transportation

Accommodations

Personal Itinerary

Arrival *Date*   *Time*

Departure *Date*   *Time*

Transportation

Accommodations

Arrival *Date*   *Time*

Departure *Date*   *Time*

Transportation

Accommodations

Arrival *Date*   *Time*

Departure *Date*   *Time*

Transportation

Accommodations

Arrival *Date*   *Time*

Departure *Date*   *Time*

Transportation

Accommodations

Addresses

Name

Address

Telephone

Name

Address

Telephone

Name

Address

Telephone

Name

Address

Telephone

Name

Address

Telephone

Name

Address

Telephone

Name

Address

Telephone

Name

Address

Telephone

Name

Address

Telephone

Name

Address

Telephone

Name

Address

Telephone

Name

Address

Telephone

Name

Address

Telephone

Name

Address

Telephone

Name

Address

Telephone

Name

Address

Telephone

Addresses

Name

Address

Telephone

Name

Address

Telephone

Name

Address

Telephone

Name

Address

Telephone

Name

Address

Telephone

Name

Address

Telephone

Name

Address

Telephone

Name

Address

Telephone

Name

Address

Telephone

Name

Address

Telephone

Name

Address

Telephone

Name

Address

Telephone

Name

Address

Telephone

Name

Address

Telephone

Name

Address

Telephone

Addresses

Name	*Name*
Address	*Address*
Telephone	*Telephone*
Name	*Name*
Address	*Address*
Telephone	*Telephone*
Name	*Name*
Address	*Address*
Telephone	*Telephone*
Name	*Name*
Address	*Address*
Telephone	*Telephone*
Name	*Name*
Address	*Address*
Telephone	*Telephone*
Name	*Name*
Address	*Address*
Telephone	*Telephone*
Name	*Name*
Address	*Address*
Telephone	*Telephone*
Name	*Name*
Address	*Address*
Telephone	*Telephone*

Notes

Notes

Fodor's Travel Guides

U.S. Guides

Alaska
Arizona
Atlantic City & the
  New Jersey Shore
Boston
California
Cape Cod
Carolinas & the
  Georgia Coast
The Chesapeake Region
Chicago
Colorado
Disney World & the
  Orlando Area

Florida
Hawaii
Las Vegas
Los Angeles, Orange
  County, Palm Springs
Maui
Miami,
  Fort Lauderdale,
  Palm Beach
Michigan, Wisconsin,
  Minnesota
New England
New Mexico
New Orleans

New Orleans (Pocket
  Guide)
New York City
New York City (Pocket
  Guide)
New York State
Pacific North Coast
Philadelphia
The Rockies
San Diego
San Francisco
San Francisco (Pocket
  Guide)
The South

Texas
USA
Virgin Islands
Virginia
Waikiki
Washington, DC

Foreign Guides

Acapulco
Amsterdam
Australia, New Zealand,
  The South Pacific
Austria
Bahamas
Bahamas (Pocket
  Guide)
Baja & the Pacific
  Coast Resorts
Barbados
Beijing, Guangzhou &
  Shanghai
Belgium &
  Luxembourg
Bermuda
Brazil
Britain (Great Travel
  Values)
Budget Europe
Canada
Canada (Great Travel
  Values)
Canada's Atlantic
  Provinces
Cancun, Cozumel,
  Yucatan Peninsula

Caribbean
Caribbean (Great
  Travel Values)
Central America
Eastern Europe
Egypt
Europe
Europe's Great
  Cities
France
France (Great Travel
  Values)
Germany
Germany (Great Travel
  Values)
Great Britain
Greece
The Himalayan
  Countries
Holland
Hong Kong
Hungary
India,
  including Nepal
Ireland
Israel
Italy

Italy (Great Travel
  Values)
Jamaica
Japan
Japan (Great Travel
  Values)
Kenya, Tanzania,
  the Seychelles
Korea
Lisbon
Loire Valley
London
London (Great
  Travel Values)
London (Pocket Guide)
Madrid & Barcelona
Mexico
Mexico City
Montreal &
  Quebec City
Munich
New Zealand
North Africa
Paris
Paris (Pocket Guide)
People's Republic of
  China

Portugal
Rio de Janeiro
The Riviera (Fur. on)
Rome
Saint Martin &
  Sint Maarten
Scandinavia
Scandinavian Cities
Scotland
Singapore
South America
South Pacific
Southeast Asia
Soviet Union
Spain
Spain (Great Travel
  Values)
Sweden
Switzerland
Sydney
Tokyo
Toronto
Turkey
Vienna
Yugoslavia

Special-Interest Guides

Health & Fitness
  Vacations
Royalty Watching

Selected Hotels of
  Europe

Selected Resorts and
  Hotels of the U.S.
Shopping in Europe

Skiing in North America
Sunday in New York